Challenging Oppression

Challenging Oppression

A Critical
Social Work Approach

BOB MULLALY

OXFORD
UNIVERSITY PRESS

OXFORD

UNIVERSITY PRESS

70 Wynford Drive, Don Mills, Ontario M3C 1J9
www.oup.com/ca

Oxford University Press is a department of the University of Oxford.
It furthers the University's objective of excellence in research, scholarship,
and education by publishing worldwide in

Oxford   New York
Auckland   Bangkok   Buenos Aires   Cape Town   Chennai
Dar es Salaam   Delhi   Hong Kong   Istanbul   Karachi   Kolkata
Kuala Lumpur   Madrid   Melbourne   Mexico City   Mumbai   Nairobi
São Paulo   Shanghai   Singapore   Taipei   Tokyo   Toronto

with an associated company in Berlin

Oxford is a trade mark of Oxford University Press
in the UK and in certain other countries

Published in Canada
by Oxford University Press

National Library of Canada Cataloguing in Publication Data
Mullaly, Robert P.
Challenging oppression : a critical social work approach

Includes bibliographical references and index.
ISBN 0-19-541695-3

1. Oppression (Psychology) 2. Equality. 3. Social work with minorities. I. Title.

HM821.M84 2002   305   C2002-900632-5

1 2 3 4 – 05 04 03 02

This book is printed on permanent (acid-free) paper ⊚.

Printed in Canada

Contents

Acknowledgements

Although I am indebted to all authors cited in this book, I am especially grateful to several contemporary writers who have significantly influenced my thinking. They include Barry Adam, Ben Agger, Anne Bishop, Frantz Fanon, David Gil, Stuart Hall, bell hooks, Douglas Kellner, Geraldine Moane, Neil Thompson, Steven Wineman, and Iris Marion Young. A special tribute goes to my good friend Peter Leonard, whose writings never fail to stimulate me intellectually and inspire me politically. At a personal level, my appreciation goes to my valued social work colleagues at Victoria University—Ronnie Egan, Marty Grace, Lesley Hoatson, and Lis Starbuck. Each read my first draft in its entirety and together at several meetings we discussed, analyzed, and critiqued the material in terms of its implications for scholarship, social work practice, our curriculum, and our personal lives. I received much encouragement and support from this progressive group of four strong women. My thanks go also to my students at Victoria University, who were the first to engage with me in a dialogue about much of the material in the book and to give me critical feedback on it. I wish to thank Victoria University for granting me a six-month leave of absence, which allowed me uninterrupted time to carry out research for the book and to write the first few chapters. I spent this research leave as a guest of the School of Social Work and Social Policy at Dalhousie University in Halifax, Canada, and am most grateful for their hospitality.

I also wish to thank the two anonymous reviewers who read and commented on the book in its proposal stage and the two reviewers who read and commented on the original draft. Their suggestions have made it a much better book. I am very grateful to Megan Mueller of Oxford University Press Canada, who worked with me throughout the entire project. She was quick to respond to my questions and concerns and always provided me with helpful advice and feedback on my drafts. Somehow, she knew just what to say (or not say) when I would have the occasional little temper tantrum because things were not going well with the book. I am also very appreciative of the excellent work carried out by my editor, Richard Tallman. This is the third project on which we have worked together. He not only manages to turn my rough manuscripts into polished form, but his wit and sense of humour help get me through the final part of the publication process, a part that many authors experience as a sort of tedious, toilsome, ignoble, and anticlimactic affliction.

Finally, I want to express my special appreciation to Heather Fraser. Throughout the project she managed to carry out the dialectic of being my sharpest critic and my biggest supporter at the same time. A scholar in her own right, I always knew that when she approved of a section or chapter of my book it was ready for publication. As a feminist from a working-class background, she has helped me to understand better the everyday practice of confronting and resisting oppression.

Bob Mullaly
Melbourne

Preface

Over the past couple of years, I have been asked two questions by many people when they learned that I was writing a book about anti-oppressive social work. (1) What is anti-oppressive social work? (2) Why am I adopting oppression as the major explanation for social problems and anti-oppressive practice as the major approach in dealing with these problems?

With respect to the question of what is anti-oppressive social work, I am convinced that it is whatever one wants it to be (this is no different from social work practice in general). I came to this conclusion having read extensively on what people say about anti-oppressive social work and having had many discussions about it with both academics and practitioners. Many social workers today recognize that there are identifiable (oppressed) social groups who have historically lived and presently live a second-class type of citizenship because they are excluded from certain social opportunities and benefits and who do not receive fair institutional treatment that mainstream groups take for granted.

However, although oppression may be recognized, the causal explanations for its existence vary among social workers—just as do the causal explanations for social problems. For example, some social workers attribute oppression not necessarily to individual weakness or pathology (though some do) but to an inferior culture or race or other social group. Rather than blaming the individual victim for his or her travails, a whole social group is blamed because of its perceived inferior or pathological nature, culture, race, and so on. The solution to oppression in this case is to assimilate as much as possible these inferior groups into the mainstream.

Other (probably most) social workers have adopted a more liberal-humanist approach to oppression. They would not blame victims on either an individual or group basis, but would attempt to compensate victims of oppression by distributing or redistributing society's goods and services to them. This notion of (re)distributive justice does nothing, however, about the social practices and processes that caused the maldistribution in the first place. A liberal-humanist approach does nothing to transform the social institutions and cultural practices that produce and reproduce inequality.

Neither of the above approaches is consistent with my view of oppression or anti-oppressive social work. In this book, I present my views and understandings of oppression, oppressed persons, and my approach to anti-oppressive social work practice. These views are framed within a critical social theory that is informed by postmodernism, post-structuralism, cultural studies, and post-colonialism. The approach in this book does not blame people (either individuals or groups) for the oppression they experience and it goes beyond merely compensating victims of oppression.

Elsewhere (Mullaly, 2001), I have answered the question of why I have adopted oppression as the major explanation for social problems and an anti-oppressive social work practice as the means of dealing with these problems. I repeat it here. First, an understanding of oppression and anti-oppression fits the lived reality of millions of people who find themselves in difficult circumstances because of social forces beyond their direct control. It does not blame victims of social problems, nor does it subscribe to the notion that minor social reform (i.e., liberal-humanist system-tinkering) is all that is required to deal with social problems. Oppression is systemic and is produced and reproduced in everyday social practices and processes in ways that serve the dominant group. It is not a technical problem amenable to technical solutions, but a moral and political problem requiring transformation of the entire constellation of society's oppressive rules, processes, and practices.

Second, an understanding of oppression automatically links the personal with the political. To see service users as victims of classism, patriarchy, racism, ageism, heterosexism, and so on requires an understanding of the structures of oppression and how they impact on individuals.

Third, knowledge of oppression eliminates any claim or pretense that social work is not a political activity. By defining social problems in terms of dominant-subordinate relationships, an anti-oppressive practice must clearly work towards: (1) changing the personal attitudes and behaviours that portray a negative image of marginalized groups; (2) combatting those cultural stereotypes, values, and thought patterns that endorse superior/inferior group relationships; and (3) eliminating institutional patterns, practices, and policies that discriminate against subordinate groups. An anti-oppressive practice is a politically saturated practice.

Fourth, an understanding of oppression provides us with a view of social justice that goes beyond our traditional notions of distributive or redistributive justice (i.e., simply distributing goods and services to resource-poor persons) because it includes the institutional contexts and the social practices and processes that caused the maldistribution of goods, services, and opportunities in the first place (Young, 1990).

Fifth, an anti-oppressive practice based on critical social theory and informed by postmodern insights helps to bridge the modernist ideals of equality, social justice, and solidarity with postmodernist concerns for diversity, difference, and cultural relativity (Pease and Fook, 1999; Thompson, 1998).

Sixth, a critical understanding of oppression helps to expose the Eurocentric biases of the traditional welfare state and of traditional social work practice (Bishop, 1994; Leonard, 1994; Young, 1990).

This book begins in Chapter 1 by taking social work to task for not paying enough attention to causal explanations of social problems. The necessity of sound theory for good social work practice is emphasized, and the theoretical framework used in the book to analyze and explain oppression and to develop anti-oppressive social work practice is presented. The concept and nature of oppression are discussed in Chapter 2, including its origins, its causes and sources, its various forms, its dynamics, the social processes and practices that produce and reproduce it, the political functions it carries out for dominant groups, and the three levels of society at which it occurs. Oppression at the personal level in both its overt and covert forms is discussed in Chapter 3, along with some of the ways that oppressed persons cope with their oppression. Chapter 4 examines several cultural contexts for oppression, including the mass media, entertainment, and advertising, as well as negative stereotypes and dominant discourses. Chapter 5 looks at oppression at the structural or institutional level and shows how oppression at this level is actually a form of violence perpetrated on oppressed persons. The psychology of oppression and the concepts of internalized oppression and domination are examined in Chapter 6. An attempt is made to explain why oppressed persons will often behave in self-harming ways that contribute to their own oppression. Chapter 7 considers the notion of multiple oppression and presents a model showing the complex interactive nature of oppression. The heterogeneity that exists within any oppressed group is also discussed. Using the material from the previous chapters, Chapter 8 articulates an anti-oppressive social work practice at the personal and cultural levels. Similarly, Chapter 9 presents an anti-oppressive social work practice at the structural level. In addition, Chapter 9 outlines a number of principles that are prerequisites for or correlates of anti-oppressive social work practice. The chapter (and the book) ends with what I believe to be the most important ingredient of anti-oppressive social work practice—the constructive use of anger.

Chapter One

Theoretical and Conceptual Considerations

The Imperative of Theory

Unfortunately, many of those who work and study in the helping professions too often view theory as esoteric, abstract, idealistic, and something people like me discuss in universities. Practice, on the other hand, is seen as common-sense, concrete, and occurring in the real world (i.e., outside the ivory towers of universities). Social work is seen by many as essentially carrying out pragmatic and practical tasks. Theory has little direct relevance and actually may obscure the practical nature of social work. Spontaneity and personal qualities of the worker are often considered to be more important than theory. New graduates from social services educational programs and students in field placements are often described by experienced practitioners as naive, idealistic, and in need of 'seasoning' (i.e., practical experience). These experienced practitioners are skeptical of the theory being taught in educational programs and emphasize instead the value of experience (Barbour, 1984).

Howe (1987) contends that this tendency to elevate theoretical ignorance to a level of professional virtue is wrong for two main reasons: (1) theory is part of everyday life—we all use theory; and (2) theoretical ignorance is not a professional virtue but a convenient excuse for sloppy and dishonest practice. We often use theories in our everyday life without being aware that we are doing so. If we see dark clouds and tell ourselves it is going to rain, we have expressed a theory about the relationship between dark clouds and rain. Without such a theory we would often get wet when we saw clouds and did not prepare for rain because we would have no conclusion that it would rain (Williams and McShane, 1988). Just as we often use theory in our personal lives without realizing it, so, too, do social workers often use theory in their professional lives without realizing it.

David Howe (1987) takes to task those 'practical folk' social workers who declare that their practice is not related to theory by showing how all social work practice is related to theory. Everyone (including social workers) sees people and their situations in one way or another. These perceptions are never theory-free because they are based on certain fundamental beliefs and assumptions about people, society, and the relationship between the two. These beliefs and assumptions enable workers to make sense of any situation, and making sense is a 'theory-saturated activity'. And just because a social worker cannot imagine how else to view a situation does not mean that it is unrelated to theory. It just means that this one taken-for-granted reality (theory) is the worker's entire world of sense. In other words, those social workers who call themselves eclectic, pragmatic, or commonsensical base their practice on personally constructed theory (i.e., based on one's own experiences) rather than scientifically constructed theory. A review of the literature by Howe on what social services users want in workers and a review of the literature by Fischer (1978) on what makes social workers effective converge on two aspects of practice: (1) workers must create the conditions conducive to a trusting, caring, and accepting relationship; and (2) workers must make use of well-articulated theories and methods that organize and direct practice in a way that is systematic and recognized by both worker and service user.

Personally Constructed Theory

Lesley, a social work student, was placed in a child protection agency as her final field placement. Part of her orientation to the agency was to meet with several staff members individually to hear what they did in the agency. Dan, an experienced practitioner, told Lesley in a somewhat patronizing manner that she should forget all the theory that the School of Social Work taught her. Dan said that he had been practising for years using only his common sense and his experience and that they had served him well. Lesley asked Dan in a respectful way where his common sense came from. Dan looked perplexed and asked, 'What do you mean?' Lesley replied, 'I was just wondering if your common sense and experiences would be the same for persons who are not male, white, middle-class, and English-speaking.'

Theory carries out four basic functions: description; explanation; prediction; and control and management of events or changes. Social work is practice-based and pursues all four of these functions: it describes phenomena; it attempts to explain what causes them; it predicts future events, including what will happen if certain interventions occur (or do not occur); and it attempts to control and manage events or changes at all levels of human activity (Reynolds, 1971). Howe (1987: 17) asserts that 'If drift and purposelessness are to be avoided, practice needs to be set within a clear framework of explanation, the nature of which leads to a well-articulated practice.'

It is important to remember that theories are not laws. They do not contain iron-clad guaranteed explanations of social phenomena because the human condition and social conditions are too complex to formulate universal laws. The social sciences do not have any laws (in spite of some economists and members of the business establishment presenting market forces as economic laws), but they do have some very good theories. We are at a point in our history where there is much discussion on the nature, dynamics, forms, functions, and causes of oppression, but there is no dominant theory of oppression or dominant approach to anti-oppression. Indeed, an examination of the current literature on the subject, along with a look at the curricula of social services educational programs and just listening to practitioners talk about the subject, could lead one to conclude that everyone believes he or she is writing about or teaching or practising anti-oppressive social work. I am not suggesting that there should be only one theory of oppression or one anti-oppressive approach to practice, but at present anti-oppressive practice seems to be whatever one wants it to be (similar to the concept of 'empowerment' in the 1980s and 1990s). This unfocused analysis of oppression on the part of social work involves a tacit recognition by most social workers that oppression does indeed exist, but consistent with social work in general, three broad approaches are used to deal with this oppression: (1) helping oppressed persons cope with their oppression; (2) attempting to modify/reform the system so that oppressed persons can better fit into it; and (3) contributing to a total transformation of society. Although the three approaches are not inherently mutually exclusive, most social workers have adopted either the first and/or the second approach, while a minority have adopted the third approach.

I agree wholeheartedly with Macey and Moxon (1996), who call for more theoretical and analytical rigour in developing anti-oppressive practice and, conversely, for less attention to theoretical fashion. It is in this spirit that I write this book. It will reflect a particular theoretical position (i.e., critical social theory), which is not intended to be the only or definitive treatment of the subject. It is meant to be analytical and rigorous in its development, however.

Social Problems: The Great Paradox of the Helping Professions

The work of the social services sector is to treat, ameliorate, and/or attempt to eliminate the causes and consequences of social problems such as poverty, crime, alienation, homelessness, child abuse/neglect, spouse abuse, runaway adolescents, and so on. However, although there is a long and voluminous social science literature on social problems, there is no agreed-upon definition or explanation of what a social problem is or why it occurs. For example, in their frequently cited book, *The Study of Social Problems*, Rubington and Weinberg (1995) present seven competing sociological perspectives on social problems (outlined below).

In spite of the plurality of views, a review of the sociological literature reveals that attempts to define social problems contain several common elements (Fleras, 2001; Jamrozik and Nocella, 1998). There has to be: (1) a condition that is societal in nature (2) that affects a significant number of people (3) in ways considered undesirable (4) about which something can be done to rectify the condition. These elements are not self-evident, however, as many questions are left unanswered. Is the condition real or imagined? Does it affect a significant number of people or a number of significant people? Who considers the condition undesirable? What can be done to rectify the condition and who decides this? Should a social problem imply the primacy of human agency, or should it focus on values and social structures? Should the enormity of an event or condition be the criterion for calling it a social problem? There are, of course, no standard answers to these and other similar questions. Like all social phenomena, social problems are, in whole or in part, social constructs based on subjective, objective, and ideological factors (Berger and Luckman, 1966). As such, social problems will have different definitions, interpretations, and proposed remedies.

Evidence of the contentious and pluralistic nature of social problems lies in Rubington and Weinberg's (1995) presentation of seven current theoretical perspectives on social problems that have been developed over time. They are: (1) the social pathology view; (2) the social disorganization perspective; (3) the value conflict perspective; (4) the deviant behaviour perspective; (5) the labelling perspective; (6) critical theory; and (7) the constructionist perspective. Although a comprehensive explanation of these perspectives on social problems is well beyond the limits of this book, a brief outline of each is presented here.

1. *The social pathology view* originated at the end of the nineteenth century. It attributes social problems to character flaws in the individual experiencing the social problem and uses the medical analogy of a sick or maladjusted person who must be treated.
2. *The social disorganization perspective* developed in the 1920s. It ascribes social problems to the social disorganization that emanates from large changes in people's living and work environments, such as rapid industrialization and urbanization or globalization of the economy. This social disorganization, in turn, causes personal disorganization that is often manifest in alcoholism, family breakdown, domestic violence, and so on. The approach to social problems from this perspective is to provide humanitarian social care to persons disrupted by large changes and to bring equilibrium back to the system by way of minor social reforms. In other words, its purpose is to fine-tune rather than overhaul the system.
3. *The value conflict perspective* developed in the 1930s as a result of the Great Depression. It attributes social problems to competing interests, differential access to resources, and other social conflicts that arise in a pluralistic society. As with any competition, there are winners and losers. The resolution to social problems from this perspective is to ensure that no group in society is deprived of opportunities and resources and that everyone is subject to the same rules (even though the rules are made by the dominant group).
4. *The deviant behaviour perspective* became popular in the 1950s and 1960s, when law and order seemed to be the dominant social problem. It explains social deviance as the means for many (disadvantaged) people to overcome the structural barriers to achieving culturally propagated and cherished social goals such as the American (or Canadian or Australian, etc.) 'dream'. Social deviance, then, is seen as a form of adaptation to structural arrangements that preclude the achievement of social goals and expectations by legitimate and

acceptable ways. The strategy to combat social problems from this perspective is to open up the opportunity structures to persons who are disadvantaged by social structures.

5. *The labelling perspective* developed in the 1950s. It turned attention away from deviant acts or deviant people towards those who had the power to define or label certain conduct or people as deviant. The study of social problems from this perspective focuses on how powerful people (including professionals) can preserve their privileged social positions by authoritatively defining (i.e., labelling) social reality as good/normal or bad/deviant.

6. *Critical theory* has its origins in the 1930s, but became prominent in the 1970s with respect to the study of social problems. It attributes social problems to social structures that favour certain groups in society and oppress others along lines of class, race, gender, and so on. The oppressed or subordinate groups are susceptible to all sorts of social problems. The solution is to transform society to one where social equality replaces the present system of dominant-subordinate relationships.

7. *The constructionist perspective* is an elaboration and extension of the labelling perspective. It is applied to a wide range of social phenomena today, including social problems. However, it does not focus on the social condition that is perceived to be a social problem, but on the processes through which social phenomena and social problems are constructed and interpreted. Much attention is given both to the social actors who make claims that a particular condition constitutes a social problem and to the effects of such claims. The identification of social problems is, therefore, a 'claims-making activity' (Fleras, 2001; Spector and Kitsuse, 1987). By identifying those who make their claims stick, the constructionist perspective enables the identification of some aspects of the power structure in society (Jamrozik and Nocella, 1998).

Although postmodernism has not developed a general perspective on 'social problems', Foucault's analysis of criminology converges with labelling theory and constructionism as he argues that criminology is a practice or discourse that creates the category of criminality (Anleu, 1999). Given postmodernism's rejection of grand theories or generalized explanations, it remains to be seen whether or not it can ever develop a 'general' perspective on social problems. Jamrozik and Nocella (1998) contend that postmodernism has limited value for the study of social problems because the notions of class division and of an overriding structure of inequality are not accepted. Conversely, postmodernists such as Bauman (1998) and Lyman (1995) would argue that the imposition of an interpretation of a social problem may not take into account the subjective awareness of those persons who are judged to be experiencing social problems. Surely, the views and experiences of those negatively affected by social problems constitute an important element in the study and treatment of social problems.

What then is the perspective of social problems adopted in this book? My approach is not to adopt one particular perspective and then to defend it to the death. Rather, it is to select aspects of different perspectives (mainly conflict and social constructionist informed by postmodern insights) without sacrificing consistency and compatibility. This approach is similar to that espoused by Fleras (2001: 3):

> Social problems are thought to involve conditions that are socially constructed and contested, yet reflect objective reality; vary over time and place; frequently exhibit a life-cycle from birth to demise to rebirth; are inseparable from the broader context in which they are located; and respond differently to treatment.

Unlike the sociological literature, the social work literature contains a dearth of discussion or explanation of the nature and causes of social problems. It is an unfortunate paradox that the helping professions in general, and social work in particular, which deal with the victims of social problems on a daily basis, tend to accept social ills as an inherently problematic given. Consequently, they fail to provide a general definition or explanation of social problems. For example, in a recent content analysis study of 14 introductory American social work textbooks[1] published between 1988 and 1997, Wachholz and Mullaly (2000) found no discussion of the concept, nature, or explanation of social problems, although most of the books contained entire chapters on working with people experiencing problems of housing, domestic violence, unemployment, poor health, poverty, racism, and so on. In the absence of any theories or discussions on the nature and causes of social problems, social workers in general, and beginning social work students in particular, will tend to adopt the prevailing lay or agency-based definitions of social problems, which have traditionally been victim-blaming (Rose and Black, 1985). This is not to say that social work or other social services areas are totally devoid of any literature or theoretical work that discusses the nature, causes, and effects of social problems. Explanatory accounts of social problems may be found in the social services literature, but only in an exceptional and inconsistent way.

Of the various theories and perspectives that do exist in the social work literature there are three major competing but unequally held explanations for the existence of social problems in liberal democratic societies such as Canada, Australia, and the United States (Coates, 1991; Mullaly, 1997a). Broadly speaking, they include the personal deficiency explanation (which corresponds to the social pathology view); the liberal-humanist explanation (which corresponds to the social disorganization and deviant behaviour views); and the social conflict explanations (which correspond to the critical and labelling views). This does not mean that other perspectives are entirely absent, but these three perspectives are currently dominant in the social work literature.

Although classification schemes of any kind tend to be arbitrary to a degree, they can be helpful in making some sense out of what Carniol (1979) calls 'the jumble of confusion' taught to social work students in the form of an eclectic knowledge base. How do students make sense out of social problems when there are so many competing perspectives but so little discussion or analysis or definition of the nature of social problems in the classroom or in the literature? Since many writers of social work textbooks seem to take societal ills as a given, the only question addressed in the books is how to tackle them. And, since there are

Parking Lots and Social Problems

A few years ago, I was involved in the social policy controversy regarding workfare programs for unemployed social assistance recipients (Mullaly, 1995, 1997b; McFarland and Mullaly, 1996). It seemed to me that the attitudes towards workfare and unemployed persons corresponded with the above three explanations of social problems. These perspectives were particularly evident in a media panel discussion on workfare in which I participated. One panel member attributed people's unemployment to unemployed persons being irresponsible, shy or fearful of work, and dependent on social assistance, and therefore advocated a tough, mandatory, and simple 'work-for-welfare' scheme. A second panel member attributed people's unemployment to lack of education and job skills and advocated a workfare program that would emphasize training and job search counselling. My position was that as long as there were more people looking and needing work than there were jobs, then workfare would not decrease unemployment or reduce welfare costs. I presented the analogy of a parking lot to make my point. If you have a parking lot that holds 100 cars and there are 120 cars wanting to get in the parking lot, then the attendants can shift cars in and out of the lot all day and there will still be 20 cars outside the lot until it is made larger. I argued that one could blame unemployed people for unemployment or blame unemployment on a lack of skills and education, but until the labour market (like the parking lot) was made large enough to accommodate everyone who needed and wanted work there would always be people left outside of it. And workfare does nothing to make the labour market bigger.

so many competing answers to this question, the student and/or worker is continuously confronted with the 'jumble of confusion'. The classification scheme used here to make sense out of social theory, in general, and social problems, in particular, consists of two competing perspectives of society and social problems: the order perspective and the conflict perspective.[2]

Order and Conflict Perspectives

Order and conflict perspectives represent two opposing views on the nature of people, society, and social problems. The former views society as orderly, stable, and unified by shared culture, values, and a consensus on its form and institutions. The latter views society as a continually contested struggle among groups with opposing views and interests. From a conflict perspective, society is held together not by consensus but by differential control of resources and political power. Individuals or groups who benefit from the maintenance of the status quo employ order models of society and social problems, whereas dissident or subordinate groups, striving to institutionalize new claims on society, favour a conflict analysis (e.g., Horton, 1966; Reasons and Perdue, 1981).

Reasons and Perdue have set forth two sets of logically interrelated and essential assumptions, one underpinning the order view of society and one underpinning the conflict view. Table 1.1 contains a modified version of these assumptions, which concern: (1) the nature of human existence, (2) the nature of society, (3) the nature of the relationship between the two, and (4) the nature of social problems. It is important to note that the order and conflict perspectives are not absolute categories in which people fall into one or the other. Most people will hold views that belong to both sets of perspectives. For example, progressive social workers can utilize psychodynamic and/or systems theories in their practice. The difference is that the progressive social workers would recognize the limitations of 'order' theories in that they do not adequately deal with structural variables such as class, race, and gender, nor do they adequately deal with power relations or conflict. Order and conflict perspectives represent two 'ideal types' or ends of a continuum where there is fluidity back and forth rather than two discrete categories with impenetrable boundaries (i.e., a dualism).

Order Perspective

The order perspective, which presently dominates social thought in Anglo democracies, is associated with Durkheim and Weber and more recently with Talcott Parsons. Parsons is usually regarded as the founder of an explicitly functionalist theory of society (McDaniel and Agger, 1984), which is synonymous with a systems analysis (i.e., structural-functional analysis) of society and social problems (Horton, 1966).

Society. Any society is comprised of people who are by nature competitive, acquisitive, self-absorbed, individualistic, and therefore predisposed towards disorder. To establish and maintain order, enduring social institutions are created and rules (laws) established so that human interaction can be regulated. In this way all parts of society can be co-ordinated so that members of society and society's organizations and institutions all contribute to the support, maintenance, and stability of the social system. The basic assumption is that there is agreement on the values and rules of society so that they, along with the social institutions regulating the system, must be learned, respected, and revered by everyone. 'We learn what is expected of us in the family, at school, in the workplace and through the media' (Howe, 1987: 35).

Social problems. If a person does not behave in ways expected of, say, a parent, a wage-earner, or a law-abiding citizen, it is assumed that something went wrong in that person's socialization process. To guard itself against disequilibrium, society will attempt to return the person to normal functioning through its social institutions. If society's official agents, such as teachers, social workers, or police, fail to correct or control the malfunctioning or out-of-step person, then he or she may have to be removed from society and the individual's behaviour neutralized by institutionalization. This removes a threat to social stability and also serves as an example to other would-be non-conformists and deviants.

Because the order view assumes that there is essential agreement among members of society on the nature of the prevailing institutions and dominant

Table 1.1 Assumptions of Order and Conflict Perspectives

	ORDER	CONFLICT
Beliefs about Human Beings	competitive, contentious, individualistic, acquisitive	co-operative, collective, social
Nature of Social Institutions	must endure and regulate human interactions (political, economic, educational, religious, family) to avoid disorder	dynamic with no sacred standing; facilitate economic co-operation, sharing, and common interests
Nature of Society	consists of interdependent and integrated institutions and a supportive ideological base; viewed as an organism or system with each part contributing to the maintenance of the whole	in a society of structural inequality the social nature of human existence is denied, with social institutions seen as serving private rather than public interests
Continuity of Social Institutions	prevail because of agreement (consensus) among society's members	prevail in a society marked by dominant-subordinate relations because of control and coercion
Nature of Relationship between People and Society	members are expected to conform and adapt to consensus-based social arrangements	acceptance, conformity, and adaptation to a coercive and hierarchical social order is questioned
Nature of Social Problems	socialization will occasionally fail whereby reverence for institutions and respect for rules will not be learned; such occurrence on a large scale is a social problem	faulty socialization is more a matter of discriminatory institutions and defective rules that promote the interests of the dominant group
Approach to Social Problems	a) behaviour must be changed through resocialization (rehabilitation, counselling) or neutralized through formal systems of state control (criminal law, prisons, asylums, etc.)	institutions, ideology, and social processes and practices must be changed to protect the social nature of human existence and promote the celebration of cultural diversity
	b) social reform can only involve minor adjustments that are consistent with the nature of the existing system	behavioural change can only involve minor adjustments consistent with co-operative and collective nature of society; massive commitment to behavioural change is a form of blaming the victim
Social Work Theories and Approaches	psychodynamic, systems, ecological	feminist, radical, structural, anti-racist, anti-oppressive

ideology, their existence is taken for granted and the existing order legitimated (Reasons and Perdue, 1981). And because these institutions and their supporting ideology fend off disequilibrium, discontinuity, and disorder of the system, their preservation becomes a social imperative. These assumptions about social institutions being good, necessary, and agreed to, as well as the belief that people are contentious and must be controlled, lead order theorists to conclude that social problems are best described and understood by focusing on lower levels or plateaus of society than on the societal or structural level. In other words, order theorists look at three levels of society for describing, analyzing, and explaining social problems: (1) the individual level, (2) the family level, and (3) the subculture level (Reasons and Perdue, 1981).

At the individual level it is believed that the source of social problems lies within the person him or herself. This is consistent with the social pathology view of social problems. A person is not conforming to the rules, norms, and expectations of society because of some individual trait. Poverty, mental illness, drug addiction, and criminal activity are blamed on supposed personal defects. As Reasons and Perdue point out, at the individual level social problems are personalized. Poverty and crime, for example, are blamed on some defect of the person and what emerges is 'a biographical portrait that separates the individual from society' (ibid., 8). Individuals are carefully scrutinized (diagnosed, assessed) to discover the explanation for the problem.

Examples of this level of explanation would include Cesare Lombroso's explanation of criminal activity being caused by persons who were physically distinct from non-criminals and Freud's psychoanalytic theory where intrapsychic phenomena were hypothesized as the determinants of maladjusted behaviour. Much of social work's earlier casework and psychodynamic practices were based on individual explanations of social problems. Sociobiology is a contemporary development of a theory that holds that genetic information explains social behaviour. For example, in 1988 a psychology professor from the University of Western Ontario in Canada created international controversy when he published an article alleging that race was connected to intelligence, sexual restraint, and personality, among other personal characteristics (Rushton, 1988).

Most order theorists (and many social workers), because they operate from a systems perspective or employ an ecological model when dealing with social problems, are not satisfied with individual levels of explanations of social problems. From this comes the liberal-humanist concept of social disorganization. This concept is based on the notion that the present liberal-capitalist social order contains some defects that create disorganization and bring harm to some people, and it is the job of social services workers to rectify these defects (i.e., to fix the parts of society not working properly so that society works better and is able to persist). Systems theory and an ecological approach to social work, however, do not try to change the fundamental (oppressive) nature of the system but deal with individuals and/or environmental influences *within* the system. The types of environmental influences most frequently dealt with by 'order social workers' are the family and the subculture.

The family as an important social unit has received enormous attention from social workers and others since the early sixties. Family disorganization has been cited as an explanation for most social problems with which social workers deal. The family is routinely analyzed in an attempt to find its contribution to situations of poverty, juvenile delinquency, mental illness, alcoholism, family violence, poor school performance, and so on. Family therapy was at one time (and still is to some social workers) viewed as almost a panacea to society's problems, and 'family dysfunction' replaced 'individual pathology' as the popular explanation for social problems (but did not eliminate individualistic explanations). Rather than blaming social problems on some defect of the person, order theorists and social workers saw the source of problems to be within the family and attributed these problems to poor parenting, undeveloped communication skills, and the like. Rather than a 'sick' individual being blamed for social problems, as neo-conservatives contend, problems are blamed on 'maladaptive' or 'dysfunctional' families. Social problems become family problems.

Explanations of social problems at the subcultural level of society focus on various categories of people who are distinct from the larger majority population by reason of such features as race, ethnicity, sexuality, and class. Subculture theorists believe these subcultural groups have distinctive values that put them at a disadvantage or in conflict with the larger or dominant culture (Reasons and Perdue, 1981). Social problems are not blamed on the individual or the family but attributed to one's culture.

An example of a subcultural theory is the 'culture of poverty' or what is often termed 'the cycle of poverty theory', which attempts to explain poverty by assuming there are common traits among poor people (feelings of inferiority, apathy, dependence, fatalism, little sense of deferred gratification). These traits are said to be passed on to subsequent generations through the process of socialization so that by the time poor children are of school age they have internalized the basic traits of poverty and are not psychologically prepared to take advantage of the opportunities available to them. Little, if any, thought is given in this theory to the possibility that many of these so-called traits of poor people are actually adaptations and adjustments on the part of the poor to cope with poverty rather than actual causes of poverty.

Another subcultural theory is the 'cultural deprivation theory', which attempts to explain the situation of Aboriginal peoples and other minority groups. This theory attributes the second-class status of indigenous people and other minority groups to an inferior culture. In other words, Aboriginal culture is inadequate to prepare Aboriginal persons to function properly (successfully) in the larger society. Examples include: Aboriginal parents do not read to their children; they do not take vacations abroad to expand their children's horizons; there is low motivation for school achievement or for work; there is no concept of the importance of time; welfare and alcoholism are part of this inferior culture. The inevitable conclusion of this subcultural theory is that children of Aboriginal ancestry are culturally deprived. Once so labelled, of course, they are expected to fail in school and often do so.

Both of the above subcultural explanations of social problems are part of a larger process of 'blaming the victim'. William Ryan (1976) outlines this process:

1. Identify the problem.
2. Study those affected by the problem and discover how they are different from the rest of society.
3. Define the differences, which are in fact often the effects of injustice and discrimination, as the causes of the social problem.
4. Assign a government bureaucrat to invent a humanitarian action program to correct the differences by *changing the people* affected by the problem.

Thus, the solution to social problems originating at the subcultural level is to try and untangle, correct, and make up for the deficiencies of these inferior cultures by altering the behaviours of the people themselves. This strategy involves counselling, resocialization, cultural enhancement services, upgrading, rehabilitation, and community education programs. In effect, people are worked on so they can better fit into the mainstream, into the culture of the majority or dominant group. This process of acculturation or assimilation leaves society's social institutions unchanged. It is better to change a minority culture than to change social institutions so that they could accommodate the minority culture.

Social work and the order perspective. Most current social work theories and practices are based on the order perspective. Major activities are personal reform, limited social reform, and advocacy, all of which are carried out in an effort to humanize capitalism, not to change it (Mullaly, 1997a). The major theories—psychoanalytic, family therapies, general systems theory, and the ecological approach—all emanate from the order perspective. In the case of psychoanalytic theory the major task, clearly, is personal reform. In the case of family therapy and general systems theory the major task is to repair the harm or disruption that has upset the healthy functioning of the family or the equilibrium of the system. The ecological approach aims to find the best fit between the person and the system. In none of these theories or approaches is any thought given to the possibility that the source of the problem lies not *within* the system but *is* the system itself. This critical omission is the Achilles heel of conventional, mainstream social work carried out in the order tradition.

This is not to say that progressive social workers would never use general systems theory or the ecological approach. These perspectives are useful in that they provide the social worker with a snapshot of the situation with which they are dealing. They can identify the relevant actors and organizations in an individual's life situation and help to clarify the relationships among them. However, by themselves, they only describe situations and do not provide any causal explanations for a problem or situation. Although these approaches may include the person's immediate environment in their examination of a particular situation, they do not deal with larger-order structural phenomena. By emphasizing only those aspects of the social environment considered amenable to social work practice, systems theory and the ecological approach ignore broader structural social forces, and this in effect reinforces social inequality (Gould, 1987).

Conflict Perspective

The harmony and consensus extolled in the order perspective as characterizing society are not recognized in the conflict perspective. Or, if they are, it is because of an illusion created by the dominant group in society to lead the less powerful into accepting an unequal social order in which the dominant group is the main beneficiary (Howe, 1987). The conflict perspective is strongly identified with critical theory, which attributes social problems to social structures, processes, and practices that favour certain groups in society and oppress others along lines of class, race, gender, age, and so on. Examples of critical theory (or theories) are feminism, Marxism, political economy, anti-racism, a structural approach, postcolonialism, and anti-oppression.

Society. Conflict theorists accept the view of society as a system of interrelated parts but do not believe the parts are held together by consensus and shared interests and values. Rather, they see society comprising inherently opposing groups with respect to interests, values, and expectations. These groups compete for resources and power and those who win exercise their control and power by imposing an ideological world view that holds capitalism as the best of all economic systems (McDaniel and Agger, 1984). The ideological climate or hegemony established by the dominant group involves the formulation of laws, the creation of social institutions, and the distribution of ideas that favour the dominant group. This results in structured inequality marked by vast differences in wealth, status, and power, and consequently the social nature of human existence is denied (Reasons and Perdue, 1981).

Conflict theorists do not accept the present social order. They want radical change. A truly just order can only come about through the radical reorganization of society, not through the extension of social control (Horton, 1966). Conflict theorists' vision of society is one where a new set of social relations is realized, with no one group dominating another (Howe, 1987).

Social problems. Conflict theorists do not believe that social problems normally[3] originate within the individual, the family, or the subculture, as do order theorists, but 'arise from the exploitive and alienating practices of dominant groups' (Horton, 1966: 704). Given the nature of a society marked by inequality and structured along lines of class, gender, race, age, and ability/disability, the explanation for social problems must lie at a higher societal plane than those perceived by order theorists. For conflict theorists the structural level is where social problems are more realistically described, analyzed, and explained (Reasons and Perdue, 1981). This level includes society's institutions and its supportive ideology. At this level a social problem is defined as:

> a condition that involves the social injury of people on a broad scale. The injury may be physical in manifestation (as with disease stemming from a health service geared to income), social-psychological (as with alienation), economic (as with poverty),

political (as with the oppression of dissident groups), or intellectual (as with nonexistent or inadequate education). Social problems ensue from institutional defects and are not to be best interpreted or understood through individuals, families, or subcultures. Thus, the social problem as such is not an aberration but rather a normal consequence of the way in which a society is organized. (Ibid., 12)

Reasons and Perdue point out that the above definition of social problems does not mean that conflict theorists ignore individuals, families, and subcultures as areas for study. The difference is that conflict theorists will always connect these societal planes with the broader structural order of society. In other words, the conflict theorist will always look to public issues (i.e., social institutions and their supportive ideology) as the source of private troubles. And because social problems are rooted in the social order they cannot be resolved by technical or administrative reforms. They can only be resolved by a massive reorganization or transformation of the social system. In sum, the major postulates of the conflict perspective are:

- Society is the setting within which various struggles occur among different groups whose interests, values, and behaviours conflict with one another.
- The state is an important agent participating in the struggle on the side of the powerful groups.
- Social inequality is a result of coercive institutions that legitimate force, fraud, and inheritance as the major means of obtaining rights and privileges.
- Social inequality is a chief source of conflict.
- The state and the law are instruments of oppression controlled and used by the dominant groups for their own benefit.
- Classes are social groups with distinctive interests that inevitably bring them into conflict with other groups with opposed interests. (Ibid., 13–14)

Social work and the conflict perspective. The conflict-oriented social services worker must fight for change at all social, economic, and political levels. A conflict analysis of society reveals who is benefiting from established social arrangements; it shows how domination is maintained; and it suggests what must be done to bring about changes in power and resources. To assist the victims of an oppressive social order the social worker needs to know who holds the power, whose interests are being served by maintaining the status quo, and what devices are being used to keep things as they are (Howe, 1987).

As suggested above, the conflict perspective of social problems does not preclude social intervention at the individual, family, and subcultural levels. The difference between the mainstream and conflict social services worker is that, instead of dealing with each of these levels separately, the conflict worker in every case would search for a connection between people's private troubles and the probable structural source of these troubles. Rather than looking to the individual or family or subculture for the source of distress, the conflict worker— with the person or group experiencing the distress—would seek to understand how the larger social order perpetrates and perpetuates problems. Although the conflict practitioner would do many of the same things as the order practitioner, many differences emanate from the different explanations each holds about the nature of society and of social problems. These differences will be highlighted throughout this book.

Whereas the order perspective underpins much of traditional social services work, the conflict perspective underpins progressive forms of social work practice. For example, most feminists subscribe to the view that society is set up and operates in ways that privilege males (the dominant group) over females (the subordinate group). Correspondingly, anti-racist social workers hold that our laws, social institutions, and ideological climate favour white people as the dominant group over people of colour. Similar positions of privilege are enjoyed by dominant groups with respect to class, sexuality, age, ability, and so on. Conversely, the subordinate groups experience social problems in greater number and with more severity than their privileged counterparts. In other words, dominant groups enjoy their privilege at the expense of subordinate groups by way of an oppressive system of social relations and an unjust set of social conditions (Gil, 1998).

The fundamental argument underpinning the conflict perspective of society in general, and anti-oppressive social work in particular, is that 'the contemporary social order is characterized by a range of social divisions (class, race, gender, age, disability and so on) that both embody and engender inequality, discrimination and oppression' (Thompson, 1998: 3). In their development of anti-oppressive practice using the law, Dalrymple and Burke support this argument. They point out that we live in a society characterized by difference, but that differences are not always regarded positively. 'Differences are used to *exclude* rather than include. This is because relationships within society are the result of the exercise of power on individual, interpersonal and institutional levels' (Dalrymple and Burke, 1995: 8). From the conflict perspective, then, oppression—not individual deficiency or social disorganization—is the major cause of and explanation for social problems. This, of course, necessitates an anti-oppressive form of social work practice to deal with these problems in any meaningful way. Such a practice requires an understanding of the nature of oppression, its dynamics, the social and political functions it carries out in the interests of the dominant groups, its effects on oppressed persons, and the ways that oppressed people cope with and/or resist their oppression. These are some of the topics discussed in the next chapter.

Critical Social Theory

The conflict perspective is part of a larger body of social theory known as critical social theory (or critical theory). One of the foremost writers on critical social theory today, Douglas Kellner, contends that the job of critical theorists is to provide criticisms and alternatives to traditional or mainstream social theory. Critical theory is motivated by an interest in those who are oppressed, is informed by a critique of domination, and is driven by a goal of liberation (Kellner, 1989). It concerns itself with moving from a society characterized by exploitation, inequality, and oppression to one that is emancipatory and free from domination.

Karl Marx is arguably the founder of critical social theory. His ideas and emancipatory intentions have been extended by such notable theorists as Lukacs, Gramsci, the Frankfurt School, and its heir apparent, Jürgen Habermas (see Agger, 1998; Jay, 1973). One writer defines critical social theory in the following way:

> A critical theory of society is defined as a theory having practical intent. As its name suggests, it is critical of existing social and political institutions and practices, but the criticisms it levels are not intended to show how present society is unjust, only to leave everything as it is. A critical theory of society is understood by its advocates as playing a crucial role in changing society. In this, the link between social theory and political practice is perhaps the defining characteristic of critical theory, for a critical theory without a practical dimension would be bankrupt on its own terms. (S. Leonard, 1990: 3)

Critical theory, then, is different from most social science theory constructed according to the canons of scientific inquiry. Traditional social theory may describe and explain social processes and practices, but it is quite independent of any attempts at political practice to change those social processes and practices that are exploitative and discriminatory. Its commitment is to the advancement of knowledge by attempting to *understand* the world as it really is. Conversely, critical theory is committed to change the world 'in ways that can help "emancipate" those on the margins of society' (ibid., xiii). Agger (1998: 15) sums it up best when he says that critical social theory 'conceives human liberation as the highest purpose of intellectual activity'.

Stephen Leonard (1990) outlines three undertakings of a critical social theory: (1) it must locate the sources of domination in actual social practices; (2) it must present an alternative vision (or at least an outline) of a life free from such domination; and (3) it must translate these tasks in a form that is intelligible to those who are oppressed in society. Agger (1998) argues that for a theory to be considered a critical theory, it must have (to some degree) the following features:

- It opposes positivism because knowledge is an active construction by scientists and theorists who necessarily make assumptions about the worlds they study and thus are not strictly value-free.
- It attempts to raise consciousness[4] about present domination, exploitation, and oppression and to demonstrate the possibility of a future society free from these phenomena.
- It argues that oppression is structural—that people's everyday lives are affected by politics, economics, culture, discourse, gender, race, and so on.
- It also argues that structures of oppression are reproduced through the internalization of dominant-subordinate relationships and it attempts to cut through this internalization of oppression by emphasizing the power of agency, both personal and collective, to transform society.

- It avoids determinism and endorses voluntarism by arguing that social change begins in people's everyday lives—in their family roles, workplace, consumer patterns, and so on.
- It rejects economic determinism by conceptualizing a dialectical relationship between structure and agency—structure conditions everyday life, but knowledge of structure can help people change social conditions.
- It holds people responsible for their own liberation and warns against any revolutionary expediency of oppressing others in the name of some future liberation.

Critical social theory is not a singular or unified body of thought. Rather, it is a theory cluster. Several current examples of theory contain enough of the above characteristics to be considered a critical theory—liberation theology, Freire's pedagogy of the oppressed, some forms (i.e., transformative forms) of feminist theory, structural social work theory, and post-colonial theory. My own treatment of oppression and anti-oppression falls unambiguously in the critical social theory cluster. No attempt is made to formulate an overarching (or totalizing) theory of oppression because one theory cannot possibly account for the many forms and sources of oppression, their dynamics and impacts, their interactions and internalizations, their subjective and objective aspects, and so on. And, as Chris Weedon (1997) points out, theory itself is constantly in process. This book is focused on theories and ideas that seem to have explanatory power at this point in time to help us better understand the oppressive social structures, processes, and practices within which we live, and our position within them. In the critical social theory tradition, the political aim of this understanding is to change them.

Modernism and Postmodernism

Modernism has been defined as 'a particular view of the possibilities and direction of human social life [that] is rooted in the Enlightenment and grounded in faith in rational thought' (Johnson, 2000: 232). A modernist perspective holds that truth and knowledge exist as objective reality (as do morality and beauty) that can be discovered, examined, understood, and explained through rational and scientific means and then controlled, used, and exploited for the betterment of the human condition (Howe, 1994; Johnson, 2000). Postmodernism, a rival perspective to modernist thought, has assumed major attention in the past three decades (Harvey, 1989). It proposes that truth, beauty, morality, and social life have no objective reality beyond how we think, talk, and write about them. No social units are fixed entities, and although some representations of social life are more privileged and/or given more legitimacy than others, ultimately no one version of reality is better or truer than another. The debate between these two perspectives strikes at the heart of two basic sets of competing assumptions that underpin the attempts of each to understand the world and our experience of it (Johnson, 2000).

For over a decade and a half now a substantial literature on postmodernism and post-structuralism has developed in both the humanities and social sciences.

However, there is still the tendency on the part of some to impose a complete, clear, and time-defined break (i.e., a great divide) between anything written in the period now known as modernity (which includes most critical theory writings) and writings in the era of postmodernity. Such a position is, of course, neither informed nor critical nor scholarly. Although there are major differences and antagonisms between the two, often ignored, overlooked, or not known in the first place is the fact that postmodernism and critical social theory share a common intellectual heritage. The postmodern writers Baudrillard, Derrida, Foucault, and Lyotard all wrote within the period of modernity, none rejected leftist causes, and all based their critiques of the Enlightenment on the thinking of Nietzsche and Heidegger. The latter is seen by many to be the archetype and trend-setter of postmodernism. Similarly, Nietzsche and Heidegger influenced the Frankfurt School's critique of civilization. Both sets of critiques reject the Cartesian philosophy of identity (with its omission of the Other), the emancipatory myth of teleology, and positivism (Nietzsche declared not only God dead, but all impostor gods such as science and philosophy).

Homi Bhaba (1994: 4–5) takes to task those people who would use the prefix 'post' in the jargon of our times—postmodernism, post-structuralism, post-colonialism, post-feminism—to indicate sequentially 'after' (e.g., after-feminism) or polarity (e.g., anti-modernism). He contends that these uses of 'post' are profoundly parochial. Bhaba takes up Heidegger's (1971) view that a boundary (such as that inherent in the concept of 'post') is not the point at which something stops, but from which something begins its 'presencing'. For example, Bhaba argues that the broader significance of postmodernism is not that we recognize the fragmentation of the grand narratives of post-Enlightenment rationalism, but that the epistemological limits of such ethnocentric ideas are also the 'enunciative boundaries' where a range of other dissonant and dissident voices and histories begin—women, people of colour, colonized nations, and so on.

There are many books now worth consulting for general overviews and critiques of postmodernism (e.g, Agger, 1998; Bauman, 1992; Best and Kellner, 1991; Harvey, 1989), and it is not my intention to reproduce these overviews and critiques here. It is important to note that postmodernism includes but is not restricted to postmodern social theory (Agger, 1998). It also encompasses postmodern architecture, art, and design as well as postmodern literary and cultural theory. With respect to postmodern social theory, there are a variety of perspectives. At one end of the continuum postmodernism is a conservative, individualistic, and nihilistic doctrine, which holds that there is no potential for solidarity among oppressed persons or for social change efforts because every person is his or her own moral agent—a position that Ife (1996) calls an 'anything goes brand of politics' and what Geertz (1986) calls 'witless relativism'. At the other end of the postmodern social theory continuum are those writers who have taken postmodern analyses and criticisms of modernity on board and are attempting to use them as essential ingredients in a necessary (in my view) revitalization of critical social theory. Examples of such social theorists are Ben Agger, Stanley Aronowitz, Nancy Fraser, David Harvey, Frederic Jameson, Douglas Kellner, and

Timothy Luke. Examples of such theorists within the social work and social welfare areas include Jim Ife (1996), Peter Leonard (1997), Bob Mullaly (1997a), and Bob Pease and Jan Fook (1999). This book and its treatment of oppression/anti-oppression follow this 'critical postmodernist' approach. It is informed mainly by the critical theories of Marxism, the Frankfurt School, transformative forms of feminism, black liberation philosophy, the Birmingham School of Cultural Studies, critical postmodernism, and post-colonialism.

Because I am developing a framework of oppression/anti-oppression based on two bodies of social thought (modernist and postmodernist) that are often antagonistic towards one another, it is necessary to explicate some of the major concepts that will become part of this framework. These concepts will be used regularly in subsequent chapters of this book.

Structures of Oppression

All societies set up organizations to carry out certain functions necessary for them to maintain themselves. Examples include an economic system to ensure the production, distribution, and consumption of needed (and desired) goods and services; a legal system to protect people's rights and to facilitate peace and order; a welfare system to attend to the plight of economically deprived people; an education system to provide persons with the knowledge and skills required to participate in the labour force; and religious organizations to tend to the spiritual needs of the population. These organizations are called social institutions. With their patterns of organization, their procedural rules of operating, their policies governing the delivery and use of their services, and their social practices, they constitute what are known as social structures. These structures affect everyone in society.

Traditional critical social theory has always emphasized social structures as a major source of oppression. Because they were originally established by and for the most part are presently dominated by a particular social group—bourgeois, Christian, heterosexual males of European origins—they will primarily reflect and reinforce the assumptions, views, needs, values, culture, and social position of this group. Furthermore, this group enjoys its privilege at the expense of other groups in society—people of colour; the working class; non-Christians; gays, lesbians, and bisexuals; women; and so on. Our social structures are imbued with racism, sexism, patriarchy, and classism in that there is a privileged or dominant group within each one of these social divisions that has more political, social, and usually economic power than the subordinate groups. The dominant relations of men over women, white people over persons of colour, affluent people over poor people, heterosexual over homosexual and bisexual persons, physically able persons over physically and mentally challenged persons 'have been so internalized into the structures of society that they have also become intrinsic to the roles, rules, policies and practices of [social] institutions' (Haney, 1989: 37).

In other words, this domination is not necessarily a conscious or intentional choice on the part of the dominant group as few people in society would consider themselves to be oppressors. Freire (1994) argues that it is more a matter that the dominant group does not see or is not aware of any viable alternative social, economic, or political structures that may be antithetical to dominant-subordinate social relations. Members of the dominant group perceive their monopoly on 'having more' not as a privilege that may dehumanize others but as their inalienable right for having taken advantage of the opportunities that exist for everyone (in their view) in society. Those who do not take advantage of opportunities are either lazy or incompetent, and it is only right that they occupy a subordinate position in society. Little thought is given in this perspective to the possibility that access to opportunities and resources is largely based on one's social position or location rather than strictly on merit or effort. Awareness of the oppressive nature and functions of our current social structures is an essential element of anti-oppressive theory and practice.

Structural Determinism and the Autonomous Subject

Is the individual a relatively autonomous moral agent who is able to act on the surrounding world either to maintain or to change it? Or is the individual's sense of self, of identity, and of autonomy a product of dominant structures and their supportive ideologies? In other words, are human subjects the *creators* or the *products* of the social structures that surround them? Whereas traditional critical social theory has tended to emphasize the significance of structural determinants in forming subjectivity and constraining individual agency (i.e., structural determinism), postmodernism has tended to focus on the micro-processes of people's lives and the everyday choices they make (i.e., human agency).

To be sure, there are extremists in both the modernist and postmodernist camps. For example, some Marxist theorists (e.g., Althusser) reject the human actor as a significant factor in any social change and see changes as the results of impersonal historical factors—even though Marx himself argued that humans produce change and that all history could be seen as the 'history of class struggle', that is, as a result of human agency (P. Leonard, 1997). Conversely, some postmodern writers, in my view, overemphasize the role of human agency in social change and thereby reinforce the conservative notion that people are self-directed individuals able to act in societies with relative freedom of choice and will make decisions to maximize their well-being. The danger here is that people who are resource-poor or living on the margins of society will be viewed as irresponsible, deviant, and not worthy of any assistance because they did not make use of their human agency.

The position taken in this book is that an emphasis on one position only is reductionist in that either micro or macro issues are overlooked, ignored, or rejected. Consistent with the approaches of such writers as Peter Leonard (1997) and Neil Thompson (1998), my approach here is that both structural forces and human agency are integral in developing an understanding of oppression and anti-oppressive practices. To adopt one position as the only viable approach is to create a 'false dichotomy' in critical social theory terms and to see them as 'either/or' oppositionals is to create an 'invalid binary' in postmodern terms.

Sibeon (1991: 24) states the case for including both in any understanding of society, human action, and social change:

> To attempt to account for 'structure' *in terms of* agency is (micro) reductionist . . . equally, to attempt . . . to 'explain' human agency *in terms of* structure is (macro) reductionist. . . . Social life is not reducible to a single reductionist principle of 'micro' or 'macro' explanation. Neither is it possible to arrive at an 'accommodation' or 'compromise' based on a *synthesis* of both of these forms of reductionism. (cited in Thompson, 1998: 48)

Power and Resistance

Related to social structures and human agency are the concepts of power and resistance. Traditional critical social theory tended to view power as a social phenomenon that resided or was concentrated mainly in large structures (e.g., institutions of the state, big business, the Church) and was used/abused by powerful individuals and institutions to maintain dominant-subordinate relationships. To counteract or overcome this use of power, critical theorists advocated for large-scale social movements to mobilize and change the power structures (e.g., the civil rights movement, the suffragette movement, the trade union movement). A corollary to this belief in collective action to bring about social change is that the individual, by him or herself, has no power and thus has to collectivize to obtain some power. Much of the community organization or development literature is predicated on these assumptions of power.

Postmodern theorists have a different view of power than that outlined above. They do not believe it is ultimately concentrated in large structures; rather, power is to be found in different localities, contexts, and social situations. The prison, the school, the hospital, the social worker's office are all examples of where power is dispersed and built up independently of any systematic strategy of class or gender or ethnicity. What happens at each locality cannot be explained by some overarching meta-theory (Harvey, 1989). Foucault saw power not as something that people either did or did not possess, but as an aspect of all social relations, a feature of the interactions between individuals, groups, and organizations. It is a fluid phenomenon open to constant influence and change (Thompson, 1998). Because power can be either constraining or enabling (Rojeck et al., 1988), an ongoing assessment must be made of who is exercising the power, in whose interests, and who has defined the interests (Healy and Leonard, 2000).

Foucault, in his later writings (e.g., 1988), argued that power is always faced with resistance, that every exercise of power is contested, and that resistance itself is an act of countervailing power. This idea has enormous potential for anti-oppressive practice. It challenges the view that individuals or subordinate groups are helpless to do anything about the dominant discursive practices that subjugate and oppress them. Such dominance can be challenged through acts of resistance (i.e., through the use of countervailing power) to undermine the ideas, assumptions, paradigms, and discourses that constitute the dominant discursive practices.

Given the above two competing or contrasting views of power—that it is concentrated within large structures or that it is dispersed and is a critical part of every social relationship—which view is most appropriate for an understanding of oppression and for developing strategies to overcome oppression? My position here is that both views have merit and must be considered in developing anti-oppressive social work practice. Both social structures and individuals are able to exercise power. However, it is patently obvious that a social institution will be able to exercise more power than an individual, and that an individual from the dominant group will, for the most part, be able to exercise more political, social, and economic power than a member of a subordinate group. Power may be dispersed throughout society, but it is not dispersed equally. The notion of 'acts of resistance' would seem to be a powerful tool for anti-oppressive workers (especially, but not exclusively, in the micro-practice area), but one must still be sensitive to the need for collectivization and mobilization as social change strategies. We will return to these issues in the final chapter of this book when an anti-oppressive social work practice is outlined.

Discourse and Language

Traditional critical social theory tended to believe that language simply reflected reality and that knowledge (obtained or given through language) was empowering. The task of progressive social services work from this perspective was to increase one's knowledge of oppression and use this knowledge when working with oppressed groups. However, postmodernism has helped to show us that there is no one universal reality but that there are many realities, and that language does not have the properties of absolute truth but is historically, culturally, and socially contextualized and largely reflects the interests and world views of dominant groups (Mullaly, 1997a). Language is not politically neutral, as evidenced by Howe's (1994: 522) summary of the relationship between power and language:

> Whereas modernity believes that increasing knowledge of the essential and true nature of things produces power, postmodernity reverses the formula, recognizing that the formation of a particular discourse creates contingent centres of power which define areas of knowledge, passing truths and frameworks of explanation and understanding. Those with power can control the language of the discourse and can therefore influence how the world is to be seen and what it will mean. Language promotes some possibilities and excludes others; it constrains what we see and what we do not see.

A related concept to language is that of 'discourse'. Discourse includes not only language, but the rules governing the choice and use of language and how the ideas and language will be framed. A discourse is a framework of thought, meaning, and action (Thompson, 1998), which does not reflect knowledge, reality, or truth but creates and maintains them. 'Knowledge', according to Foucault, is produced by discourse—it is 'the way in which power, language and institutional practices combine at historically specific points to produce particular ways of thinking' (Featherstone and Fawsett, 1994, cited in Stainton and Swift, 1996: 77). Although there is always more than one discourse at any point in time, there is usually one dominant discourse. The current dominant discourse consists of a set of assumptions about the social world that largely reflects the interests of capitalism, patriarchy, and people of European descent. As Agger (1989) points out, even our textbooks are largely written within this dominant discourse. The knowledge that appears in the social science literature assists in the reproduction of the existing social order through: (1) the incorporation of ideas that support the current socio-political order; and (2) the suppression and/or marginalization of scholarship that seeks to challenge or transform it (Agger, 1989, 1992; Wachholz and Mullaly, 2000).

The concept of 'discourse' is another important tool for understanding oppression and for developing anti-oppressive practices. For example, in our own personal and work lives we can avoid language and discourses that reflect and reinforce inequality (Thompson, 1998). By understanding a dominant discourse we can deconstruct it and expose any discriminatory or oppressive assumptions, ideas, and beliefs that may underpin it. And we can develop counter-discourses based on the ideals of equality, fairness, and social justice. These ideas and practices will be examined at greater length in Chapter 8.

Ideology

A concept related to discourse is that of ideology. The meaning of ideology here goes beyond the narrow Marxist view of ideology as a set of ideas that serve to hide the exploitative and alienating aspects of capitalism. An ideology is defined here as *any* consistent set of social, economic, and political assumptions, beliefs, values, and ideals[5] (Mullaly, 1997a). Ideologies provide frameworks for making sense of the social world; in other words, they provide us with a world view. Our thoughts, actions, and interactions are filtered through one or more ideologies (Thompson, 1998). Donald and Hall (1986: ix-x) refer to ideologies as 'frameworks of thought' that 'enable us to make sense of perplexing events and relationships—and, inevitably, impose certain "ways of looking" . . . on those events and relationships which we are struggling to make sense of' (cited in Thompson, 1998: 20). Through the process of socialization, dominant ideologies become so ingrained that we consider them to be taken-for-granted views or common-sense knowledge. An ideology will determine the nature and causal explanations given to social problems, as well as the solutions to these problems, including the types of social interventions and social work activities to be used (Mullaly, 1997a). Thompson (1998) defines ideology as the power of ideas that sustains or confronts discrimination, oppression, and inequality. Although there is some overlap between the two, a discourse may be viewed as the linguistic embodiment of an ideology (Foucault notwithstanding).

More than one ideology tends to exist at any one time, but as with the concept of discourse presented above, there is usually one 'dominant' ideology with the others being 'subordinate' to it. A dominant ideology is the one that represents the position of the dominant groups. For example, capitalism as a social and economic system serves the bourgeoisie more than it does the working class. A subordinate or countervailing ideology is not as prominent as the dominant ideology and is usually in opposition to it. Ideologies based on collectivism and equality (e.g., various forms of socialism, anarchism, non-Soviet Union forms of communism) are subordinate to capitalist ideology (based on individualism and inequality), which is found in all Anglo democracies. Because the dominant ideology is so ingrained, both within the dominant group and within many in the subordinate groups, any other ideology or world view is seldom given credence as containing a workable social or economic system. The existing systems are seen to be natural, normal, and inevitable. Any alternatives are either not seen or are deemed to be mystical, unrealistic, or too problematic to be worth the effort of even considering.

Obviously, ideology is an important component in understanding oppression and developing strategies of anti-oppression. An analysis of the dominant ideology enables us to identify and expose those thought structures that rationalize oppression and, conversely, to promote countervailing ideologies based on social justice and equality. It also helps us better to understand 'internalized oppression', which is why people will often develop loyalty to and defend a social system that discriminates against them. This is not to say that ideological analysis is straightforward today, if it ever was. Critical social theorists have always argued that ideology has been routinized in everyday life through various discourses and practices that suggest the inevitability and rationality of political conformity (Agger, 1998). In talking about the dominant group's preferential access to social opportunities, Adam (1978: 10) says, 'The privileged develop ideologies and the coercive means to protect the[ir] hierarchy of access.' Ideology in postmodern capitalism has become even more dispersed into the symbols and discourses of everyday life (to be taken up in Chapter 4). Featherstone (1991) argues that postmodern ideology is so deeply implanted in daily popular culture that it is difficult to differentiate truth from falsehood and reality from illusion, which is required by any program of consciousness-raising. However, Agger argues that the interpretative tools of deconstruction (another postmodern concept) should be invaluable at detecting and debunking oppressive ideologies.

A Politics of Difference and a Politics of Solidarity

Traditional critical theory emphasizes solidarity among oppressed people, but does so through various meta-narratives and by assuming the notion of a fixed identity. For example, orthodox Marxism calls for solidarity of the working class against capitalism and early second-wave feminism called for solidarity among women against sexism and patriarchy. Solidarity among those who have had common experiences of oppression has been the essence of critical social theory's political practice. Solidarity has underpinned all significant social movements. It is the glue that holds alliances and coalitions together and provides them with their strength as measured by the numbers of people participating.

Without solidarity among oppressed people, resistances to the dominant social order are dispersed and weakened.

However, the politics of solidarity have often neglected the politics of difference by reflecting in their own organizations and culture the very forms of domination and exclusion that existed in the wider society (P. Leonard, 1995). Marxism, for example, has often overlooked other forms of oppression such as patriarchy and racism, and has tended to view the working class as a homogeneous group whose members possess a fixed identity (i.e., an exploited and alienated worker) and who are all equally exploited, not recognizing stratification, ethnicity, gender, and other types of differences among them. Similarly, early second-wave feminism also called for solidarity and unity among oppressed 'sisters' without regard to differences in race, social position, and so on, and without recognizing or acknowledging other forms of oppression experienced by many women. These examples show the need to reject the notion of an essential subjectivity (e.g., women, workers) and to substitute the concept of 'fractured identities' to refer to individual diverse subjects. The notion of fractured identities also helps us in anti-oppressive work to avoid the common practice of identifying and classifying people as either oppressors or oppressed. Everyone in society occupies both roles (identities) at various points in time, although one's principal status will tend to be one or the other. This notion of fractured or multiple identities and the multiplicity of oppression (and domination) are the subjects of Chapter 7.

Postmodernism has been especially important in acknowledging the multiple forms of 'otherness' as they emerge from differences in subjectivity, gender, class, race, and the like. It is this aspect of postmodernism that Stephen Leonard (1990) says gives it a radical edge. Postmodernism helps the anti-oppressive worker develop a new politics of solidarity—one that pursues the idea of fractured identities where differences within particular oppressed groups 'are always given attention, contextualized with reference to their specific geographical location in the world, their class position, and their places within the structures of race and ethnicity . . . age, sexuality, and differences of ability' (P. Leonard, 1995: 7). As an early writer on oppression argued, identities are social constructions whereby 'the minority situation is more a matter of social definition than of social difference' (Adam, 1978: 10). Traits such as gender, skin colour, sexuality, and class are seized upon as bases for inequality. Differences of skin colour, class, gender, and age are today's social realities, but how we deal with these differences is one of the great issues of the day. So far, we (Western society) have tended to use them to rationalize situations and practices of oppression and social inequality. In sum, solidarity within and among oppressed groups is crucial in the struggle for emancipation, but to avoid various forms of oppressive inclusions and exclusions that have occurred in the past it must incorporate a progressive politics of difference (to be discussed in subsequent chapters).

Conclusion

In this chapter I have emphasized the necessity of having clear theoretical frameworks of explanation in which to locate good (informed and well-articu-lated) social work practice. Without analytically and rigorously developed social work theories, practitioners are left with their own personally constructed theo-ries that reflect only the individual worker's particular experiences, social posi-tion, and associated biases. The particular school of social theory adopted in this book is critical social theory informed by postmodern, post-structural, feminist, and post-colonial insights. As opposed to the victim-blaming assumptions inher-ent in the order perspective of society, critical social theory is consistent with the conflict perspective, which locates social problems in systems of dominant-sub-ordinate relationships. Critical social theory is concerned with people who are oppressed, is informed by critical analysis of oppression, and is driven by a goal of emancipation from oppression.

Although this book follows in the critical social theory tradition of advancing our knowledge and understanding of the world of oppression *in order to change it*, it moves beyond the critical theory that belongs to a historical period known as modernity. It makes no claims to universality, reason, and order—claims that in the past have often masked the interests of those making them. This book is consistent with the 'critical postmodernist' approach that has been adopted and developed in the 1990s by several social theorists and social work theorists. This approach represents an attempt to revitalize critical social theory using some of the insights of postmodernism, post-structuralism, and post-colonialism.

Chapter Two

Oppression: An Overview

The Nature of Oppression

Oppression is generally understood as the domination of subordinate groups in society by a powerful (politically, economically, socially, and culturally) group. It entails the various ways that this domination occurs, including how structural arrangements favour the dominant over the subordinate group. However, 'oppression', as a term, is not wholly satisfactory because it implies, for some people (e.g., Lerner, 1986), forceful subordination or evil intent on the part of oppressors. It also assumes a 'fixed identity' on the part of both oppressors and oppressed—that the world is divided into two groups and people belong to either one or the other, but never to both. The position taken here is similar to that of Caroline Ramazanoglu (1989), who argues that although a single term is limited, 'oppression' is a relatively loose concept that can be qualified in different situations or at different historical moments. It does not need to entail, for example, evil intent on the part of men with women as passive victims. Nor does it necessarily deny that persons can be both oppressors and oppressed (the subject of Chapter 7). For example, poor people over the course of history have been exploited and oppressed by affluent persons, yet poor people do not comprise a homogeneous group, as evidenced by the fact that there are 'working' and 'non-working' subgroups of poor people. Although both subgroups are dominated by affluent groups and are oppressed in the form of classism, the working poor also oppress the non-working poor in that they have been among the most vocal critics of the non-working poor and the welfare benefits that go to this latter group.

Oppression, then, is not a static concept but a dynamic and relational one. Gil (1998: 11) argues that once oppression is 'integrated into a society's institutional order and culture, and into the individual consciousness of its people through socialization, oppressive tendencies come to permeate almost all relations.' He points out, however, that the intensity of oppression is not constant, but varies over time as a result of acts of resistance and the emergence of liberation movements based on solidarity to overcome oppression (Freire, 1970, cited ibid.).

To understand what oppression is, it is necessary to know what oppression is not. As discussed in Chapter 1, no one in society is free from social structures. Such structures consist of boundaries, barriers, expectations, and regulations. One could make a loose argument that everyone in society is oppressed because one's choices or freedoms are restricted by the facts of social structures. For example, when a person drives an automobile she/he is obliged to buckle up the seat belt, to drive on one particular side of the road, and to obey all traffic laws and regulations. These restrictions on our freedom cannot be regarded as oppressive. Not everything that frustrates or limits or hurts a person is oppressive. So, if one wishes to distinguish between what oppression is and is not, one has to look at the social context of a particular restriction, limit, or injury (Frye, 1983).

Everyone suffers frustrations, restrictions, and hurt. What determines oppression is when a person is blocked from opportunities to self-development, is excluded from full participation in society, does not have certain rights that the dominant group takes for granted, or is assigned a second-class citizenship, not because of individual talent, merit, or failure, but because of his or her membership in a particular group or category of people. Examples of such groups in Western society are people of colour, women, poor people, and gays and lesbians. 'If an individual is oppressed, it is by virtue of being a member of a group or category of people that is systematically reduced, molded, immobilized. Thus, to recognize a person as oppressed, one has to see that individual as belonging to a group of a certain sort' (ibid., 8).

What Is Oppression?

A group of social work students were overheard one day discussing the 'oppressive actions' of their faculty. 'They have all the power and they abuse it. They expect us to read all kinds of material, write papers, attend classes, participate in discussions, and they evaluate everything we do. On top of this they are always asking us what areas we want to focus on, what methods of evaluation we should have, what our learning objectives should be, and what do we think about everything. Jeez, they want us to do their job for them. There is just too much pressure on students in this program. It is so oppressive!' At another school, a group of social work students were overheard discussing the oppressive actions of their faculty. 'They never ask what we want to learn or how we can learn it or what ways of evaluation we think would be most valuable and helpful. They have rules and policies for everything and if we don't follow them—watch out! They never ask our opinions. They think just because they are the faculty that they know everything and that students have nothing to offer. It's so oppressive in this program!'

Arguably, not all groups in society are oppressed. Nor are all oppressed groups equally oppressed. Those in the dominant mainstream of society are less likely to be oppressed and more likely to be among the oppressors. Women are more likely to be oppressed (by men) as women. Men are less likely to be oppressed as men. People of colour are more likely to be oppressed (by white people) as people of colour. White people are less likely to be oppressed as white people. Gay, lesbian, and bisexual persons are more likely to be oppressed (by heterosexuals) as gay, lesbian, and bisexual persons. Heterosexual persons are less likely to be oppressed as heterosexual persons. This is not to say that oppression is a simple matter of dividing society into two groups: bad people (i.e., the oppressors) and victimized people (i.e., the oppressed). It is much more complex. As indicated above, given the relational nature of oppression, people may be oppressed in some relations and oppressors in others, while some relations may involve mutual oppression (Gil, 1998). These issues are addressed in some detail in Chapter 7.

There is also a danger in presenting oppression as based on a singular group characteristic. Postmodernism cautions us in reducing oppression to monocausal structural explanations (Agger, 1998), for as Lyotard (1988) points out, such explanations simplify the complexities and varieties of social reality by not acknowledging the incredible diversity inherent in people's differing gender, class, race, age, and sexuality positions. So, although women may be oppressed as women, for example, there is great diversity among women that will result in more or less oppression. Yes, all women are oppressed by patriarchy (though there is no agreement among feminists as to how much), but many women are also oppressed by race, class, age, sexuality, standards of beauty, and so on. Oppression is a multi-faceted social phenomenon.

In addition to the fact that oppression is group-based (i.e., dominant groups tend to be the oppressors of groups outside the mainstream), another feature of oppression is that it is not accidental (nor is it usually intentional).

> The experience of oppressed people is that the living of one's life is confined and shaped by forces and barriers which are *not accidental or occasional* and hence avoidable, but are systematically related to each other in such a way as to catch one between and among them and restrict or penalize motion in any direction. (Albert et al., 1986: 19)

Given that oppression is perpetrated and perpetuated by dominant groups and is systematic and continuous in its application, a logical question is: why does it occur? Freire (1994) argues that oppression occurs because it benefits the dominant group. It protects a kind of citizenship that is superior to that of oppressed groups. It protects the oppressors' access to a wider range of better-paying and higher-status work as well as preferential access to and treatment from our social institutions. Oppressed people serve as a ready supply of labour to carry out the menial and dangerous jobs in society, and they also serve as scapegoats for the dominant group during difficult times, often being blamed for inflation, government deficits, crime, recessions, social disruptions, and so forth. In short, oppression carries out certain social or political functions for the dominant group, ensuring that society reproduces itself and maintains the same dominant-subordinate relationships.

The dominant group in society probably does not subscribe to the idea that it uses oppressive behaviour as a means of protecting its favourable position. Most people would not consider themselves as oppressors. In fact, most people would probably believe that oppressive behaviour should not be a part of a democratic society. Why, then, do they engage in oppressive practices? Paulo Freire (1970: 45) eloquently answers this question:

> The oppressors do not perceive their monopoly on *having more* as a privilege which dehumanizes others and themselves. . . . For them, *having more* is an inalienable right, a right they acquired through their own 'effort', with their 'courage to take risks'. If others do not have more, it is because they are incompetent and lazy, and worst of all is their unjustifiable ingratitude towards the 'generous gestures' of the dominant class. Precisely because they are 'ungrateful' and 'envious', the oppressed are regarded as potential enemies who must be watched.

Thus, the view that most oppressors tend to hold of oppressed groups is that they constitute potentially dangerous classes that must be controlled for the good of the whole society. This view is underpinned by a number of myths detailed by Bishop (1994) and summarized below. These myths are part of a larger ideology of oppression that rationalizes it as necessary for the preservation of society.

• *Myth of scarcity*:	There is not enough to go around, which deflects attention from the fact that a small minority owns most of the world's resources.
• *Myth of objective information*:	It is possible for one group (mainly white, Anglo-Saxon, bourgeois males) objectively to observe humanity, thus becoming the authoritative knower.
• *Myth of might is right*:	The majority rules even if it means tyranny of the minority.
• *Stereotyping*:	All members of a group are the same.
• *Blaming the victim*:	People are responsible for their own oppression.
• *Separation, competition, and hierarchy*:	Human beings are competitive by nature and aspire to be ahead/above others.

To this set of myths that supports oppression, Haney (1989) adds two others:

• *Myth of supremacy*:	The dominant educational system, with its emphasis on Western civilization, leads to a belief in the supremacy of a white, Western, male culture
• *Myth of class*:	Most people belong to the middle class, which lives in harmony with a 'higher' (superior) class—this belief mandates and then sanctions a dominant class and a subordinate class.

I would add one more myth to the above list—the *myth of equal opportunity (or meritocracy)*. Because civil and political rights have been equalized under the law, it is believed that if one works hard and takes advantage of the opportunities (education, job market, etc.) available to all, one can succeed in life. If a person fails, the judgment made is that the person did not take advantage of available opportunities (and, therefore, should not be helped). This myth overlooks or does not recognize the fact that not all people are in the same position to take advantage of so-called opportunities, as social position and resources will give some people preferred access to these so-called 'equal' opportunities. And, of course, since the majority of those people who 'fail' are disproportionately from historically disadvantaged and subordinate groups, the notion of superior/inferior groups is reinforced—an example of a process that Ryan (1976) calls 'blaming the victim' (outlined in the previous chapter).

Dominant-subordinate relations form part of a social hierarchy marked by differences in power, status, and resources. A hierarchy is often shaped as a pyramid, with small numbers (a privileged elite) near the top and large numbers (less-privileged subordinate people) near the bottom (McGregor, 1997; Moane, 1999). Most major systems in Western societies are hierarchically organized and male-dominated—politics, economics, religion, art, culture, health, and education (Seager, 1997). However, this male domination is more prevalent in some countries (e.g., France, Portugal, and Greece) and less prevalent in others—the Scandinavian countries have the highest number of women in the top positions of these hierarchies (Karl, 1995). Also, the males at the top of the hierarchies are primarily of a particular race (white), religion (Christian), class (bourgeois), sexual orientation (heterosexual), and tend to be able-bodied (Moane, 1999). It must be noted here that hierarchies also exist *within* subordinate groups themselves (Walkerdine, 1996; Wineman, 1984), a theme that will be explored in Chapter 7.

When a hierarchy becomes established, a dynamic of superiority-inferiority or domination-subordination is inevitable, and there is difficulty maintaining the conceptualization of the lesser (inferior) person having as much intrinsic worth or value as the superior person (Miller, 1986). Once a group is defined as inferior, the label tends to become permanent (Gil, 1998). The superior group judges members of inferior groups to be incapable of performing roles or functions that the dominant group values, and therefore assigns them roles and functions that are poorly valued (such as providing unpaid or ill-paid services). The inferior capacities of members of subordinate groups are considered to be innate or natural (Miller, 1986). For example, women are considered by many men to be biologically inferior and emotionally weak, but also natural caregivers. Therefore, it is believed, the best place for a woman is in the home (of a man) looking after it and (his) children—functions that are not valued. Such stereotypes reinforce, in the dominant group's eyes, the need for hierarchies because they reflect normal and natural social divisions and relations.

Using anthropological studies Gil (1998) shows that relations of domination, subordination, and exploitation within and among human societies were never, nor are they now, normal, natural, and inevitable. Rather, they were, and are, the results of human choices and actions. An essentialist argument sometimes is made that domination and subordination are natural and inevitable outcomes of our human nature because the evidence is all around that we naturally compete and try to gain dominance over others and pursue our own individual interests in almost all activities. However, 'human nature' is a slippery concept. Gil (1976b) argues that you can make an argument that human nature is whatever you want it to be by use of selective evidence. A counter-argument, for example, is that a preponderance of evidence shows it is natural for people to co-operate with each other and work towards the collective good of society. In other words, it may be human nature (if there is a human nature) to be both competitive and co-operative and the society will emphasize one or the other. That is, human nature is socially produced and changeable, not universal, innate, and essential. Gil (1998) also argues against the inevitability thesis of oppression by referring to (1) societies in the past that were not characterized by oppression and inequality; and (2) liberation movements throughout history that have emerged to challenge and overcome oppression and injustice.

Oppression as a Social Justice Issue

David Gil (1994: 98) makes the point that although social work professional codes of ethics require social workers to 'promote social justice', these codes do not specify the meaning of social justice, instead treating it as if it were self-evident. Yet social justice cannot be promoted unless its meaning is first clarified, and we must also examine its relationship to oppression/anti-oppression.

In *Justice and the Politics of Difference*, Iris Marion Young presents a concept of social justice that goes beyond mere distributive/redistributive notions of social justice. Because it encapsulates such elements of oppression as social practices and processes that cause inequitable distributions in the first place, I believe Young's concept of social justice has much more potential for understanding oppression than any distributive notion of social justice. In defining social justice as 'the elimination of institutionalized domination and oppression', Young (1990: 15) contends that contemporary philosophical theories of justice do not conceive justice so broadly. Instead, they restrict themselves to an interpretation of social justice as the morally proper distribution (or redistribution) of benefits and burdens among all of society's members. The benefits to be distributed would include both material resources, such as wealth and income, and non-material social goods, such as rights, opportunities, and power. Issues of distributional justice are analogous to persons dividing a stock of goods and comparing the amount or size of the portions individuals have. Injustice, according to this distributive notion of social justice, would be defined as a situation where one group has a monopoly over a particular good. Even explicitly socialist discussions of social justice fall within the distributional theory, as the principles of distribution (need vs market) are considered paramount to social justice. What distinguishes the distributive perspective of social justice, then, is the tendency to see social justice and distribution as co-extensive concepts.

Welfare capitalism and conventional social work have also adopted the distributional concept of social justice in that the focus has been on the distribution and redistribution of income and other resources (often defined in terms of some kind of social minimum). Discussion has tended to centre on inequalities of wealth and income and the extent to which the state can or should alleviate the suffering of the poor and disadvantaged. Even progressive social work and social welfare writers tend to equate social justice with a redistribution of goods and services. An example is Lena Dominelli, who has written landmark books on feminist social work (Dominelli and McLeod, 1989) and on anti-racist social work (Dominelli, 1988). She contends that 'those endorsing an emancipatory approach to social work have an explicit commitment to social justice' (ibid., 4). She then criticizes the law as limited in pursuing social justice: 'Its [the law's] tendency to individualise collective problems can only mean that *redistributive justice* remains beyond its scope. Yet it is precisely this *form of justice* which black activists, women, and other oppressed groups are demanding' (ibid., 14, emphasis added). It may be that some oppressed groups are demanding this form of justice, but, again, this is limited justice because it does nothing to alter the processes and practices that allow for an unjust share of society's resources to go to one group in the first place.

Obviously, the immediate provision of basic goods and services for people suffering severe deprivation must be a first priority for any group or program seeking social justice. Any conception of justice must take into account the vast differences in the amount of material goods that exist in our society, where thousands starve and live on the streets while others can have anything they want (Young, 1990). From an anti-oppressive perspective, Young identifies a major limitation of the distributional notion of social justice. Equating the scope of social justice with distribution only is misleading in two ways: (1) the social structures, processes, and practices that caused the maldistribution in the first place are ignored; and (2) the limits of the logic of extending the notion of distribution to such non-material goods and resources as rights and opportunities are not recognized. Let us examine these two limitations.

1. *Ignoring social structures, processes, and practices.* Young notes that the distributional view of justice assumes a social atomist or individualist perspective of people in that they are externally related to the goods they possess and only related to one another in terms of a comparison of the amount of goods they possess. The institutional contexts within which distribution occurs are ignored. These institutional contexts go beyond a narrow Marxist account of the mode of production and include all social structures, processes, and practices, the rules and norms that guide them, and the language and symbols that mediate social interactions within them. It is this institutional context that affects distribution—what is distributed, how it gets distributed, who distributes it, who receives it, and what the outcome is. An example presented by Young is economic inequality. Distributive discussions often omit the decision-making structures that determine economic relations in society. Young writes:

Economic domination in our society occurs not simply because persons have more wealth and income than others, as important as this is. Economic domination derives at least as much from the corporate and legal structures and procedures that give some persons the power to make decisions about investment, production, marketing, employment, interest rates, and wages that affect millions of other people. Not all who make these decisions are wealthy or even privileged, *but the decision-making structure operates to reproduce distributive inequality and the unjust constraints on people's lives.* (Ibid., 23, emphasis added)

2. Limits of extending the notion of distribution to non-material goods and resources. Advocates of the distributive theory of justice claim that any issue of justice, including such non-material goods as rights and opportunities, may be treated as some thing or aggregate of things to be possessed and/or distributed and redistributed. Young argues that such treatment produces a misleading conception of the issues of justice involved as it reifies aspects of social life that are better understood as functions of rules, relations, and processes than as things.

Because rights and opportunities are not possessions, distributing or redistributing rights and opportunities is not the same as distributing or redistributing income. Some groups may have rights and opportunities that other groups do not have, but extending them to the groups that do not have them does not entail the formerly privileged group surrendering some of its rights and/or opportunities as it does with a redistribution of income. Rights are not things but relationships, institutionally defined rules specifying what people can do in relation to others. 'Rights refer to doing more than having, to social relationships that enable or constrain action' (ibid., 25). In other words, people may have certain rights but still be unable to exercise them because of particular social constraints based on class, gender, race, and so on. For example, a person living in poverty may have a right to a fair trial but be unable financially to hire proper legal counsel.

Similarly, opportunity connotes doing rather than having. It is a condition of enablement rather than possession, which usually involves a system of social rules and social relations, as well as an individual's skills and abilities. Having opportunities may lead to securing material goods such as food, shelter, and a job, but it is no guarantee that these goods and services will be secured. Just as people may have certain rights but are unable to exercise them, so, too, might people have certain opportunities but because of particular social conditions and practices be constrained from using them. For example, in Australia or in North America we may say that Aboriginal persons have the opportunity to obtain an education, but education occurs in a complex context of social relations. Aboriginal communities tend to have inferior schools, fewer material resources, and less access to tutors and computers. As well, Aboriginal children often experience a degree of culture shock in schools outside Aboriginal communities. This is not to say that distribution is irrelevant to educational opportunities, but opportunity has a wider scope than distribution (ibid.).

The above discussion of the distributive theory of social justice shows that it contains a major limitation. By focusing on something that must be identifiable and assignable it reifies social relations and processes and institutional rules. It gives primacy to substance over relations, rules, and processes by conceiving of people as social atoms, which fails to appreciate that individual identity and capacities are themselves the products of social relations and processes (Taylor, 1985, cited ibid.). Such an atomistic social ontology ignores or obscures the importance of institutional contexts and rules and social relations and processes for understanding issues of social justice. An adequate conception of social justice must be able to understand and evaluate these social phenomena as well as the substance of distribution.

Heller (1987) suggests a conception of justice that includes the above social phenomena that are absent from the distributional concept. She views justice as primarily the virtue of citizenship wherein persons collectively deliberate about problems and issues facing them within their institutions and actions, under conditions free from oppression and domination, with reciprocity and mutual tolerance[1] of differences. Young argues that this conception of justice shifts the focus from distribution issues to procedural issues of participation in deliberation and decision-making. A norm would be just only if people who follow it have an effective voice in its consideration and acceptance. A social condition would be just only if it enabled all people to meet their needs and exercise their freedoms. A social process would be just only if it were an inclusive process with respect to different social groupings. A social practice would be just only if it is in accordance with the way that people carrying it out would like to be treated themselves. Social injustice from this perspective entails not only an unfair distribution of goods and resources, but includes any norm, social condition, social process, or social practice that interferes with or constrains one from fully participating in society, that is, from becoming a full citizen.

This concept of social justice is empowering because it goes beyond a concern with distribution to include the institutional conditions necessary for the development and exercise of individual capacities and collective communication and co-operation (Young, 1990). Oppression consists of institutional conditions that inhibit or prevent one from becoming a full participant in society. A society may be evaluated as just to the degree that it contains and supports the institutional conditions necessary for the promotion of the universal value that everyone has equal intrinsic worth. For all those concerned with developing an adequate conception of social justice and for those committed to social justice in practice, oppression must be a central concern.

The Genealogy of Modern-Day Oppression and the Politics of Identity

It was pointed out above that most members of a dominant group would not consider themselves to be oppressors. Rather, their oppressive and exploitative behaviours, policies, and practices make sense to them because these are largely compatible with the pursuit of socially sanctioned goals and with the internal logic of established social institutions. Gil (1998: 233–4) asks 'how and why did human societies evolve ways of life in which oppression and injustice came to be taken for granted and considered legitimate, and appropriate?' Looking for a single, universal causal explanation for oppression is of course futile, given its complexity and its historical and contextual variability. However, a number of writers have attempted to develop genealogies of oppression. A review of a few of them increases our understanding of oppression as a social phenomenon.

By using anthropological, historical, and archaeological sources, Gil contends that oppression is not inevitable since it only became firmly established in human societies within the past 10,000 years (out of a history of 300,000 years) following the development and spread of agriculture, animal husbandry, and crafts, which gradually generated a stable economic surplus. These new conditions facilitated the emergence of complex divisions of work, social castes, and the spatial and social differentiation of societies into rural and urban areas—all of which set the conditions for oppression and injustice. Gil divides the oppression following the development of agriculture into two types: exploiting strangers (other societies and their people) and exploiting fellow citizens within societies. He then attempts to show how these two types of oppression are the ancient sources for such contemporary manifestations of oppression as racism, classism, sexism, ageism, and heterosexism.

There are other genealogies of oppression in the literature as well. For example, Sidanius and Pratto argue that comparative cultural studies show that before economic systems began to produce and sustain surpluses and wealth, social structures were relatively flat with the exception of gender and age hierarchies that they claim are essentially universal across all known societies. 'As soon as a society can produce an economic surplus, this surplus facilitates the development of role specialization, coalition formation among males, and the creation of an arbitrarily-set hierarchy' (Sidanius and Pratto 1999: 299). Arbitrarily set hierarchies include such social characteristics as class, race, ethnicity, tribe, and nation. Although these hierarchies are established arbitrarily, Sidanius and Pratto contend that once a particular system of group dominance becomes established, it is remarkably stable and resistant to change.

Haney (1989) presents another historical analysis of oppression. She cites four formative events between the fourteenth and nineteenth centuries in Europe and England that shaped contemporary patterns of racism, sexism, classism, and other expressions of oppression. The first was the slave trade that took place between the sixteenth and nineteenth centuries, when millions of African people were forcibly taken from their continent and brought to Europe, England, and what became the United States. The second was the 'enclosure movement', whereby men with money began to regard land as a commodity to make more money, and thus began to evict people from the land they owned to make quicker and bigger profits—creating masses of poor people who had to work for wages. The third formative event was the rise of the modern family and the 'invention of childhood', whereby patriarchy became entrenched and the home became the private, intimate space (the king's castle) separated from both the public sphere and the workplace. Finally, during this same period, nature became increasingly viewed as an object to be subdued and mastered rather than simply understood or lived with—leading eventually to an imagery of nature being penetrated or raped; that is, nature became feminized.

Whatever genealogical account is presented of oppression, there is agreement in the anti-oppression literature, especially among feminist writers, that oppression today was most influenced by post-Renaissance 'man', his science, and his theories (Weedon, 1997). Modern-day forms of oppression are not superstitious carry-overs from the Dark Ages. On the contrary, Young (1990) states that nineteenth- and early twentieth-century scientific and philosophical discourse explicitly proposed and legitimated formal theories of race, sex, age, and national superiority. Also, she contends that the methods of science and the attributes of the scientist have, in part, contributed to the formulation of these theories of superiority/inferiority.

The social construction of a white, bourgeois male as a superior being should not be surprising. In Western thought the philosopher and the scientist, that is, the knower and the producer of knowledge, both came from the same social context—from bourgeois and male-dominated European families. Only children of bourgeois or aristocratic families had the resources to pursue education and scholarship (among other opportunities such as politics, commerce, or leadership of the armed forces). Not only did this group of people control the economy, the political system, the army, and the culture, but also the production of ideas and knowledge. And, as will be argued below, the ideas and knowledge they produced under the banner of science both reflected and reinforced their claims of superiority and their positions of power and dominance.

There has been much criticism of modern scientific reason by critical theorists, feminists, and postmodernists. These criticisms, which were summarized in the previous chapter, have, in part, punctured the authority of modern scientific reason. A major aspect of this criticism has been directed at the construction of the scientist and philosopher as a knower or subject standing outside the objects of knowledge—autonomous, objective, and neutral. The subject is a socially detached observer, standing in the immediate presence of reality but without any involvement in it. Moreover, as Foucault (1977) notes, these observations are not mere passing looks, but are normalizing gazes that assess their object according to some hierarchical standard. Some of the particulars or attributes of the object are then defined as deviant or are devalued in comparison to the norm.

Young (1990) cites recent scholarship revealing the bourgeois, male, and European biases that have been attached to the notion of rationality. That is, the virtues of science have also become the virtues of masculinity—detachment, careful measurement and the manipulation of instruments, comprehensive generalizing and reasoning, and authoritative speech supported by evidence (Keller, 1986, and Merchant, 1978, both cited in Young, 1990). Those articulating and carrying out the code of modern scientific reason were white, bourgeois males speaking for themselves and unmindful that there might be other positions. In other words, they became not only the knowers or truth-seeking subjects, they also became the standards against which all other groups (objects) were measured. This already privileged group assumed the privilege of the authoritative subject of knowledge, and groups they defined differently became the objects of their distancing and mastering observations.

> The imposition of scientific reason's dichotomy between subject and object on hierarchical relations of race, gender, class, and nationality . . . has deep and abiding consequences for the structuring of privilege and oppression. The privileged groups lose their particularity; in assuming the position of the scientific subject they become . . . agents of a universal view from nowhere. The oppressed groups, on the other hand, are locked in their objectified bodies, blind, dumb, and passive. The normalizing gaze of science focused on the objectified bodies of women, Blacks, Jews, homosexuals, old people, the mad and feeble-minded. From its observations emerged theories of sexual, racial, age, and mental or moral superiority. (Young, 1990: 127)

This superior/inferior, normal/abnormal, good/bad distinction did not guarantee respectability and superiority for all white bourgeois men, however, as even they were subject to disease and deviance, especially if they succumbed to sexual impulse. The nineteenth-century medical and moral literature is replete with male fears of becoming effeminate. Therefore, manly men must protect their health and beauty (i.e., their manly virtues) by exercising control over sexual urges. Bishop (1994) contends that every oppressed group has been assigned at least one negative sexual myth, usually that the oppressed group is sexually out of control, immoral, or perverted. All women secretly want to be raped. Gays and lesbians are perverts who engage in unnatural sex acts and want to seduce children. Poor people breed like rabbits. Black men want to rape white women. Black women are sexier than white women. Aboriginal women cannot say no. Disabled and old persons have no sexuality. These stereotyped attributes, of course, reinforced the socially constructed and scientifically legitimated belief that groups other than young, white, bourgeois males were inferior and degenerate.

Scientific legitimation of inequality along lines of gender, class, race, and other social divisions is by no means an artifact of the nineteenth century. The last few decades have seen a resurgence of attempts to define human nature as the product of biological inevitability and assertions that biology determines destiny—including capitalist competition, gender roles, race relations, national and international antagonisms, and so on, and so on (Rose, 1982). 'Biological determinism' is an attempt at a total explanation of human social existence based on two principles: (1) social phenomena are the direct results of the behaviours of individuals; and (2) individual behaviours are the direct results of inborn physical characteristics (Lewontin et al., 1984). Biological determinism has been adopted as a social theory by some sociologists and is known as sociobiology. It has provided the dominant group in general, and the New Right in particular, with a reductionist theory of human nature that ascribes all inequality or social differences to perceived physical differences such as gender, skin colour, and class. There is nothing biologically intrinsic, however, in being, for example, black, Jewish, gay or lesbian, poor. In addition, biological determinism is more than a theory. It is politics as well, for if social inequalities are the results of our biologies, then no social intervention can significantly alter social structures or the positions of people within them. Indeed, we should not even try, because differences among human beings are biologically determined and, therefore, natural and fixed.

Lewontin et al. (1984) cite some examples of studies where biological explanations of social phenomena were used by policy-makers to reject or terminate social programs. The difference in IQ scores between black and white persons was attributed in one American study (Jensen, 1969) to the genetic inferiority of black people (and not to any cultural or linguistic biases of the instruments) and suggested they would be better served if they were educated for mechanical tasks to which their genes predisposed them. This claim of genetic inferiority was extended from blacks to the working class in general in a subsequent study by psychologist Richard Herrnstein (1971). The Nixon administration in the United States seized upon these genetic arguments to make cuts in education and welfare. In the 1970s claims of intellectual inferiority associated with (non-white) race by a psychologist (Eysenck, 1971, 1973) in the UK became an integral part of the campaign against Asian and black immigration in order to curb demands on the welfare system. Claims of basic biological differences between men and women with respect to temperament, cognitive ability, and 'natural' social roles (i.e., claims for the immutability of male supremacy by such academic biologists as E.O. Wilson) contributed to the rejection of the Equal Rights Amendment to the Constitution of the United States in the mid-1970s. In spite of being discredited time and again, biological determinism is still used by dominant groups and their allies to legitimate domination and social inequality.

Biological determinism or sociobiology is really an ideology of oppression, or what Rose (1998) calls 'ultra-Darwinism', rather than science. Feminists and postmodernists, among others, have shown us that social categories are by no means self-evident and unproblematic. The production of social identity changes for any group over time with respect to its defined membership, its relationship to the mainstream, and its position of privilege or punishment (Adam, 1978). In addition, the essentialism of biological explanations infers that there are no differences within social categories—all women are the same, all black people are the same, and so on. Social inequality requires the means to distinguish between sameness and difference, self and other, among people. And biological determinism helps to provide such means.

In a pre-figurative work to postmodernism, Adam (1978: 10) stated:

> A moment's reflection will reveal the extraordinary triviality of traits per se by which disqualification from social opportunities is achieved. A momentous world of meanings accrues about, for example, gender, skin tone, erotic preference [sexual orientation], etc., as these qualities are seized upon as bases for social inequality. The minority [subordinate] situation is more a matter of social definition than of social difference.

Once a social definition is constructed, various social practices and psychological responses come into play to contribute to its institutionalization. In effect, an aggregate of differentiated individuals are categorized (constructed) as a distinct group and consequently share a common status assigned to them by others and are subject to categorical treatment. They become united only by a negative identity.

The Dynamics of Oppression

As argued above, racial, gender, class, mental, and other theories of superiority generated by biological determinism and by nineteenth-century scientific reason have been discredited by twentieth-century research and social movements. There are now considerable pieces of social legislation and social rules in the form of civil, political, and human rights, and affirmative action and employment equity programs that express a commitment to equality among social groups. Ideologies of natural superiority and group domination no longer seem to hold the influence they once did in our society. Nonetheless, various forms of oppression are still rooted in contemporary society, but they appear in different manifestations, having both continuities and discontinuities with past structures.

In its current form, oppression does not mean the exercise of tyranny by a ruling group (at least not in democratic societies). Oppression does not usually occur today through some coercive rule of law (although sometimes it does, as in cases of anti-union legislation) or because of the evil intentions of a dominant group. It mostly occurs through the systemic constraints on subordinate groups, which take the form of unquestioned norms, behaviours, and symbols, and in the underlying assumptions of institutional rules. Oppression is more effective in achieving its apparent function of maintaining the privileged position of the dominant group when both victims and perpetrators are unaware of the dynamics of oppression. When people perceive their situation as natural and inevitable, and there is an illusion of freedom and opportunity, no other weapons are necessary to defend and legitimate unjust ways of life that benefit the privileged groups at the expense of the oppressed groups.

Much of modern-day oppression in Western democracies is structurally systemic, covert or hidden, and unintentional.

> In this extended structural sense oppression refers to the vast and deep injustices some groups suffer as a consequence of often unconscious assumptions and reactions of well-meaning people in ordinary interactions, media and cultural stereotypes, and structural features of bureaucratic hierarchies and market mechanisms, in short, the normal processes of everyday life. We cannot eliminate this structural oppression by getting rid of the rulers or making new laws, because oppressions are systematically reproduced in major economic, political, and cultural institutions. (Young, 1990: 41)

For us to understand the meaning and practice of oppression, Foucault (1977) suggests that we go beyond viewing oppression as the conscious and intentional acts of one group against another. Instead, oppression is often found in such areas as education, the production and distribution of goods and services, public administration, the delivery of health and social services, and the like. In other words, many people contribute to maintaining and reproducing oppression in carrying out many of their day-to-day activities, but they do not understand themselves to be agents of oppression. This is not to say that members of oppressed groups are never intentionally harmed, as evidenced by the rape of women, physical attacks on gay men, locked out workers, and the harassment of people of colour. Nor does it mean that members of oppressed groups never oppress others, as indicated by the verbal attacks of the working poor on the non-working poor, by physical attacks of youth gang members belonging to one oppressed group against youth belonging to another oppressed group or attacks on members belonging to the same oppressed group. In spite of these acts of intentional oppression the contention here is that most oppression today is systemic and unintentional because it is built into our social institutions and carried out unconsciously in our day-to-day activities.

'I have never been oppressed'

One day in a class on anti-oppressive social work, a discussion was occurring on gender oppression. Fiona, a young, single, upper middle-class, white student exclaimed in an animated tone, 'I think all this talk on how women today are downtrodden is grossly exaggerated. I can honestly say that I have NEVER experienced oppression. I had all the things I needed while growing up. No one has ever told me that because I am a woman I could not do whatever I wanted. I am in university today and will be a professional social worker when I am finished. This is not to say that some women don't have it hard, but so do other people. To say that society oppresses women today is a "crock".' The instructor asked the other women in the class if they agreed with Fiona. A lively and awareness-raising discussion ensued.

What are some of the systemic and unintentional daily activities that contribute to oppression in today's society? Bishop (1994) outlines several components that appear to be common to all forms or sources of oppression and help to maintain oppression. First, a position of supremacy is held by the dominant group, and this is backed by 'power over' *others*. This power can include greater material resources, physical strength, weapons, information, decision-making, and control of the media. Both groups internalize this hierarchy and act it out, thus reproducing the hierarchy with minimal resistance. Second, all social groups incur stereotypes. Although stereotypes can be positive, they are most often hurtful and used in a damaging way against subordinate groups. The more powerful groups in society cannot be hurt by stereotypes as much as those with little power. Third, all oppressed groups are susceptible to violence or its threat in society. Beatings, threats, vandalism, and harassment are activities sometimes perpetrated on subordinate groups to keep them in their place whenever they step out of it or think of doing so. Fourth, as mentioned above, all oppressed groups have been assigned at least one negative slur about their sexuality. Usually, it is a belief that members of the oppressed groups are sexually out of control, perverted, or immoral. Fifth, subordinate groups are at a greater risk of being separated from their children than are members of the dominant group. Poor people, Aboriginals, single mothers, blacks, gays and lesbians, and immigrants are all suspect in terms of their abilities to care properly for their children, and consequently they experience more surveillance and intrusions and have less protection of their rights than do those of the dominant group. Fear of losing one's children is, of course, a powerful social control mechanism in obtaining compliance or conformity from subordinate group members.

Forms of Oppression

Although all oppressed groups experience some obstacles to developing their capacities and to participating fully in society, it is impossible to give one essential or universal definition of oppression. Iris Young (1990) has developed a set of five categories or forms of oppression (summarized below) that encompass both distributive issues of injustice and social structures, relations, and practices that go beyond distribution. The first three forms or 'faces' of oppression emerge from the social division of labour, the fourth from culture, and the fifth from violence. Although not all oppressed groups experience all five forms of oppression, they do experience at least one of them and usually more than one.

1. Exploitation

As a form of oppression, exploitation refers to those social processes whereby the dominant group is able to accumulate and maintain status, power, and assets from the energy and labour expended by subordinate groups. Exploitation is primarily experienced by working-class persons, women, and people of colour. With respect to workers, capitalism systematically transfers powers from workers through the private ownership of the means of production and through markets that allocate labour and the ability to buy goods. As well, the powers of workers are diminished by more than the amount transferred, because workers also suffer material deprivation and a loss of control over their work, which results in a loss of self-respect.

The injustice of class division goes beyond the fact that a few people have enormous wealth while many people have little. Exploitation is realized through a structural relationship between the have and have-not groups. Social rules about what work is, who works for whom, how work is to be compensated, and how the results of work are to be distributed and used all operate through a systematic process to produce and reproduce relations of power and inequality.

Women are exploited not only in the Marxist sense that they are wage workers or that their domestic labour is covered by the wages a family receives, but also in terms of their sexual labour, nurturing, caring, and smoothing over workplace tensions (Alexander, 1987; Young, 1990). These tasks, which are often unnoticed and unacknowledged, involve women expending energy in jobs to enhance the wealth, status, or comfort of others, usually men who are released to carry out what is often considered to be more important and creative work. In other words, the power, freedom, and status of men is often attributable to women who work for them, which constitutes a systematic and unreciprocated transfer of power and energy from women to men (Young, 1990).

Along with class and gender, Young argues that there is also a race-specific form of exploitation resulting from members of non-white groups performing *menial* labour tasks for white people. Wherever there is racism in a predominantly white society there is an expectation that members of non-white groups will carry out servant roles for the dominant group—domestics, bellhops, maids, non-professional nannies, porters, busboys, janitors, dishwashers, and the like. In addition to servile, unskilled, minimum-wage, and low-status work with little autonomy, these jobs involve a transfer of energy whereby the servers enhance the status of the served.

Besides Young's contention that menial labour constitutes a form of exploitation, dangerous work can also be considered exploitative. During times of war it is usually poor white and black working men who are on the front lines of the battle, while white bourgeois males—high-ranking officers and officials in departments of defence—direct operations far from the front lines and take credit for victory. Aboriginal men are often recruited as construction workers on skyscrapers and bridges. Female workers are subject to sexual harassment on the job, a type of corporate violence to which men are not typically exposed. Many female workers who earn a living by making repetitive wrist, arm, and back movements, such as secretaries and other keyboard operators, are subject to repetitive strain injuries such as tendonitis and carpal tunnel syndrome (Dekeseredy and Hinch, 1991).

The above forms of exploitation cannot be eliminated by a redistribution of material resources. As long as current structural relations and institutionalized practices remain unaltered, the process of transferring energy and labour from the exploited to the dominant group will reproduce an unequal distribution of goods and benefits. 'Bringing about justice where there is exploitation requires reorganization of institutions and practices of decision-making, alteration of the division of labor, and similar measures of institutional, structural, and cultural change' (Young, 1990: 53).

2. Marginalization

Marginalization affects primarily people of colour, old and young persons, many single mothers and their children, physically and mentally disabled people, unskilled workers, and Aboriginal people. These groups constitute a growing underclass permanently confined to the margins of society because the labour market cannot or will not accommodate them.

Young suggests that marginalization is perhaps the most dangerous form of oppression because it excludes whole groups of people from useful and meaningful participation in society, and this, in turn, may lead to severe material deprivation. Even though advanced capitalist societies have put in place modern welfare systems to deal with the material deprivation, in Anglo democracies, at least, welfare redistribution has not eliminated large-scale suffering, and in the present political climate there is no assurance that the welfare state will continue. As well, the welfare state in liberal democracies has been criticized for denying those who become dependent on it of certain rights and freedoms that others take for granted (Galper, 1975, 1980). Welfare bureaucracies have often treated poor people, the elderly, and disabled individuals who rely on them for support and services with punitive, demeaning, patronizing, and arbitrary policies and regulations that interfere with their basic rights to privacy, respect, and autonomy.

Even when material deprivation is not present, marginalization may still occur. Many old people, for example, have the material means to live comfortable lives, but they are excluded from meaningful social participation and cannot exercise their capacities in socially defined and recognized ways. Most of society's productive and recognized activities are age- and work-related. Thus, older people are often subject to marginality in the form of feelings of uselessness, boredom, and a lack of self-respect. Marginalization constitutes a basic feature of injustice and oppression. To overcome it requires both restructuring productive activity to address a right of participation within the wage system and establishing some socially productive activity outside the wage system.

3. Powerlessness

Powerlessness consists of inhibitions in the development of one's capacities, a lack of decision-making power in one's working life, and exposure to disrespectful treatment because of the status one occupies. It affects primarily non-professional workers, but also people of colour and women to a lesser extent. It is based on the social division of labour but is more complex than the traditional Marxist model of class exploitation in that it recognizes the distinction between the 'middle class' and the 'working class' to be a social division of labour between professionals and non-professionals.

Most workplaces in advanced capitalist societies are organized hierarchically, so that direct participation of workers is rare and decisions (in both the private and public sectors) are imposed on workers and citizens. However, this decision-making power is often mediated by agents who may have no say in the decision, but do exercise power and authority over others in carrying out decisions and policies. The powerless are those who do not have power or authority even in this mediated sense; they 'exercise little creativity or judgement in their work, have no technical expertise or authority, . . . and do not command respect' (Young, 1990: 58–9). Non-professionals suffer this type of oppression; professionals (white males at least) do not.

The status privilege of professionals has three aspects (Sennett and Cobb, 1972, cited in Young, 1990). First, a professional develops her or his capacities and obtains recognition by obtaining a university education and through subsequent professional advancement with an accompanying rise in status. Second, professionals have considerable work autonomy relative to non-professionals and usually have some authority over others, whether subordinate workers or clients. Third, the privileges of the professional extend beyond the workplace to a whole way of life or culture associated with *respectability*. The norms of respectability in our society—in terms of dress, speech, tastes, and demeanour—are those of a professional culture. If one wishes to make a good impression, whether seeking a bank loan or applying for a job or appearing in court, one will often try to look 'professional' or 'respectable' as part of his or her efforts. Typically, professionals receive more respectful treatment in our society than non-professionals.

Allies or Enemies?

Carolyn and Heather, although from different geographical locations, have similar backgrounds. Both were raised in poverty and were exposed to abuse and alcoholism in their families. They and their families received constant visits from child and family services workers, police, and representatives from other regulatory agencies. They were victims of harsh and discriminatory treatment at their respective schools. Both also worked hard, struggled to get an education, received a few breaks, and eventually graduated from social work programs. Here the similarities end. Heather would bend over backwards for the service users with whom she worked, especially if they came from conditions of poverty. She had tremendous empathy for them and a keen understanding of their situations. Carolyn, on the other hand, became one of the most punitive and moralistic social workers in the agency, especially towards those who were poor. She also treated the clerical staff and others in subservient positions in the agency in an overbearing and heavy-handed manner. It is easy to understand Heather's position as an ally and advocate for poor people, but what about Carolyn's?

The power and respectability aspects that accompany the privileged status of being a professional also involve racist and sexist dynamics. People of colour and women who are professionals must prove their respectability again and again. When it is not known that they are professional persons they often are not treated with respect or deference, but when it is revealed that they are, for example, a university teacher or a business executive, they will often receive respect. Conversely, working-class white men are often accorded respect until their non-professional, working-class status is discovered.

The injustices of powerlessness are fundamentally issues of the division of labour and bring into question the social status of those who make decisions and those who carry out these decisions. This social division of labour provides a plausible explanation for why so many social workers are co-opted by our present social system that oppresses many people. As professionals, social workers are able to exercise their capacities through their university training and through the professional development that occurs throughout their careers. In addition, they are able to exercise considerable power over others and get the respect that goes with the privilege of professionalism. It requires considerable commitment as well as energy to work at transforming the society that has given the social worker some amount of power and privilege.

4. Cultural Imperialism

Exploitation, marginalization, and powerlessness all refer to relations of oppression that occur through the social division of work. Feminists, post-colonial theorists, and black liberation philosophers, among others, have identified a different form of oppression—cultural imperialism. This form of oppression comes about when the dominant group universalizes its experience and culture and uses them as the norm. Through a process of ethnocentrism the dominant group, most often without realizing it, projects its experience and culture as representative of all humanity. Our social institutions are based on the culture and experiences of the dominant group, and our educational system, the media, the entertainment industry, literature, and advertising reinforce this notion of a universal culture. We are socialized into this ethnocentric view of the world. Cultural imperialism is experienced in varying degrees by all oppressed groups.

The dominant group reinforces its position by measuring other groups according to the dominant norms (which are the dominant group's own norms). Thus, the differences of women from men, black people or Aboriginal persons from white people, Jews from Christians, gay men, lesbians, and bisexual people from heterosexuals, and workers from professionals become largely constructed as deviance and inferiority. These 'Other' groups experience a double and paradoxical oppression. Stereotypes are used to mark them at the same time their own experiences and perspectives are rendered invisible.

The stereotypes applied to the culturally imperialized, which brand them as deviant and inferior, are so pervasive in society that they are seldom questioned. Examples are that Aboriginal persons are alcoholic and lazy, gay men are promiscuous and perverted, women are good with children, black people are drug addicts and criminals. The fact that culturally dominated groups tend to be defined from the outside not only renders their own experiences and perspectives invisible to the dominant group, but forces oppressed groups to always look at themselves through the eyes of a dominant group that views them with contempt and amusement (Du Bois, 1969, cited in Young, 1990). 'This, then, is the injustice of cultural imperialism: that the oppressed group's own experience and interpretation of social life finds little expression that touches the dominant culture, while the same culture imposes on the oppressed group its experience and interpretation of social life' (Young, 1990: 60). To overcome cultural imperialism it would seem that a necessary step would be for culturally oppressed groups to take over the definition of themselves and assert a positive sense of group difference. This and other matters related to cultural imperialism are the subjects of Chapter 4.

5. Violence

Almost all oppressed groups suffer systematic violence simply because they are subordinate in the social pecking order. Violence includes not just physical attack, but harassment, ridicule, and intimidation, all of which serve the purpose of stigmatizing group members. The oppression of violence lies not only in direct victimization, but in the constant fear that violence may occur, solely on the basis of one's group identity.

Women have reason to fear rape, people of colour have reason to fear harassment, gays and lesbians have reason to fear unprovoked assaults, striking workers have reason to fear attacks by police or strikebreakers. Violence is structural when it is tolerated, accepted, or found unsurprising by the dominant group, or when perpetrators receive little or no punishment, or when structural inequalities lead to morbidity and mortality (this last point is discussed in Chapter 5). Violence is a social practice when people from the dominant group set out looking for people from oppressed groups to beat up, rape, or harass or when members of a subordinate group carry out acts of violence on other members of the same group. This latter form of violence is called 'horizontal violence'. To reform institutions and social practices that encourage, tolerate, or enable violence against members of specific groups will require a change in cultural images, stereotypes, and the day-to-day reproduction of dominance and aversion. Strategies for such change are outlined in the final two chapters of this book.

The above summary of Young's (1990) five faces of oppression avoids the problems associated with either a unified (i.e., there is one form of oppression that is dominant over all others) or a pluralistic account of oppression (there are a number of oppressions that run parallel to one another). The former tends either to omit groups that even the theorist thinks oppressed or to leave out important ways in which groups are oppressed. The latter fails to accommodate the similarities and overlaps in the oppressions of groups on the one hand, and falsely represents the situation of all group members as the same on the other.

Young's framework avoids the above reductions and exclusions. Rather than a full theory of oppression, the five forms of oppression function as objective criteria for determining whether or not individuals and groups are oppressed. Each criterion can be operationalized and applied through the assessment of observable behaviour, status relationships, distributions, texts, and culture. Although the presence of any one of these five conditions is sufficient for calling a group oppressed, different oppressed groups exhibit different combinations of them, as do different individuals within these groups. Comparisons can be made of the ways a particular form of oppression occurs in different groups, or of the combinations of oppressions that groups experience. Obviously, this framework has significant potential for helping social workers understand better the oppressions of people with whom they work in their professional practice.

Some writers have presented sets of control factors or mechanisms (some of which overlap with Young's five forms of oppression) that they believe are characteristic of systems of domination and oppression. For example, Bartky (1990) argues that stereotyping, cultural domination, and sexual objectification are central to maintaining oppression, and Ruth (1988: 438) refers to 'circles of control'—economic control, cultural control, and psychological control (the latter is manifested in internalized oppression, which is the subject of Chapter 6). Geraldine Moane (1999) proposes the following six mechanisms of control that she argues are characteristic of oppression and have important implications for psychological functioning: violence, exclusion from power, economic exploitation, sexual exploitation, control of culture, and fragmentation or 'divide and conquer'. All of these mechanisms are addressed and discussed in various sections of this book.

Personal, Cultural, and Structural Levels of Oppression

At least since 1972, writers have identified specific forms of oppression such as racism (Bromley and Longino, 1972; Dominelli, 1997), violence (Galtung, 1990), and oppression or discrimination in general (Thompson, 1997, 1998) as occurring at three levels: the personal or individual level, the cultural level, and the institutional or structural level. These three levels or locations of oppression are in dynamic interaction with one another, with each level supporting, reinforcing, and influencing oppression on the other two levels and, in turn, being supported, reinforced, and influenced by the other two levels. Thompson (1997) has termed this multi-dimensional perspective as the 'PCS' model of analysis (P for personal, C for cultural, and S for structural). This model, which extends oppression beyond the individual to individual interactions or practitioner-service user encounters, is adopted here as the working model of oppression/anti-oppression.

In some respects, the PCS model of analysis is an elaboration of 'the personal is political' analysis of feminists, social activists, and progressive social workers

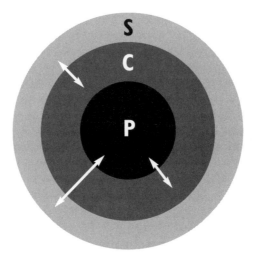

Figure 2.1 PCS Levels of Oppression

(Mullaly, 1997a). It retains the 'personal' and the 'political' as it recognizes that social problems are political or structural by nature and that they cause personal difficulties for many people. Furthermore, just as structural forces affect people, so, too, do people affect structures. This insight is behind all social change movements, ranging from small acts of resistance or protest on an individual level to large social movements such as the civil rights and environmental movements. What is added to this perspective is an intermediary level—the cultural level. Culture (values, norms, and shared patterns of thought) tended to be lumped in with other structural forces in the 'personal is political' model. However, thanks to one of the most important contemporary theoretical movements, cultural studies (to be discussed in Chapter 4), we now have greater understanding of how, by endorsing the idea of a superior culture, the dominant culture of a society reflects and reinforces oppression on the other two levels. Cultural imperialism was outlined above in the section on Young's five forms of oppression.

The individual or personal level is located within both the cultural and structural contexts of society, and the cultural level is located within the structural context (see Figure 2.1). Thus, although we may examine oppression at only the personal level or at one of the other levels, it will be an incomplete examination because one's thoughts, attitudes, and actions can only be understood in the larger context(s) with an awareness that the three levels continuously interact with one another.

Oppression at the personal level comprises those thoughts, attitudes, and behaviours that depict a negative pre-judgment of a particular subordinate social group. It is usually based on stereotypes and may be overt or covert. Without institutional or structural backing these negative thoughts, attitudes, and behaviours constitute prejudice (Dominelli, 1997; Thompson, 1998). Oppression at the personal level and the responses of individual oppressed persons to their oppression are the subjects of Chapter 3.

Oppression at the cultural level consists of those values, norms, and shared patterns of seeing, thinking, and acting, along with an assumed consensus about what is right and normal, that, taken together, endorse the belief in a superior culture. It refers to the ways and discursive practices used by the dominant group to portray subordinate groups in history, literature, the media, stories, movies, humour, stereotypes, and popular culture. It acts as a vehicle for transmitting and presenting the dominant culture as the norm, the message being that everyone should conform to it. Ultimately, it can lead to ethnocentrism, that is, to a narrow view of the world only from within the narrow confines of one culture (Thompson, 1998). It is the cement of cultural oppression that reinforces the personal and structural oppression (Dominelli, 1997). Oppression at the cultural level is the subject of Chapter 4.

Oppression at the structural level refers to the means by which oppression is institutionalized in society. It consists of the ways that social institutions, laws, policies, social processes and practices, the economic and political systems all work together primarily in favour of the dominant group at the expense of subordinate groups. At this level oppression is often given its formal legitimation. An analysis of how social structures produce oppression, including structural violence, is the subject of Chapter 5.

Conclusion

This chapter examined the concept of oppression along several dimensions. Oppression was described as a second-class citizenship that is assigned to people, not on the basis of failure or lack of merit, but because of one's membership in a particular group or category of people. Oppression exists because it carries out a number of positive functions for the dominant group at the expense of subordinate groups. A number of myths that rationalize oppression as necessary for the preservation of society were presented. It was argued that the (re)distributional concept of social justice that has historically underpinned social welfare and social work practice only compensates victims of oppression. It does nothing to alter the social processes and practices that produce and reproduce inequality. A few competing accounts of the genealogy of oppression were presented, with the common element among them being that although oppression is remarkably stable and resistant to change once it is established, it is not a fixed, essentialist, or natural social condition.

Although there are different forms, sources, levels of severity, and experiences associated with oppression, there is a common set of dynamics between dominant and subordinate groups. Iris Marion Young's five categories of oppression, of which all oppressed groups experience at least one (and usually more), were presented. This categorization is adopted here because it encompasses both distributive issues of social injustice and practices that go beyond distribution. Finally, a model of oppression that locates oppression at three levels—personal, cultural, and structural or institutional—was outlined. A more in-depth look at oppression at each of these levels is the subject of the next three chapters.

Chapter Three

Oppression at the Personal Level

Normalizing Gaze and Objectified Bodies

In the last chapter it was pointed out that the scientific discourse of the nineteenth century gave legitimation to a white, male, bourgeois, body type and facial features as the norm or hierarchical standard against which all other groups were measured (Young, 1990). Using this measuring stick, the autonomous, neutral, and objective subject of knowledge, who typically fit these characteristics, observed by way of normalizing gazes (Foucault, 1977) that all other bodies were degenerate or less developed. Whole groups of people came to be defined as different, as the Other, and members of these groups became locked or imprisoned in their bodies.

In addition to a superior body type the nineteenth-century ideal of health and beauty was primarily an ideal of manly virtue[1]—a strong, self-controlled rational man distanced from sexuality, emotion, and everything disorderly or disturbing (Mosse, 1985; Young, 1990). Those groups of people referred to above—among others, people of colour, Jewish persons, and women—came to be defined as the Other because they did not possess the ideal body type, and they also were considered (by white bourgeois males) not to possess these virtues, which affirmed their degeneracy. The notion of whiteness was identified with reason, while blackness was associated with body (Kovel, 1984). This allowed people who were white to identify themselves as possessing reason and, therefore, to be the subject of knowledge, and to identify people of colour as the objects of knowledge (Said, 1978). Nineteenth-century discourse often extended the concept of black to depict Jews and gays and lesbians. A new discourse on old age also occurred at this time, shifting it from an association with wisdom and endurance to an identification with frailty, incontinence, and senility (Cole, 1986, cited in Young, 1990). All groups that did not meet the norm of the young, white, strong, self-controlled, rational, bourgeois man were objectified (in varying degrees) as the degenerate Others.

Subordinate groups were given negative identities by the dominant group on the basis of bodily characteristics (ugly, dirty, smelly, defiled, impure, contaminated, weak, disfigured, sick, and so on) and on the basis of inferior intellect and character (lazy, irrational, intellectually underdeveloped, mentally childlike, hypersexual or asexual, brutish, uncivilized, overly visible, criminal, and so on). This is not to say that all subordinate groups endure the same composite stereotypes (though many do), but all groups have some of these negative characteristics assigned to them by the dominant group.

Acts of Oppression at the Personal Level

As outlined in the previous chapter, oppression at the personal level consists of thoughts, attitudes, and behaviours that depict negative prejudgments of subordinate groups. Oppression at the personal level is usually based on stereotypes and may be manifest in conscious acts of aggression and/or hatred, but today it tends to be in the form of unconscious acts of aversion. Let us look at both types of oppression.

Conscious Acts of Aggression and/or Hatred

Many acts of oppression at the personal level reflect the notion of an inferior and/or ugly body type. African North Americans have experienced a number of derogatory names imposed on them by white people in reference to the colour of their skin—nigger, coon, spade, darky, smokey, shadow. Similarly, North American First Nations people have been subject to the names 'redskin' or 'savage' or 'Chief', people of Asian origin to the degrading labels of 'Japs', 'gooks', or 'slanty-eyes', and physically challenged persons to 'crip' or 'spaz' (the former is an abbreviation of 'cripple' and the latter an abbreviation of 'spastic'). It is still common to hear males address or talk about women in vulgar versions of their sexual characteristics. This insulting type of labelling may be made directly to a member of a subordinate group or it may be found in locker-room humour or in graffiti. Whatever form it takes, name-calling devalues members of subordinate groups by accentuating differences between the dominant and subordinate groups in a negative way. It reflects the belief that the characteristics of the dominant group (skin colour, eye shape, male body) represent the norm or universal standard and that anything not meeting the standard is open to ridicule and insult. The message to the subordinate group is that they are inferior because they do not match up with these standards or norms.

Although legislation today aims to protect people from harassment and codes of behaviour make these actions socially unacceptable, they still occur too often. One just has to visit the men's washrooms in any *university* to find some of the most extreme racist, sexist, homophobic, and anti-Semitic sentiments written on the lavatory walls and doors. These anonymous expressions of hatred towards persons who are defined as different and as having ugly or fearful bodies constitute clear evidence that those thoughts, beliefs, and attitudes, which portray a negative prejudgment of subordinate groups, still exist today in spite of a discursive commitment to equal respect and consideration for all.

Objectified and socially constructed ugly and degenerate bodies are not the only objects of conscious acts of oppression; after all, nineteenth-century biological and medical science held that the superior body type directly determines the intellectual and character superiority of persons in this group (West, 1982). Conversely, the inferior body type directly determines the intellectual and character inferiority of persons in this group. With the universal standard being a rational, strong, self-controlled, and autonomous white, bourgeois male, whole groups of people were and are classified as intellectually and morally degenerate (Young, 1990). For example, women were considered to be physically delicate and weak because of the specific constitution of their bodies and subject to madness, irrationality, and childlike behaviour (Astbury, 1996).

The Iron Lady

A common response in the US in the 1970s and 1980s to the question of whether or not a woman could or should ever become President was: 'No, because at the first indication of a war a woman President would likely start to cry' (rather than exercise the manly virtues of decisive, strong, and strategic leadership). There are exceptions to this gender-exclusive rule, however. Margaret Thatcher, former Prime Minister of the United Kingdom, was often portrayed as 'male-like' or 'a pseudo male' (possessing strength, reason, and able to make the hard decisions, etc.) as evidenced by the label of 'the *iron* lady' that was given to her.

Other characteristics often assigned to members of subordinate groups include: sexual licentiousness (women and people of colour), sexual degeneracy (gay and lesbian persons), asexuality (older persons and disabled people), childlike stupidity (people of colour, women, older persons), irresponsibility (most subordinate groups), laziness (most subordinate groups), criminality (most subordinate groups), and intellectual deficiencies (most subordinate groups).

These and other characteristics, which are defined by the dominant group as part of the identity of subordinate groups, are used in the same way as derogatory names—to harass, ridicule, defame, intimidate, and, in effect, remind subordinate populations of their second-class status. At the same time the definition of subordinate groups as degenerate and intellectually and morally inferior provides a convenient rationale for reserving most of life's opportunities for the dominant group. Decent income and jobs, education, good health, supportive networks, social and political inclusion, and adequate housing in nice neighbourhoods ought to go to members of the dominant group, who are considered to be more deserving and worthy. Otherwise, opportunities would only be squandered away. Members of the dominant class will often point to the vandalizing of public housing as evidence of a lazy, irresponsible, and ungrateful group of people.

The most extreme form of a conscious act of aggression and hatred is violence against members of oppressed groups. The fear and loathing of socially

Ungrateful or Unjust?

John, a 14-year-old boy, and his family lived in a relatively new public housing neighbourhood. It seemed to John that as soon as the parents of friends he made outside his neighbourhood learned where he lived, he was not invited back to their homes. He also had applied for a number of part-time jobs, but whenever the person taking his application noticed John's address, the tone of the interview changed and John never received a call to come to work, although others outside the neighbourhood did. At school he did not seem to receive the same favourable treatment from certain teachers that other children did. One day he overheard one of his teachers referring to 'the troublemakers who come from that welfare neighbourhood'. It seemed to John that his home address caused him a lot of problems. He soon became a willing and regular participant in vandalizing the property and grounds of the public housing estate.

constructed ugly bodies, in concert with cultural stereotypes, have much to do with harassment and physical violence perpetrated on members of oppressed groups. In the previous chapter an overview of violence was presented as one of Young's (1990) five forms or faces of oppression. Young notes that violence is: (1) systemic when it is directed at members of a subordinate group just because they are members of that group; (2) a social practice when members of a subordinate group are sought to beat up, rape, or taunt; (3) legitimized when it is tolerated or found to be unsurprising because it happens frequently, or when perpetrators receive light or no punishment; (4) mostly irrational and xenophobic; and (5) a form of injustice that a theory of distributive justice does not capture.

All members of subordinate groups must live with the fear of random and unprovoked physical attacks on their person, family, or property. African Americans may not fear lynching and public whipping to the extent they once did, but they still experience a high incidence of racial violence, including beatings and rape by on-duty police officers. Gay-bashing is common today, as is the physical abuse of children and the elderly. Physical violence (beatings, sexual assault, murder) against women continues at epidemic levels. Ethnic violence is prevalent against Jews, as is government-sanctioned violence by police against striking workers on picket lines. The terrorist attacks of 11 September 2001 in the United States have resulted in wide-scale violence in many Western countries against people of Middle Eastern extraction and persons of the Islamic faith, with public harassment, damage and destruction of mosques, beatings, and even murders reported in the media. Even when there is no violence, the threat is ever present, and this threat and the accompanying fear rob oppressed people of freedom, dignity, and peace of mind.

Unconscious Acts of Aversion and Avoidance

It is probably true today that theories and ideologies of superiority do not exercise the influence in society that they once did. After much struggle on the parts of all subordinate groups there is a formal commitment in most Western democracies to some sense of equality, as evidenced by civil rights and human rights codes and legislation regarding affirmative action, equal pay, and other policies of equal treatment. And, as Young (1990: 132) notes:

> Commitment to formal equality for all persons tends also to support a public etiquette that disapproves of speech and behavior calling attention in public settings to a person's sex, race, sexual orientation, class status, religion, and the like. . . . The ideal promoted by current social etiquette is that these group differences should not matter in our everyday encounters with one another.

This is not to say that committed racists, sexists, and so on are relics of the past, but such people must be more careful today of how and when and where they exhibit overt acts of oppression and prejudice. Many (maybe most) acts of oppression at the personal level today are not of the open and aggressive type but occur as aversive behaviour that emerges in everyday interactions between persons in dominant and subordinate groups. In other words, much oppressive behaviour at the personal level has gone underground. Hostility, fear, avoidance, and feelings of superiority are expressed by dominant group members in mundane contexts of interaction in terms of their gestures, speech, tone of voice, and body movements (Brittan and Maynard, 1984). For example, dominant group members may show that they are uncomfortable or nervous around persons of a subordinate group by avoiding eye contact, increasing the physical distance between them, using kinetic gestures of defence and aversion, or going out of their way to avoid interaction or sharing the same approximate space.

It is not uncommon, for example, for men to be nervous around a group of women, or for white people to cross the street when they see two or more black people coming down the street towards them. It is not unusual for a loving heterosexual couple to recoil in horror upon seeing a gay or lesbian couple displaying the very same affectionate behaviour that they themselves display, or for a black person to be followed around a store by security people, or for people to shout at and talk in baby terms to an older person, or for the noise level in a room of white people to diminish when a person of colour enters, or for a salesperson to look at and address the male partner of a couple, only asking the woman what she thinks about the colour of the car or the kitchen in a house that is being shown to them.

Rather than overt sexism, racism, and so on, the above are examples of covert acts of oppression or of oppression having gone underground. Many members of the dominant group exhibiting these aversive and unconscious acts would deny that they are prejudiced or that they acted in an oppressive way. In fact, many of these same people may be consciously committed to equality and respect for members of all social groups. This shows how entrenched sexism, racism, ageism, classism, and the like are in our individual, collective, and cultural psyches, and why unconscious oppression is so difficult to counteract and eradicate. Unlike explicit acts of aggression and exclusion, acts of aversion and avoidance cannot be legislated against. There is no legal or policy remedy to this kind of oppression.

Effects of Oppression on the Individual

Thus far, this chapter has looked at acts of oppression that occur at the personal level, that is, those acts of aversion or avoidance directed specifically (though not necessarily intentionally) at subordinate group members personally by dominant group members. The remainder of this chapter discusses the impact and effects of oppression on the individual who is oppressed. Of course, oppression at any level (personal, cultural, or structural) is felt eventually by subordinate persons at the individual level. In effect, what exists is a three-headed monster (i.e., personal, cultural, and structural forms of oppression) that treats subordinate groups in an inhumane, unjust, and discriminatory manner. The oppressed person experiences the full impact of multiple-level oppression every day. Therefore, questions to be addressed here include: How does oppression affect one's identity or sense of self? How does it impact on one's sense of location in society? And what effect does it have on the individual's self-esteem and other facets of the personal psyche?

Impact on Identity

Oppression at the personal level reinforces the privileged social position of the dominant group and the disadvantaged position of the subordinate group in a number of ways. First, the group identity of the subordinate group is defined by the dominant group and subordinate group members have no say in this definition. It is imposed on them, marking them as different and inferior—as the Other, and there is no escape from it because the behaviour and reactions of members of the dominant group and other subordinate groups (and members of one's own identity group in some cases) are constant reminders of it. Conversely, dominant groups have no need to think about their group identity because they occupy an unmarked, neutral, normative, and universal position (Young, 1990). The identity as inferior that is imposed on subordinate groups on a personal level is reinforced by the ways they are portrayed in the dominant culture, through the media, the education system, advertising, literature, movies, and so on, as will be discussed in the next chapter.

When members of subordinate groups experience aversive and avoidance behaviour from the dominant group they are reminded of their group identity and feel either marked (when the behaviour is aversive) or invisible (when the behaviour is avoidance) or not taken seriously or demeaned. This presents a double bind for them. They can either protest aversive or avoidance behaviour, or they can suffer its humiliation in silence. Because we live in a society where an aspect of the dominant culture is to avoid conflict and confrontation, it tends to be seen as tactless and in poor taste to draw attention to covert and often unintentional acts of racism, sexism, ageism, and so on. If a member of a subordinate group protests against such acts, it may lead to his or her exclusion from public or social events. As well, one who does protest against this kind of oppression is often accused of being too sensitive, or making something out of nothing, or overreacting. Thus, the subordinate group member is left with the choice when experiencing oppressive behaviour of either suffering it in silence or protesting such behaviour and then being made to feel crazy.

The above, of course, begs the question, 'What is identity, what are its functions, and why is it so important?' 'Identity' is one of those loose and slippery terms with no universal agreement on its precise meaning. Breakwell (1986) says that what one theorist calls 'identity' another will call the 'self', even though both are attempting to understand the same fundamental phenomena. Some writers view identity to be one of a set (along with character, self-concept, personality, status) of social, psychological, and behavioural characteristics that differentiate one person from another. Breakwell points out that one's theoretical orientation will largely determine the meaning one gives to identity. For example, in the psychoanalytic tradition identity is a global awareness (i.e., awareness of oneself in relation to others) achieved through crisis and sequential identifications in social relations; the behaviourist talks in terms of personality; the symbolic interactionist might talk of the self-concept; and to the role theorist identity is any label applied consistently to a person. The concept of identity adopted here is social-psychological, and links socio-political with intrapsychic phenomena in the belief that both contribute to the establishment of or changes to one's identity or identities. In other words, this concept of identity focuses on the dialectical relationship between social context and personal psychology and considers how they both contribute to a person's identity.

There is a voluminous psychological literature on identity and no attempt will be made here to summarize it. Instead, a selection of ideas, which are consistent with a social-psychological perspective of identity, will be presented. It is hoped that these ideas will contribute to an understanding of what an identity is; how oppression affects identity; what some of the negative intrapersonal and interpersonal consequences are for oppressed persons of having a negative identity; and how they might respond on intrapersonal, interpersonal, and intergroup levels.

Structure of Identity

In its simplest terms, identity refers to the conditions or distinguishing features that mark or characterize or identify an individual. A person may be identified by his or her name, history, present social status, gender, race, personality, age, appearance (height, weight, etc.), religion, and so on. Some of these identity characteristics are obviously associated with one's physical being; others are invisible (e.g., sexual orientation, religion); still others are psychological (e.g., personality); and yet others are social characteristics (e.g., class) or social roles (e.g., parent, academic).

Obviously, many factors contribute to identity. In fact, 'identity' is probably an inaccurate or incorrect term as each of us has many identities. Each of the above markers or identity characteristics may constitute an identity in itself. For example, *part* of my identity to those who know me or know of me is that of a male. However, for people who do not know me but see me on the street my *total* identity may be that of a male, or at least a white male. This point touches on the legitimate concern of postmodernists—that we should not assume that individuals have only one identity. Each component of identity may be considered to be an identity in itself, or what some writers refer to as a 'sub-identity'. These characteristics or defining properties of identity (or sub-identities) are known in the literature as the *content* of identity (ibid.). Even though many of these characteristics are shared with other people, the particular constellation or configuration attached to a person makes that person distinctive and gives him or her a unique overall identity. It should be noted that the contents of identity are not static. The characteristics of identity will shift in relation to each other according to the *context* in which the identity is located.

My Shifting Identity

While living in Australia I found myself emphasizing my Canadianness more than I ever did living in Canada. Similarly, when I was attending university in central Canada in the late 1970s, I had emphasized (some would say overemphasized) my 'Atlantic Canadianness'. Waddell and Cairns (1986) explain such shifts in emphasis as being determined by different situations or contexts. That is, identity components (or sub-identities) will be highly relevant or emphasized in one context (e.g., my being Canadian in Australia) and irrelevant or inappropriate to emphasize in other contexts (e.g., my being Canadian in Canada).

In addition to the contents of identity not being static, Breakwell points out that the organization of the contents are not static either. Some people will have a relatively fixed hierarchy of identity components while others will have no level of fixed connectedness among the characteristics of their identities. Although it is not known exactly what causes this variation, to some extent the organization of components must depend on the value attached to them. The *content* dimension is one part of the structure of identity. The *value* dimension is the other. A positive or negative value attached to each component of identity is based on current social beliefs and values in interaction with previously established value codes (ibid.). And, of course, those components that have a positive value attached to them correspond highly with the identity characteristics of the dominant group, whereas the negatively valued identity components tend to be associated with subordinate groups. Although the value attached to various contents of identity is socially determined, the powerful and dominant group largely determines the value and, as argued in Chapter 2, they do this in a way that protects and reproduces their privileged social position.

The individual learns his or her social and personal worth through interactions with others in the context of dominant ideologies. And, as Tajfel (1981) reminds us, the determination of self-worth or social worth cannot occur free from stereo-types. This is not to say that an absolute systems determination of values occurs, for self-reflection and evaluation may lead to a rejection of current dominant social values. There should be no assumption that identity is without agency—an important point for anti-oppressive practice. However, the tendency is for domi-nant ideologies to influence the individual's choice of personal values and beliefs about one's identity and its value.

Any viable exploration of identity must differentiate between *personal identity* and *social identity*. The latter is that part of the self-concept derived from group associations, interpersonal relationships, and social position or status, whereas the former is free of such role or relationship determinants (Breakwell, 1986). There is considerable disagreement in the psychological literature about the rela-tionship between these two concepts and whether or not the person does experi-ence or can differentiate between both types or aspects of identity. The position taken here is that personal identity is how the person views him or herself, whereas social identity is how society or the world surrounding the person views him or her. As mentioned above and argued in more detail below, how society views (and responds to) the individual will have an effect on, but not necessarily totally determine, how the individual views him or herself. With respect to the question of whether or not the individual experiences both types of identity and/or can differentiate between them, the history of oppression and oppressed persons answers this question in the affirmative.

Oppressed persons learn early in their lives how society views and treats them, and throughout their lives this learning is reinforced. The (dominant or subordi-nate) individual actively accommodates to and assimilates portraits of the self supplied by the social world. When one's personal identity matches the negative portrait or social identity provided by the social world, then we have a case of internalized oppression. When there is incongruence between the personal iden-tity and social identity of a subordinate person, there is also potential for resis-tance and change. In the case of incongruence between both sets of identities, however, there is also the likelihood of uncertainty, insecurity, guilt, and anguish on the oppressed person's part—and this must be confronted before any efforts at social change can occur.

Processes of Identity Formation

Consistent with the social-psychological approach (and with phenomenological and historical materialist philosophies and critical social theory), identity is the process and product of an individual's interactions with influences in the physi-cal and social worlds. These influences include, among others, one's history, one's family, and the dominant ideology at the particular point of history in which the individual is going through the process of identity formation. For example, many people who experienced the Great Depression of the 1930s are still influenced by this event in their current lives, as evidenced by an extreme caution and frugality with money and purchases. Part of our identity is our his-tory and culture—who we are, where we came from, the social status and other characteristics of our family and/or social group. The family is a significant determinant of identity because it is the actual location in which people are socialized in the first instance and learn about their place in the world, how to behave in it, and what to expect from it based on personal and family characteristics. The dominant ideology of a society, which is transmitted to the individual through interactions with others and through the dominant culture (see Chapter 4), identifies and legitimates an individual's position of dominance or subordination in society according to the person's class, gender, race, age, sexuality, and so on. Persons develop and internalize a picture of themselves, in large part, according to how society views them, which, in turn, is determined largely by ideology, stereotypes, myths, and ethnocentrism.

The notion that identity may totally be a product of dominant ideologies is, of course, overly simplistic and crudely deterministic. At any one time, the social context contains many competing ideologies or explanations of social events, conditions, relationships, and dynamics. In other words, the individual is presented with many competing and contradictory explanations and interpretations of social reality. There is no doubt that the dominant ideology will significantly influence the formation of one's identity, but it will not necessarily be the sole determinant of one's identity. The individual is not without agency. For Peter Leonard (1984) these contradictions provide the individual with choices and it is these choices that form part of the dialectic between the individual and the social order. The individual, on the one hand, is shaped, influenced, and penetrated by the social order—its institutions, ideologies, and social practices. On the other hand, the individual will mediate the conflicting messages and ideologies and engage in acts of resistance (often unconsciously) to the dominant ideology and attempt to change the social order. The individual both shapes and is shaped by the social order. Identity is both a social product and a social process.

Unfortunately, there is no satisfactory or comprehensive explanation or theory of how choices among competing ideologies and contradictory messages are made by persons and incorporated into their structure of identity. Breakwell (1986) proposes three goals that are inherent in the identity process and that give it purpose and direction. The identity processes work to produce: (1) uniqueness or distinctiveness of identity for the individual; (2) continuity of identity across time and context; and (3) a feeling of personal worth and social value. There is little known about how these three relate to each other and it is obvious that there will be occasions where they conflict with one another. Apter (1983) would add a fourth goal to identity formation, which would also guide the processes of identity—the desire for autonomy. These goals suggest that a healthy identity is one that, at a minimum, has its own distinct nature and character; is relatively stable over time and in different social contexts; reflects a positive self-image on the part of the person and a sense of value to society; and allows the person to be self-determining and able to act with purpose on his or her own behalf.

It has already been argued that many or most members of subordinate or oppressed groups will not have healthy identities as defined by the above criteria. To be viewed and treated as second-class, sub-human, expendable, and the like and to have an identity imposed by another group based on stereotypes and Eurocentric ideas and sentiments of an inferior Other does not facilitate the development of a healthy identity. In other words, oppression interferes with the development or maintenance of a healthy identity—and a healthy or strong sense of identity would seem to be essential for tackling one's oppression and oppressors. Building and strengthening identity would seem to be essential activities in an anti-oppressive social work practice.

Coping with Threats to Identity

As mentioned above, oppression presents a serious threat to the development or to the existence of a healthy identity. Because a healthy identity is part of what it is to be an autonomous and self-directing human, the individual will develop and employ coping strategies to protect his or her identity. A coping strategy is any action the individual believes will protect the self (i.e., physical, psychological, or social self). Breakwell (1986) outlines a number of coping mechanisms that operate at the intrapersonal or intrapsychic, interpersonal, and group (inter and intra) levels, with strategies at one level having repercussions for events at the other levels. These mechanisms may be recognized and intentional on the part of the individual or they may be employed unconsciously. They can have as their targets: (1) the removal of certain (material or ideological) aspects of the social context that contain threat; (2) the movement of the person into a different social position that is not as threatening; and (3) the revision of the content or value dimensions of identity structure. Although an overview of each coping mechanism is well beyond the scope of this book, a brief overview of the levels at which these coping mechanisms occur is presented below.

Intrapsychic coping mechanisms operate at the cognitive and emotional levels rather than at the action level, although they have implications for action. There are a number of groups of intrapsychic strategies; (1) those that deflect the implications of the threats to identity; (2) those that accept the threat as real and attempt to modify parts of one's identity to escape from or reduce it; and (3) those that re-evaluate and change (excising part of or adding to) the contents of identity because one or more aspects of the identity may engender threats. *Interpersonal* coping strategies rely on changing relationships with others to cope with threats. Examples are isolating oneself from others and its opposite strategy, negativism, where the person confronts anyone who threatens his or her identity structure. *Group* coping strategies include joining a number of different groups simultaneously to ameliorate the threat or stigma of being a member of one's identity group only. Another group strategy is to come together with others who are experiencing the same threat or form of oppression (either as an information-exchange group or a self-help group). A different version of some of these coping mechanisms is presented below.

Effects of Oppression on the Psychological Functioning of the Oppressed Person

Moane (1999), in reviewing a series of studies, found that oppression negatively affects psychological functioning because it leads to a loss of personal identity (discussed above), a sense of inferiority or low self-esteem, fear, powerlessness, suppression of anger, alienation and isolation, and guilt or ambivalence. A discussion of some of these effects of oppression is presented below.

Positivist psychological literature claims that self-esteem is positively related to one's identity as a dominant group member and negatively related to one's identity as a subordinate group member. However, Adam (1978) points out a number of problems with such findings. First, measures of 'general self-esteem' often run aground in a conceptual fog. All assume a universal absolute standard of esteem and anxiety and ignore the general level of anxiety tolerance of the group of which the individual is a member. Heightened insecurity may be normal in a particular context. For example, one study (Powell, 1973, cited in Adam, 1978) found higher self-esteem among black citizens in a southern US city with a large black population, a historically black university, a militant student population, and an active desegregation program than among a small ghettoized black population in a northern city with a conservative Protestant majority and an apathetic city administration. Second, exclusive focus on psychological states incorrectly equalizes their macro-social conditions. For example, McCarthy and Yancey (1971) and Rosenberg and Simmons (1971) found that many of the studies carried out in the 1960s, which compared black and white levels of self-esteem, ignored the white hegemony of earning a living, going to school, reading, watching television, participating in the consumer society, and so on. Finally, such measures ignore the situationality of the phenomenon because they are based on the concept of a unitary, fixed, or essential identity. A black person's personal self-esteem and his or her racial self-esteem, for example, may differ dramatically, and the self-esteem among black people ranges from high to low levels.

What the self-esteem studies are likely reflecting is the fact that a subordinate person's social environment is one where insecurity is normal. Lack of control over one's destiny and the unpredictability of one's world contribute to a general insecurity, anxiety, fear, and restlessness. Black children, for example, perceive their environments as more threatening than do white children (Baughman, 1971, cited in Adam, 1978). The gay or lesbian person does not know what to expect from family, friends, and workmates if and when he or she 'comes out'. The verbal bashing of poor people and social assistance programs by bourgeois politicians and the mainstream media contributes to unrest and worry among people in receipt of financial assistance. The objective insecurity of members of subordinate groups is often mirrored in a heightened sense of personal insecurity and anxiety (Adam, 1978). This may lead to lowered self-esteem, but it may not. And, if it does, it may not mean lower self-esteem in every area of the subordinate person's psyche.

Another psychological effect of oppression referred to above is that members of subordinate groups will often assume ambivalence or guilt for the systemically constricted life chances available to them. The post-colonial revolutionary and writer, Frantz Fanon (1967: 139), says, 'All those white men in a group, guns in their hands, cannot be wrong. I am guilty. I do not know of what, but I know that

I am no good.' Oppressed persons will often ask themselves, 'What have I (or my identity group) done to attract the hostilities of society?' In the absence of anything obvious on which to blame the oppressive situation, coupled with the continuous message from the dominant group that he or she and other similar people are ugly, degenerate, and morally inferior, the subordinate person will often blame him or herself. Women who are sexually assaulted may ask, 'What did I do to bring on this assault?' Black parents will teach their children not to do anything to attract negative attention and then berate their children when they are harassed or beaten even if these attacks have been unprovoked. Concentration camp victims often acquired profound guilt about events completely beyond their control. Gay and lesbian persons may suffer enormous guilt (especially in disappointing their parents), given religious teachings that homosexuality is an abomination and, until recently, its classification by the medical establishment as a mental illness (Greenberg, 1988). Suffering, it seems, permits the growth of guilt. Suffering may be experienced as 'guilt anxiety' rather than social injustice. Over time it develops a logic of its own in that it emerges as an ingrained, reflexive mechanism to cope with oppression (Adam, 1978). Sometimes it is easier to accept blame and punish oneself for something one did (but in reality did not do) than to believe that the hostile environment is due to who you are and beyond one's control. In this way, social order is assured.

Alienation is another outcome of oppression. In fact, Bulhan (1985: 186) argues that it is the key to understanding oppression: 'there is hardly a concept as pertinent to the situation of oppression as alienation.' It has a long history and has gone through many reformulations, most notably by Rousseau, Hegel, and Marx. Bulhan argues that it is a dynamic concept with synthesizing power. It not only relates experience to social conditions; it also entails a critique. And, consistent with critical social theory, this critique implies a solution. Marx's concept of alienation is probably the best known. Marx argued that capitalism resulted in the alienation of the worker and that this alienation had four aspects. The first was the worker's alienation from the product of his or her labour, which, according to Meszaros (1970), meant alienation from that which mediates the worker's relationship to the external world and hence to the objects of nature. The second aspect of Marx's concept of alienation was the worker's alienation from him or herself because the worker is coerced, controlled, and regimented and, therefore, derives no intrinsic satisfaction from work activities. The worker is alienated from his or her own activity, which is also alienation from his or her body, mind, and spirit, which, taken together, constitute the self. The third aspect refers to alienation from human essence as the worker is denied realization of his or her inherent human potential through work activity. The final aspect of Marx's concept of alienation is alienation from other people in that capitalism divides society into antagonistic classes (owners and workers) to the point where degradation and violence ensue (Bulhan, 1985).

Obviously, Marx's concept of alienation is that of 'alienated labour' and his focus was on economic and class oppression. Fanon (1967), the black Algerian psychiatrist, revolutionary, and intellectual, adopted alienation as a central and synthesizing concept. Bulhan, in his book on Fanon and his ideas, points out that although Fanon was greatly influenced by the Marxian formulation of alienation, as a psychiatrist he was interested in a psychological perspective of the concept. As well, his exposure to existentialism (he was a personal friend of Jean-Paul Sartre), phenomenology, and psychoanalysis enriched his perspective on alienation. His reformulation of the concept of alienation, which occurred in a developmental way over years of observing and experiencing colonization first-hand and gathering clinical data, emphasized some variables (i.e., cultural and psychological) more than others (i.e., economic and class).

Bulhan outlines Fanon's concept of alienation, which contains five aspects: (1) alienation from the 'self' or from one's corporality and personal identity; (2) alienation from 'significant others', that is, from one's family and group; (3) alienation from the 'general other', illustrated by the violence and paranoia characterizing relations between the white colonizers and black colonized; (4) alienation from one's 'culture' or from one's language and history; and (5) alienation from 'creative praxis', which involves the denial and/or abdication of self-determined, socialized, and organized activity. Fanon's concept of alienation obviously contains more relevance for more groups of oppressed people than does that of Marx, as it extends alienation beyond class and economics. Fanon himself emphasized alienation from self and alienation from culture as the most significant aspects of alienation.

The following section looks at how oppressed persons might respond to oppression and its effects. However, an overview of the role of an anti-oppressive social worker in dealing with the above effects of oppression is left until the final two chapters.

Surviving Oppression: Responses of Oppressed People at the Personal Level

Frantz Fanon (1967, 1968) proposed a theory of identity development among oppressed people. Under conditions of prolonged oppression, Fanon presented three models of psychological defence and identity development: the first involved a pattern of compromise; the second, flight; and the third, fight. Bulhan (1985) developed these three models into stages of colonization (but they have relevance to most oppressed groups). Although the notion of stages is fraught with practical difficulties because it implies a linear track of progress (see the discussion in Chapter 8 on the limitations and dangers of adopting linear developmental models), Bulhan's model sheds some light on the shifting relationship between oppressed people and their oppressors. The first stage (capitulation) involves an identification on the part of the oppressed with the oppressor, which results in increased assimilation into the dominant culture along with a simultaneous rejection of one's own culture. The second stage (revitalization) sees a reactive repudiation of the dominant culture and a defensive romanticization of the subordinate (or indigenous culture in post-colonial terms). The third stage (radicalization) is characterized by synthesis and an unambiguous commitment to radical change.

Adam (1978) outlines a similar model of responses made to oppression. He presents two major sets of responses that oppressed people may make with respect to their lived oppression: (1) accommodation and compliance through a process of accepting one's externally imposed inferior status; or (2) rejection through a process of collective resistance and a politics of difference (Adam, 1978; Young, 1990). Although presented here in binary form, some oppressed persons may adopt both sets of responses and shift from one to the other depending on the context. Accommodative responses are discussed below, while rejection of inferior status and resistance are considered in Chapters 5 and 8. It should be noted that although the responses that seem to reflect an inferiority on the part of subordinate persons are outlined here, the concept and various theories or explanations of 'internalized oppression' comprise the subject material of Chapter 6.

The point has been made previously that members of oppressed groups are defined by the dominant group in ways that often devalue, objectify, and stereotype them as different, deviant, or inferior. Their own experiences and interpretation of social life find little expression that touches the dominant culture (Young, 1990). Because they find themselves reflected in literature, the media, formal education, and so forth either not at all or in a highly distorted fashion, they often will suffer an impoverished identity (Adam, 1978). The paradox of this situation for oppressed populations is that at the same time they are rendered invisible by the dominant group they are also marked as different.

This lack of a strong self-identity will, in many cases, lead to an internalization of the dominant group's stereotyped and inferiorized images of subordinate populations (Young, 1990). This internalized oppression, in turn, will cause some oppressed people to act in ways that affirm the dominant group's view of them as inferior people and, consequently, will lead to a process of inferiorized persons reproducing their own oppression. Through a process of cultural and ideological hegemony many oppressed people believe that if they cannot make it in our society, that if they are experiencing problems, then it is their own fault because they are unable to take advantage of the opportunities that the dominant group says are available to everyone. It is, as Paulo Freire (1994) said, as if the oppressor gets in the head of the oppressed. People understand their interests in ways that reflect the interests of the dominant group.

When people internalize their oppression, blaming themselves for their troubled circumstances, they will often contribute to their own oppression by considering it as unique, unchangeable, deserved, or temporary (Adam, 1978), or they may blame other significant people in their lives, such as parents or family. Oppressed persons often contribute to their own oppression also by psychologically or socially withdrawing or engaging in other self-destructive behaviours, thereby causing them to be rejected by others. This, in turn, confirms the low image they may have of themselves (Moreau and Leonard, 1989). The radical psychiatric movement of the 1970s considered all alienation to be the result of oppression about which oppressed people have been mystified or deceived. That is, the oppressed person is led to believe that he or she is not oppressed or that there are good reasons for his or her oppression (Agel, 1971).

Paulo Freire (1994) discusses several positions that oppressed people may adopt that either reinforce or contribute to their own oppression. Fatalism may be expressed by the oppressed about their situation—'There is nothing I can do about it' and 'It is God's will' are common expressions of fatalism. However, this fatalistic attitude is often interpreted as docility or apathy by the oppressor, which reinforces the dominant group's view of the oppressed as lazy, inferior, and getting all that they deserve. Horizontal violence often occurs among oppressed people whereby one Aboriginal person, for example, may strike out at another for petty reasons, which again reinforces the negative images held by the dominant class of subordinate groups. Self-depreciation also occurs when a group hears so often that they are good for nothing that in the end they become convinced of their own unfitness. Moreau and Leonard (1989) and Adam (1978) call this process 'inferiorization'. Another characteristic of some oppressed persons is that they feel an irresistible attraction towards the oppressor and his or her way of life, which is rather similar to the Stockholm Syndrome, whereby hostages over time often come to feel affection and even admiration for their captors. This affirms, of course, the belief that oppression is legitimate and that it is more desirable to oppress than to be oppressed.

It must be noted that such responses are not irrational on the part of those oppressed persons who use them. Although they may appear to be peculiar, unnatural, or neurotic, they are actually rational coping mechanisms employed in everyday life to lessen the suffering of oppression. Their irrationality lies in the fact that they also function to sustain domination. Adam (1978) identified seven such responses. An overview of each follows.

1. *Mimesis*. One response to oppression is for a member of a particular oppressed group to mimic or imitate the behaviours and attitudes that the dominant group displays towards that group in an attempt to gain a slightly more privileged status. For example, the harshest critics of the non-working poor often are the working poor (who repeat all the punitive and moralistic accusations held by the dominant group), even though both groups suffer the oppression associated with poverty. Similarly, an organized women's group in Canada called 'REAL Women' has been unrelenting in its attack on the efforts of the women's movement to obtain more gender equality in society, and 'Uncle Tom' black persons who are given positions of authority over other black persons not infrequently treat their subordinates as inferiors rather than as compatriots.

Each oppressed group has a small class of converts and apologists who assist the dominant group in the preservation of the status quo by conforming to the values of their 'masters'. Impressed with the small privileges that go with their 'borrowed status', they savour these privileges and will often defend them with fear and harshness. Over time, the converts often will identify more with the dominant group than with their own community, thus presenting it with a chronic threat or destabilizing force from within.

2. *Escape from identity*. To avoid or ease the burdens of oppression some

inferiorized persons will attempt to escape from the 'composite portrait' (with its accompanying range of social penalties) used by the dominant group to define their particular place in society. Although this may be regarded as neurotic behaviour in that one cannot escape from what one is (or is constructed to be), to the person attempting to flee from his or her identity, escape from one's identity is viewed as an attempt to move into another social category—one that has fewer social penalties attached to it. However, escaping one's identity isolates the individual from others in the same subordinate group by denying or not recognizing that one is a member of that group. Examples are Jews who convert to Christianity solely to escape their primary identity, gay and lesbian persons who enter into heterosexual marriages to be socially accepted, and women who associate exclusively with men.

Escape from identity, like other inferiorized responses to oppression, functions as a form of false consciousness that subordinates the person to the rationality of oppression. As well, it successfully isolates the person from others who share the same form of oppression. This false consciousness and fragmentation of oppressed people serve to maintain the status quo with respect to dominant-subordinate relations in society.

3. *Psychological withdrawal.* Oppressed persons may adopt a cautious, low-profile conservatism as a way of decreasing their visibility (and social penalties) and compensating for a disfavoured identity. Overly visible behaviour (even though it may sometimes be deliberate acts of resistance to oppression) by fellow members may be strongly condemned because it gives the rest a bad name (for example, the 'loudmouthed' black, the 'pushy' Jew, or the 'swish' homosexual). An effort to reduce the hazards of a high-risk environment outweighs active resistance. This coping effort is often manifest in psychological responses such as passivity, lethargy, and submission. African Americans during the period of slavery and Jews in Nazi concentration camps often exhibited these psychological characteristics. Obviously, psychological withdrawal reinforces rather than threatens the oppressive order.

4. *Guilt-expiation rituals.* Sacrifice is classically conceived as the destruction of a victim for purposes of maintaining or correcting a relationship with the 'sacred' order. Some oppressed persons will see the dominant order as sacred and immutable, and to atone for the guilt of not being able to become full-fledged members they will engage in certain conscious or unwitting guilt-expiation rituals. These rituals become manifest in certain self-mutilating alterations such as black people straightening their hair and lightening their skin, gay men acquiescing to aversive therapy such as extended electroshock treatment to atone for their imputed transgressions, and the ultimate self-sacrifice of suicide by Aboriginal persons (and others) as a guilt-ridden response to oppression.

5. *Magical ideologies.* Some oppressed people will see their situation with respect to the dominant group as so immutable that they will appeal to supernatural means as a way out of their oppressed condition, such as astrology, various superstitious beliefs, messianism, and even gambling. This appeal is made to someone or something else full of power and authority to fix what is wrong.

Internal blinders shield the person from confronting the real menace causing his or her inferiorized situation and lead the person on a search for a magical solution. For example, reading the astrology section of the daily newspaper may be an interesting and harmless pastime for many people, but some people will avoid taking action on troublesome life situations because they believe their destiny is determined solely by the stars. There is nothing that they can do about their oppression because their destiny rests with a force greater than themselves. Every day becomes a new search (in an astrological chart) for a sign that their travails will be (magically) alleviated or eliminated. This kind of fatalism is also found among many people who believe that everything in life is in God's hands and that no amount of human endeavour can change what Divine Providence has in store for them. Because the belief in these situations is that one's problems are determined by magical means or supernatural beings, then only a magical or supernatural solution can resolve them.

6. *In-group hostility.* Hierarchies provide a self-perpetuating dynamic that allows the dominated to console themselves through a comparison of yet more degraded people. It constructs what Adam (1978) calls a 'poor person's snobbery' that sets up a superior-inferior relationship among oppressed groups similar to that between dominant and subordinate groups. It can occur on an inter-group basis, as in the case of members of the white working class oppressing black people, or within an oppressed group, such as closet gay people ridiculing homosexuals or light-skinned black people treating their more dark-skinned compatriots with disdain. In this way the dynamics of oppression are reproduced by dominated groups themselves.

7. *Social withdrawal.* Social withdrawal is a coping strategy in which the oppressed person externalizes identity conflict into the immediate social environment. The oppressed person will develop repertoires of behaviours for different audiences. That is, he or she will behave in one way when in contact with the dominant group (usually assuming a low profile to escape attention) and another way when in contact with their own subordinated community (in a way that affirms with others their true identity). Social withdrawal does not challenge or negate the dominant view of the oppressed group as it is a means to placate the powerful other. For example, black parents will often advise their children to avoid (withdraw from) confrontation with the dominant white society as a means of coping with harassment. In effect, this behaviour contributes to a strategy of invisibility, but it also supports the dominant view that black people are by nature servile and passive.

The other side of social withdrawal is that it permits the first move towards reconciliation with other members of one's subordinate group. As the oppressed individual withdraws from the dominant group by acts of compliance and enters into communication with other members of the subordinated community, the individual may discover his or her identity with them. That is, they become acquainted with their identity as defined by their own group, as opposed to that identity that has been defined and imposed by the dominant group. A dialectical movement towards integration occurs as community members discover each other and, in the process, discover themselves. Although the discovery of self and community requires some degree of social withdrawal from an inhospitable social environment controlled by the dominant group, the danger is that it may lead to ghettoization, which, though safe from the dominant group, is also stifling and confining for the oppressed person. The ghetto or haven is a response to oppression and potentially a first assertion of community. It has the potential for developing a more genuine identity—a sense of community, solidarity, and confidence—so that members are able to assert their authentic identity and differences in ways that contravene the prevailing rationality of the dominant group.

Social withdrawal opens up the possibility of resistance to dominating power. As noted in Chapter 1, Foucault (1988) argued that power and resistance are implicated in each other—that power and oppression are never exercised without insubordination and obstinacy, that is without resistance. Resistance is the inevitable and pervasive counterpart of oppression. It can occur on an individual or collective basis. As such, social withdrawal holds the potential for consciousness-raising, community-building, and mobilization against oppressive structures, cultures, and practices. More will be said about using acts of resistance as strategies to confront and challenge oppression in Chapter 8.

Critical Social Theory and Personal Oppression

In Chapter 1 it was stated that the treatment of oppression/anti-oppression in this book would be grounded in critical social theory in general and in the conflict perspective of society in particular. Such theory explains social problems to be the result of contests or conflicts between various social groups, with a dominant group controlling most of society's resources and possessing most of the economic and political power. Society is organized to the benefit of this group (mainly bourgeois males of European descent) and is held together, not by consensus, but by the differential control of resources and power. Social structures, processes, and practices are established by the dominant group and favour its members while oppressing others along lines of class, race, gender, age, sexuality, and so on. In other words, dominant groups enjoy their privilege at the expense of subordinate groups by way of a set of unjust social conditions and a system of oppressive social relations (Gil, 1998).

But how is modern-day oppression carried out and sustained? Critical social theory answers this question in general terms by arguing that oppression is structural—that people's everyday lives are affected by politics, economics, culture, discourse, social practices, gender, race, and so on. It also argues that structures of oppression are reproduced through the internalization (by both oppressors and oppressed) of dominant-subordinate relations. The practical mission of critical social theory is to translate its developed understandings of domination, exploitation, and oppression into a political (anti-oppressive) practice of social transformation whereby society is free from these phenomena. Thus, a crucial task for critical social theory is to locate actual practices of domination wherever they occur, that is, at the personal, cultural, and structural levels.

Conclusion

An attempt has been made in this chapter to critique dominant-subordinate relations at the personal level and to locate those social practices of oppression that occur in everyday personal interactions between members of dominant and subordinate groups. The dominant group is able to mark the body of the Other as ugly and degenerate. Furthermore, this inferior body type becomes an indication of an intellectually and morally inferior character. These socially constructed differences are then used by the dominant group as the bases and rationale not only for appropriating most of society's resources and political influence but for carrying out acts of prejudice and discrimination against subordinate group members. Such acts can be either conscious and aggressive or, more likely today, unconscious and aversive. Unconscious and aversive acts of oppression are much more difficult to contravene since, given their nature, they seldom can be legislated against.

The effects of these acts of oppression at the personal level on oppressed persons include the imposition of an identity by the dominant group that is often stereotyped, essentialist, and inferior. It is also an identity in which the subordinate group had no say in its development or definition. On the surface, there appears to be no escape from this negative identity—subordinate group members are reminded of it in their interactions with the dominant group on a daily basis, and a heightened sense of insecurity and anxiety invariably accompanies it. The politics of identity include a tendency to accept and internalize this socially constructed and imposed identity and to act in ways that reinforce the stereotypical identity in the eyes of the dominant group.

However, oppressed people can and do respond to their oppression. Some are compliant with and accommodating to their subordinate status while others resist oppression, yet it is not always a simple matter of distinguishing between the two. What may appear to be compliant behaviour to the observer may actually be a coping mechanism on the part of the subordinate person to protect him or her from some of the hurt all oppressed people often experience in their daily interactions with dominant group members. Or, it may be an act that resists the image or identity that the dominant group has defined and, instead, is a preliminary step towards defining one's own identity.

Critical social theory provides a useful framework for understanding oppression in all its complexity. However, to paraphrase Marx, it is not enough to understand an oppressive society—the task is to change it. And, as noted in Chapter 1, critical social theory has a practical or political component. One must be able to translate the critical analysis of a subject into a transformative political practice. The implications of the analysis here of dominant-subordinate relations at the personal level for anti-oppressive social work practice are presented in Chapter 8.

Chapter Four

Oppression at the Cultural Level

Culture

In Chapter 2 culture was defined as a common set of values and norms, including shared patterns of seeing, thinking, and acting, that a group holds. However, there is no accepted universal definition or unitary notion of culture today. In fact, communication—the 'ways and means' of sharing culture (linguistic, non-verbal, symbolic)—is itself part of culture. For example, 'popular culture' and 'mass culture' are terms used to refer to the electronic and print media that distribute cultural messages in the form of music, television, novels, movies, and so on. Peter Leonard (1997) identifies three common meanings of culture: (1) high culture—the traditional hierarchical conception in which only the products evaluated positively by elites are counted as culture (e.g., classical music, the arts); (2) popular or mass culture, where the emphasis is on mass-produced cultural forms such as pulp fiction, genre novels, television shows, movies, and videos; and (3) as the objects of ethnographic study—cultures as ways of life of specific societies. Leonard then proceeds to deconstruct these notions in a way that opens up cultural analysis to all sorts of interpretive possibilities.

Proponents of postmodernism, post-structuralism, and cultural studies talk about multiple cultures that often intersect with one another (e.g., cultures of class, gender, race, nation). Indeed, as Agger (1992: 9) notes, 'cultural politics is [today] considered an important auxiliary of traditional class politics, more narrowly defined in economic terms.' He, like Leonard, argues that the concept of culture today is much broader than the received high culture of various literary and philosophical canons. He claims that much of the credit or momentum for expanding the notion of culture was provided by the sweeping transformations in information technology after World War II, and that a good deal of the momentum of cultural studies is due to the post-structural turn in anthropology with its reflexive focus on the impact of anthropological discourse on the cultures and peoples studied by anthropologists. Both Leonard and Agger point out that the earlier modernist notions of culture are problematic because they contain essentialist ideas about culture, making truth claims about the accuracy of descriptions and analyses of 'other' cultures and universalizing cultural domination rather than cultural pluralism.

To explore and present the complexities and various meanings of culture along with the competing theoretical, political, and methodological treatments and critiques of culture is well beyond the scope of this book.[1] The best I can do at this point is to outline the concept of culture as it is used here in an attempt to further our understanding of oppression and anti-oppression. I view culture in the broad anthropological sense as any expressive activity that contributes to social learning. This view is similar to that of the Birmingham School of Cultural Studies (discussed in a subsequent section of this chapter). Members of the Birmingham School contend that not all culture is institutionalized because, in the broadest sense, culture refers to the language we use, along with the meanings, symbols, and interpretations of social reality. It includes ideologies, religious faiths, and the texts and representations of social communication that we (as a society) produce. Seidman (1998: 200) articulates this broad view of culture: 'Culture is less the sort of thing we associate with museums, galleries, and prize-winning literature than the meanings—norms, values, beliefs, ideals—that make up the stuff of everyday life.'

As suggested above, society is saturated with culture. And, because culture involves social learning, it is inherently political since social learning both communicates and reproduces the social order. Williams (1981: 13) underscores this political function when he defines culture as 'the signifying system through which necessarily (though among other means) a social order is communicated, reproduced, experienced and explored'. Thus, culture as a system of signifiers not only provides a sense of location for individuals and communities, it is also provides a location of conflict—an important insight for anti-oppressive practice.

In Western, pluralistic society there are always multiple cultures that often conflict with one another, but usually one culture dominates and a number of cultures are subordinate. Consistent with critical postmodern thought, the dominant culture attempts to remain dominant through the suppression of difference and multiplicity inherent in a pluralistic society. In other words, one of the ways the dominant group is able to maintain hierarchical divisions of class, gender, race, age, sexual orientation, and the like is by promoting, imposing, and universalizing its own culture while repressing or suppressing other cultures. This is not to say that culture is simply imposed on people from without; rather, as the post-structuralists suggest, it is lived practice. In other words, culture is not only received by people as consumers, but it is produced and reproduced by the same people in everyday life. However, before we explore how the dominant culture remains dominant, we first must consider some of the elements of the dominant culture.

The Dominant Culture

Adam (1978: 30) states that 'Educational institutions, churches, the mass media, the publishing industry, and other [cultural] agents serve as conduits of cultural reconstitution, by continually reproducing the language and symbolic universe of a society.' But what is it exactly that is reconstituted or reproduced? In a nutshell, the dominant cultural messages, images, or products are those that present a world view or define reality in ways that privilege males over females, affluent people over poor people, white persons over persons of colour, heterosexual people over homosexual or bisexual people, young adults over children and older adults, Christians over non-Christians, able persons over persons with disabilities, anglophones over non-anglophones, employed people over unemployed people, two-parent families over other forms of families, North (industrialized countries) over South (industrializing countries), Western societies over Eastern societies, liberal democracies over social or socialist democracies, and capitalism over other economic systems. What we have is a totalizing culture with inclusions and exclusions. Most people would fall within some of the above categories of the dominant culture, but most people would also fall outside many of the categories. A white woman, for example, is a member of the dominant group with respect to race or colour, but is a subordinate member with respect to gender. A loose argument could be that the more dominant characteristics one has, the more privileged he or she might tend to be. Also, the fact that almost everyone is a member of at least one dominant group makes it difficult to challenge the dominant culture since everyone has at least a little stake in preserving it (this point is pursued in Chapter 7).

Advertising, the news, entertainment, and other mass media forms produce and distribute images and products that depict the dominant groups or social systems as the norm—the 'official definition of reality' (Adam, 1978). Every day dominant group members see their identity groups, their religion, their social systems, their language, and so on presented as the norm in the mass media, in their government bodies, in advertising, and in other cultural arenas. In effect, they see themselves seamlessly reflected in the 'official culture' of society. As Young (1990: 59) notes, 'the dominant cultural products of the society, that is, those most widely disseminated, express the experience, values, goals, and achievements of these [dominant] groups.'

In contradistinction to the dominant groups, members of subordinate groups discover themselves as symbols of the Other, manipulated in the transmission of the dominant culture. The systematic selection of particular characteristics of subordinate group members for public presentation by agents of cultural transmission constructs an image that rationalizes an inferior or fearful status for subordinate groups. For example, even before the events of 11 September 2001 people from the Middle East were constantly presented in American movies, television, and novels over the past decade as swarthy, unshaven, sinister, fanatical terrorists who were hell-bent on bringing the United States to its knees. Conversely, those fighting the evil terrorists tend to be portrayed as youthful, white (sometimes with a token African American), English-speaking, Christian, and macho males—an American cultural and stereotypical ideal.

Studies and analyses of the cultural products and messages transmitted by the media (in North America, at least) have shown that the dominant group and the status quo consistently receive favourable treatment and, conversely, that subordinate groups and their efforts to obtain social justice consistently receive negative treatment (see, for example, Gitlin, 1980). In an excellent chapter on community organizing and the media, Biklen (1983) presents an overview of how and why the media protect the status quo and undermine the legitimate aspirations and social change activities of subordinate groups. Biklen looks at the news and entertainment functions of the media separately (he does not look at advertising). He argues that both areas legitimate the status quo by defining social reality in narrow terms that are more in accordance with the lived reality of the dominant group than that of subordinate groups. The media limit audiences' viewing and reading choices to events and interpretations that fall within the prevailing institutional order. For example, crime is defined as most devastating (i.e., front-page news) when a member of the upper socio-economic group is the victim and least devastating (i.e., back-page or no coverage) when it is a subordinate group member. The media define politics in terms of political leaders and treat social movements, which are also political events, as one status step above crime. Similarly, they define power as something that a small group possesses, but do not suggest that this power is enjoyed by a few at the expense of others (usually subordinate groups). Not only do the media treat power, politics, and crime narrowly (and consistent with corporate values), but they do the same in regard to social problems and other critical social phenomena. As well, Biklen states that they treat subordinate group members and social activists who attempt to change the status quo and their issues as 'marginal, deviant, and not in the preordained set of legitimate choices' (ibid., 157).

Biklen argues that the pure entertainment part of the mass media includes many of the same characteristics as the news side. For example, television entertainment often presents a stylized and/or stereotypical portrait of North America, which defines the public's sense of reality and the nature of social conditions, social change, and viable solutions to social problems in narrow terms that do not threaten the privileged position of the dominant group. Using one of Todd Gitlin's (1979) critiques of television, Biklen (1983: 163) says of its treatment of difference:

> Television treats difference (for example, poverty, homosexuality, aging) romantically, as a vehicle for humour, individualistically, or not at all. Situation comedies portray poverty in a romantic, humorous light. Productions that deal with human tragedy tend to treat genuine differences as individual problems with individual solutions. Even when television ventures out to deal with controversial topics such as racism, prejudice is often shown as laughable. The audience is largely protected from the painful hurt and suffering that attend real-life prejudice. In more realistic shows, we usually learn that social problems and personal differences rarely can ever be solved adequately.

Many subordinate group activists find themselves presented by the media as irresponsible and incompetent militants rather than as people who have suffered first-hand from systemic and systematic discrimination, prejudice, and exploitation. Biklen also makes the point that even when the media recognize the legitimacy of a subordinate person, it is done in a way to suggest that the person is unusual or an exception—not like the others. The media treat social movements in much the same way that they do crime—overly concerned with its effects on the dominant group and with a tendency to sensationalize it. Rather than examining the issues central to public protests and demonstrations, the media will tend to focus on the dress, decorum, and size of the group.

Media Bias against Social Protest

In the mid-1980s I was involved in a number of peaceful social protests in my home province of New Brunswick. The media reporting of one demonstration (outside the legislative buildings) against cuts in health, education, and social services gave prominence to the flower beds trampled by the 'rowdy demonstrators'. (In fact, they were trampled by the rowdy reporters trying to get photos of or interviews with the leaders of the protest). One other demonstration, which I helped to organize, had one of the largest turnouts in recent memory in Fredericton, the capital of New Brunswick. In spite of the large turnout, the main question asked of me was how did I account for the lower than predicted turnout. Somehow, an inflated number of expected crowd size got floated around before the demonstration. It became the issue (and the headline)— not the concerns and suffering that led to the demonstration in the first place or even that it was the largest demonstration in recent years. Some of my Aboriginal colleagues in New Brunswick have told me that it is not unusual when they are protesting for the media to attempt to elicit a comment from them about the possibility of violence or for reporters to look through their vehicle windows for firearms and/or liquor bottles. Of course, such activities by the media are based on stereotypes of drunken, violent, irresponsible 'Indians', a stereotype often reflected in the news reports.

The above are but a few examples of one way society controls its dissidents, aided and abetted by the media—kill or defame the messenger and you effectively kill or discredit the message. Fortunately, there are many instances where the media have been used to promote the interests of subordinate groups and to bring about social change. However, given the nature of the media and those people who either own or largely control it, any attempt to use them to promote the legitimate causes of subordinate groups will require a careful plan to avoid having the message twisted or subverted. Biklen provides some helpful suggestions on how to use (and avoid being used by) the media.[2] Any practice of anti-oppressive social work cannot ignore the fact that the mass media reach more people more often than any other mode of communication.

The ethnocentric phenomenon of universalizing the dominant culture as the norm and marginalizing subordinate cultures—as the media invariably do—was identified as 'cultural imperialism' in Chapter 2. All people are socialized, in varying degrees, into the dominant culture and all social institutions are based on the culture of the dominant group. Conversely, all 'other' cultures are measured against the yardstick of the dominant culture, and the more they deviate from the dominant culture, the more they are judged to be deviant and inferior cultures. But how is this domination, along with its social reproduction and social control functions, actually carried out? And what are the cultural means whereby dominant cultures are universalized and subordinate cultures repressed and suppressed? In an attempt to answer these questions, the following four areas will be examined with respect to their contributions to maintaining oppression at the cultural level: popular or mass culture; humour and stereotypes; language and discourse; and the culture of professionalism and respectability.

Popular/Mass Culture

As noted above, popular or mass culture refers to cultural forms that are either mechanically or electronically mass-produced, such as movies, television shows, popular fiction, and popular music. Several writers or schools of writers have looked critically at the role of mass culture in reproducing dominant-subordinate relationships. Although each of their theories or analyses is an incomplete explanation of cultural oppression by itself, cumulatively they help us to understand better how the role of social reproduction is carried out. As a corollary to understanding the social control and social reproduction functions of mass culture, we also develop means of political resistance to dominant cultures and overall social change.

American critical social theorist Ben Agger (1992, 1998) has written extensively in the area of cultural studies as a form of critical theory. It is mainly from his work that I draw the following overviews of the contributions made by various critical theorists to understanding oppression at the cultural level.

Critical Social Theories of Culture

Marx and Ideology
The earliest critical social theory of culture is that of Marx (arguably the founder of critical social theory). Central to Marx's critique of capitalism and the culture of capitalism is the notion of 'ideology'. Unlike the common meaning of ideology today—a world view or a consistent set of social, economic, and political beliefs (Mullaly, 1997a)—Marx used ideology to refer to a system of mystifications that invert and distort reality and create falsehoods to protect the capitalist status quo. Much of his critique of capitalism identified ideas that justified (and mystified) its exploitative and oppressive social relations and/or obscured more egalitarian social relations. Such ideas as 'capitalism is necessary' and 'it has a life of its own' were used by the early capitalists (and are repeated by contemporary capitalists) to ameliorate class-consciousness and to prevent the working class from seeking alternative economic arrangements.

Marx and Engels (1978) argued that the ruling (i.e., dominant) ideas in a given society are those of the ruling (i.e., dominant) classes, and that these ideas, although presented in ways that make them seem to be in everyone's best interests, actually support the interests and privilege of the dominant class. Kellner (1990) notes that ideas such as competition and the right to accumulate unlimited property and wealth, which serve the interests of the capitalist class, are presented as universally valid ideas that serve the interests of everyone.

An example of how Marx engaged in a critique of capitalist 'ideology' may help to clarify this discussion. Marx identified religion (a form of culture) as part of the ideological apparatus of capitalism and referred to it as 'the opiate of the masses'. By this he meant that because religion promised relief from suffering and misery in the hereafter (by going to heaven), it helped to console and pacify people and reconcile them to material deprivation and occupational servitude here on earth. In this way religion acted as an ephemeral narcotic. Marx was much more concerned about the material conditions of 'life after birth' than he was with a spiritual concern of 'life after death', and he saw the latter acting as a diversion from the former. He perceived religious teachings such as 'Blessed are the meek, for they shall inherit the earth' as false claims about society that only serve to convince people that radical change is undesirable. Similarly, he perceived messages that capitalism was both inevitable and a rational social and economic system as false claims to divert workers away from the socialist revolution detailed in *The Communist Manifesto* (Marx and Engels, 1967). The effects of these false (ideological) claims were to divert people from their alienation and portray the existing society as rational and necessary.

Of course, Marx wrote in the period of early capitalism when the concern of many of the working class was to put food on the table. Marx tended to identify culture as a mere reflection and extension of the economic base of capitalism; in other words, his view of culture was that it simply preached the values of capitalism as doctrine. Most critical social theorists today believe that culture in late capitalism is much more subtle, complex, and pervasive than how Marx perceived it to be over 150 years ago. Rather than simply reflecting the economy or operating independently from the economy, culture today is seen by theorists as necessarily *appearing* to operate independently from the economy—otherwise, it would not so effectively maintain and celebrate the status quo. Thus, ideology continues to be an important concept in the study and understanding of culture and cultural domination, but Marxist cultural theorists have reformulated Marx's original concept in light of the above noted limitations. Agger (1992: 123) articulates this reformulated concept of ideology as 'a more complex and irrefutable system of ideas, concepts, and representations that at once close the door on radical social change and open the door on individual self-betterment, including such diverse *promises* as personal occupational mobility, vacations, weight loss, entertainment, sexual and chemical gratification, and participation in sports.' This is only a partial list, however, as will be seen below.

As well as being narrow and underdeveloped, the ideology of capitalism in Marx's time was clear and visible because it was contained in books (e.g., the Bible) or in stated assertions by capitalists. This visible and audible form of ideology made it relatively easy to address and to refute clear-cut claims that oppression and suffering in this world will be overcome in the next world (in heaven) by counterfactual claims that, for example, there is no afterlife. Similarly, a counterclaim to the assertion that capitalism is the only rational economic system can be made by appealing to socialist principles. This does not mean that the counterclaim will always prevail, as evidenced, for example, by considerable support today in North America for Christian fundamentalism with its literal interpretations of the Bible and for the continued existence (albeit in a different form) of capitalism. The point is that Marx's notion of ideology was in a visible and audible form and, therefore, easy to recognize, resist, counter, or refute. However, this early Marxist view of ideology overlooks the facts that ideology (1) is not always in the form of a clear-cut text, but is often concealed and thus difficult to refute; and (2) is not simply something that is read or received through ideological indoctrination, but is experienced in our everyday lives where subtle and subliminal messages are conveyed in ways that are so tied into cultural discourses, practices, and experiences that we lose the distinction between what is real and what is illusory. To account for these broader notions of ideology and culture we must turn to other critical social theorists.

Reification and Hegemony

Two early twentieth-century theorists who attempted to update, reformulate, and expand Marxist theory are Georg Lukacs and Antonio Gramsci. Although it was not their central focus, both addressed the concepts of ideology and culture. Lukacs was among the first Marxists to give serious attention to culture in a way that suggested that, in the form of art and literature (i.e., high culture), it was an important realm, in and of itself, for social and political investigation. In effect, he helped to free culture from its Marxist 'economistic' straitjacket (Agger, 1992).

Lukacs's main goal was to explain why the socialist revolution that Marx had prophesied did not occur. As part of his explanation, Lukacs (1971) argued that as capitalism advanced from its early form in the nineteenth century to a technological form in the twentieth, workers did not face the same dire material conditions as existed earlier, and they began to accept capitalism as an inevitable and workable social and economic system. According to Lukacs, this is exactly the image of capitalism that the capitalists wanted to nurture, and they increasingly manipulated class-consciousness to convince people that radical social change was impossible. Lukacs called this claim 'reification'—the reduction of social relations, culture, and ideas to inert processes that, like nature, appear frozen and hence unchangeable (Agger, 1998). In other words, reification supported the view of society as an immutable part of nature. Conservative religious doctrine, evolutionary biology, and 'laws' (*sic*) of bourgeois economics were used to rationalize this status quo position. Also, the development of state intervention (including the welfare state) and the emergence and growth of the middle class served to dampen any revolutionary fervour that may have previously existed among the working class.

Although Lukacs made a significant contribution to understanding how social relations under capitalism were reproduced in everyday life, his analysis was pre-dominantly a class analysis. His focus was on the relationship of workers to the economic system and how, through a process of reification, this system and its resultant dominant-subordinate relations became acceptable and intractable. This was consistent with Marx's more mechanical understanding of ideology. As well, his notion of culture was that of high culture only, which, he argued, should be examined for what it reveals about the class position and world view of the writer or artist, that is, for their ideological investment in that which they create (ibid.).

Antonio Gramsci, an Italian Marxist, extended the cultural critique beyond ideas associated with a class-based ideology or cultural political economy. He perceived culture to be a *relatively* autonomous area of experience and practice with respect to the economic system and analyzed culture to examine the con-ventional wisdom of a society promoted in everyday life through various sources of *hegemony* (Gramsci, 1971). In Gramsci's writings, hegemony refers to the unquestioned dominance of all conformist ideas that support the inter-ests of the group promoting them. These ideas embody social structures and lead to a reproduction of society. Hegemony goes beyond clear-cut texts that contain falsehoods or indoctrination about the necessity and rationality of the present society. It also refers to the ways in which domination is produced not only from outside everyday life (through the structures of capitalism), but also from within everyday life by people who are resigned to their subordinate positions and who are often supportive and enthusiastic about the 'goods' soci-ety. In fact, Gramsci and subsequent critical social theorists have made the point that the most effective hegemonic messages are those concealed in various discourses of popular culture and in people's everyday experiences and activities.

Kellner (1990) distinguishes between hegemony and propaganda. Whereas propaganda has the connotation of deliberate, planned, heavy-handed, and coer-cive manipulation, hegemony suggests a subtle process of incorporating persons into particular patterns of belief and behaviour. Hegemony functions in ways that divert people from their alienation by suggesting such relief as watching televi-sion or shopping and subtly depict current society as rational, inevitable, and necessary. This concept of hegemony goes a long way towards explaining how culture is a crucial factor in maintaining dominance and exploitation, although not necessarily in any deliberate or conspiratorial way.

Gramsci is important in another way as well. His view of society goes beyond the simplistic monolithic model of a belief that social institutions are the mere instruments of class or group domination. He recognized that in any society there is a competition over which assumptions, ideas, beliefs, and positions are domi-nant. In his view, hegemony is never established for all times, but is always open to negotiation and/or contestation—by efforts to establish *counter-hegemony* on behalf of subordinate groups (Kellner, 1990). The idea of developing counter-hegemony and contributing to a crisis of the dominant hegemony, in my view, contains enormous potential for anti-oppressive practice.

The Culture Industry

The Frankfurt School theorists—Theodor Adorno, Herbert Marcuse, and Max Horkheimer and their heir apparent, Jürgen Habermas—have made sophisticated revisions to Marx's original works and have contributed enormously to the development of critical social theory (see Jay, 1973, for an overview of the Frankfurt School). They addressed a 'later' late stage of capitalism than did Lukacs. One of their contributions was the development of the concept of the 'culture industry' to explain ideological manipulation and cultural domination. The term 'culture industry' was used by Horkheimer and Adorno to refer to the ways in which entertainment and the mass media became industries in post-World War II capitalism that distributed cultural commodities and manipulated people's consciousness. The culture industry thesis helps to explain how the commodification of culture in late capitalism contributes to both profits and social control. In effect, they argued that it is impossible to separate the economic system from the ideological or cultural dimensions of capitalism, an argument that gave critical social theory its own dialectical methodology of analyzing society at both the economic and cultural levels simultaneously (Agger, 1992).

The Frankfurt theorists viewed mass culture as a late capitalist mode of ideology that acted much like Marx's notion of religion (as ideology) in anaesthetizing the masses. Instead of presenting clear texts about the necessity and rationality of the present society, mass culture diverts people's attention away from their personal problems and the irrationality of the present system by idealizing the present and making it appear pleasurable (Agger, 1998). Watching movies or television occupies people's time, takes their minds off their troubles, and suggests that they ought to solve their problems by the same means and in the same world as those who are being viewed, that is, in ways that do not involve radical social change. And even if the viewer is unable to overcome problems in the same way as those on television or in the movies, one can vicariously enjoy the problem resolution of others by identifying with those on the screen.

The culture industry not only makes a profit from movies, magazines, and television shows; it also remedies our alienation through the processes of diversion and identification. And, as Agger (1998) points out, although the culture industry may operate in the same way as religion, it is not a structured document like the Bible or the Koran that can be studied and criticized. Nor does it offer relief in the distant hereafter as religion does; rather, it offers immediate relief. The Frankfurt theorists argued that the culture industry of late capitalism has rendered culture part of our everyday existence. Culture is not separate from us. It is us. This makes it much more difficult to critique than when it was a realm apart.

Another argument coming from the culture industry thesis is that mass culture is relatively undifferentiated because all classes and groups in society are exposed to the same advertising and entertainment. Thus, all classes and groups develop the same or similar consumer aspirations, as well as a common world view characterized by individualism, consumerism, and other capitalist values.

In this way, mass culture appears to level class differences, which, in effect, actually protects them.

The culture industry thesis also argues that mass culture, by way of advertising, creates or manufactures certain false or manipulated needs and desires in order to ensure that mass consumption matches mass production. These needs or desires are not arrived at through autonomous or rational thought; they are imposed on us. As well, the images that bombard us through the mass media not only stimulate consumption, they also deflect critical thought as people tend to identify themselves with their leisure and consumer lifestyles. In this way, according to the Frankfurt School, the reproduction of capitalism is guaranteed.

The Birmingham Centre for Contemporary Cultural Studies

The ideas of the above Marxist cultural theories and theorists set the stage for more recent critical theories of culture. Gramsci's writings on hegemony and counter-hegemony as well as his notion of the 'organic intellectual' (Gramsci, 1971) are central to most schools of cultural studies today. The term 'cultural studies' was popularized by the Birmingham Centre for Contemporary Cultural Studies, which was established in 1964. This group of interdisciplinary scholars has developed a highly original body of literature indebted to Marxist theory, but they have gone beyond Marxist approaches to culture to synthesize such diverse intellectual and political influences as critical social theory, postmodernism, post-structuralism, post-colonialism, and feminism. The work of the Birmingham School was particularly influenced by its confrontations with Margaret Thatcher and her policies that attacked intellectuals, the Left, and the working class (see, for example, Hall, 1988). Thus, much of their work, carried out closer to everyday politics and social movements, has been more concrete than that of the members of the Frankfurt School, whose theorizing reflects a certain social distance and aloofness. For example, empirical studies have been carried out by various Birmingham scholars on working-class and youth culture (see, for example, Brake, 1980; Clarke, 1990; Hebdige, 1979, 1988; Willis, 1977, 1978) and women's culture (McRobbie, 1981; Radway, 1984).

The Birmingham cultural theorists have been able to maintain theoretical integrity in their work while grounding it in political critique. Using Gramsci's theory of cultural hegemony, their studies analyze hegemony[3] at the level of everyday cultural practices with the intent of developing counter-hegemonic practices—alternative formulations of culture and everyday life that counter dominant formulations. This, of course, takes cultural studies away from being a mere academic activity and gives them a political purpose and practice. It also differentiates the Birmingham School from the Frankfurt School—the latter, for the most part, gave up on the politics of everyday life (i.e., attempting to achieve social transformation), which reflects historical differences in the contexts of the two schools more than theoretical differences.

Among the many contributions that the Birmingham School has made to the study of culture is that by insisting that working-class culture should receive attention, it has helped to broaden the study of culture to include work done by women, minorities, and non-Western writers and artists. Conversely, it has contributed to the rejection within the cultural studies movement of the values conveyed by the white, male, bourgeois, Eurocentric canon—notably capitalism, Christianity, and male supremacy. This again reflects the political or social change dimension of the Birmingham Centre for Contemporary Cultural Studies. I will look more carefully at some of their political practices in the Chapter 8, where I discuss anti-oppressive social work practice at the cultural level.

Postmodern Perspective on Culture

The postmodern theory of Baudrillard (1983) makes a significant contribution to our understanding of how today's mass culture helps to maintain the status quo. His concepts of the 'simulation society' and 'hyper-reality' show how the process of power associated with Marx's notion of the mode of production has tended to be replaced by the process of power coming from electronic means of information and entertainment. Baudrillard argues that in postmodernity (what he calls hyper-reality) we lose all distinctions between reality and 'simulations' of reality that come from advertising, journalism, and entertainment.

Simulated Family Life Today

The example of simulated family life most cited in the literature focuses on television and the family. Instead of sitting at the dinner table discussing each other's day at work, school, or home and thus bonding together, it is commonplace today for families either to eat (often fast-foods) quickly and rush to the television or to eat their evening meal in front of the television to watch/consume a simulation of family life. And, usually, these simulations present an idealized happy, harmonious, traditional, and successful problem-solving family image—at a time when the family is undergoing changes in form and structure, is experiencing attacks from domestic violence, desertion, careerism, and unattainable materialism, and when members are looking for understanding and satisfying relationships that are not present in the workplace or at school. Thus, television (in this case) provides a simulated family life to those experiencing an impoverished or oppressive family life.

In an age of hyper-reality, texts written to reveal reality, such as Marx's *Capital*, lose their capacity to educate, anger, and stimulate people to engage in social change because they are not distinguished from, nor are they as *popular* as, magazines and tabloids found on racks at grocery store checkouts. Agger (1998) contends that the most efficacious social texts of our times are popular magazines (e.g., *People*, *Seventeen*), movies, and advertisements for clothing, beer, and other consumer products because they embody everyday discourses that make simulation more real than reality. Few books today are intended to be read slowly and critically. Of this, Agger says:

Textuality loses the character of considered argument, to be perused in a sense out-side of reality, and becomes a simulation, representation, reproduction, photograph, and figure, thus subtly presenting itself to readers as reality itself (and not an authored text promoting one version of reality among many possible versions). (Ibid., 141)

This line of reasoning is similar to that of the Frankfurt School, but it gives deeper meaning to how domination is maintained by the narcotic and vicarious effects of the mass media. It is not just a matter of escaping or having people's attention diverted from social problems by popular culture, as asserted by the Frankfurt theorists; it is also the substitution of imagery for reality. This imagery is not just about selling a product either; it is about selling a lifestyle. Beer adver-tisements, for example, not only promote a particular brand of beer; they (all) promote a particular lifestyle as well—a youthful, physically attractive, popular, and affluent culture. Anyone can be a (simulated) member of this culture by sim-ply purchasing and consuming the product, thus achieving contact with the imagery in the commercial.

The loss of distinction between reality and simulations of reality is an impor-tant insight in understanding how the dominant culture reproduces itself. In addition, Agger (1998) claims that the interpretive deconstruction methods of postmodernists are useful in: (1) revealing the political positioning of various 'social texts', which comprise 'old-fashioned' doctrinal texts and various discur-sive practices from academia to advertising; and (2) suggesting reformulations of oppressive discursive practices. This will be considered further when we come to language and discourse.

Feminist Perspectives on Culture

Since the women's movement in the 1960s, feminists have sought to empower women to speak in their own voices about their own experiences in order to form their own images of themselves. This has led to a feminist cultural politics that seeks to create a feminist, non-misogynist culture. Agger (1998) contends that all feminists—liberal, socialist, radical, cultural, Marxist, and visible minority—emphasize the following issues of feminist cultural politics, although each school of feminism conceptualizes these issues differently and accords different explanatory power to each.

Feminist cultural politics seeks to: (1) make the invisible visible by drawing theoretical and critical attention to cultural works by and about women; (2) unmask and oppose the sexual objectification of women in culture, particularly through feminist film theory and a critique of pornography, both of which chal-lenge conventional representations of women and distort their real experiences; and (3) address issues of how femininity and masculinity are constructed through culture by raising the question of engendered cultural works and inter-pretation. These three goals show how contemporary feminism has thoroughly integrated its political and cultural concerns and how it has engaged in a feminist practice in a culture in which women are either invisible or sexually objectified.

An anti-oppressive practice at the cultural level has much to learn from feminist cultural studies about self-identification, developing cultural theory, politics, and practices that are in opposition to the dominant culture.

In sum, there is much to be learned from the above critical theories and perspectives on how popular or mass culture promotes, produces, and reproduces the dominant culture. Marx's concept of ideology is helpful in understanding how we are told lies about the rationality and necessity of capitalism and then made false promises to the effect that if we accept our fate within capitalism we will be rewarded by the system or in the hereafter. Lukacs's concept of 'reification' is a useful contribution as it reveals how the dominant group prevents attempts at fundamental social change by convincing us that the system is inevitable, workable, and intractable. Gramsci's theory of hegemony extends the notion of culture beyond a narrow economic interpretation to include *all* conformist ideas that are internalized and become part of people's everyday lives and practices, ultimately leading to the reproduction of society. The Frankfurt School's identification of the (mass) culture industry as a major means of manipulating people's consciousness by anaesthetizing the masses and diverting their attention away from their troubles is another major contribution in understanding cultural oppression. The cultural studies of the Birmingham School show us how the ruling hegemony is carried out at the level of everyday cultural practices—practices that support a white, male, bourgeois, Eurocentric domination. Baudrillard helps us to see how strategies for social or political change are thwarted in a society where the distinctions between reality and simulations of reality are blurred, and where imagery promotes a lifestyle more consistent with that of dominant groups than of subordinate groups. Finally, feminist cultural studies help us to see how one subordinate group has integrated analysis, theory, and practice into a politics of empowerment and emancipation. Taken together, the insights of these theories, analyses, and perspectives help us to develop anti-oppressive practices at the cultural level and to inform our anti-oppressive practices at other levels.

Stereotypes as Cultural Expressions of Oppression

One major way in which the dominant group reinforces its position of power and privilege and, coincidentally, oppresses subordinate groups is through the use of stereotypes. A stereotype is a biased, oversimplified, universal, and inflexible conception of a social group. Although stereotypes may be positive, such as the brave soldier or the smart businessman (who avoids taxation) or the friendly Atlantic Canadian or the respectable doctor or clergyperson, most stereotypes are harmful and destructive. It is no accident that most negative stereotypes are applied to subordinate groups, as they are powerful tools of ideology that help to maintain oppression. Every oppressed group is undermined by stereotypes that have been imposed on them by the dominant group. It is part of the process of the social identity of subordinate groups being determined mainly by the dominant group rather than by themselves, as noted in the previous two chapters.

As discussed in Chapter 2, the dominant group projects its own experiences and culture as representative of humanity, often without realizing it. Because encounters with other groups have the potential of challenging this claim to universality, the dominant group reinforces its position by measuring (i.e., contrasting) other groups along the lines of dominant group characteristics. As a result, the differences of women from men, non-Christians from Christians, and homosexual from heterosexual persons become reconstructed as largely deviant and inferior (Young, 1990). These groups become the Other and are marked by negative stereotypes that, in effect, reinforce notions of dominant group superiority. These stereotypes permeate society and become so ingrained that they are seldom questioned by members of the dominant group or by some members of the subordinate groups (to be discussed in Chapter 6). Some examples of seldom-questioned stereotypes are that all Aboriginal people are alcoholics, all unemployed people are afraid to work, all gay men are perverse pedophiles, all women are natural caregivers, and all black people lack any sense of sexual control. On the other hand, white, bourgeois, heterosexual males tend to escape such group stereotypes and are free to be individuals (ibid.).

Thompson (1997, 1998) maintains that stereotypes are part of the dominant culture and that all stereotypes have three characteristics. First, they defy logic or evidence, as they are based on ideology and, therefore, are resistant to challenge and change. Second, they are often unduly negative and thus hurtful and potentially oppressive. Third, they become so ingrained that we are often unaware that they affect our perceptions and actions. It should be noted that Thompson's first characteristic is debatable to a certain extent. Bishop (1994: 67) argues that stereotypes do not 'come out of the blue', that is, they are usually built on a real observation of another culture and contain a kernel of truth. Bishop notes, for example, that in North America Jewish mothers have been the subject of some cruel humour that combines sexism and anti-Semitism in that they are portrayed as simple-minded, overbearing, and possessive. This negative stereotype is based on the love, care, and concern that many women give to their children in the generally highly valued family structure of the Jewish community (which is the kernel of truth about the stereotype). In addition to interpreting a positive characteristic in a negative way outside the culture, this stereotype overlooks the fact that this group comprises millions of scientists, artists, and great minds, as well as women struggling with addictions and poverty and possessing every conceivable type of child-rearing beliefs and practices. Thus, I would add two more characteristics of stereotypes to Thompson's list: (1) a stereotype represents a perceived essential nature of members of the subordinate group (e.g., poor people are naturally lazy, women are naturally good with children); and (2) the group is homogenized within a stereotype in that it applies to all members without exception (e.g., all Aboriginals are alcoholic, all black men are violent).

Although each oppressed group may be characterized in a unique stereotypical way (e.g., Jews are greedy and cunning; black people are lazy and sexually promiscuous; poor persons drink too much and are irresponsible), Adam (1978) and Dominelli (1997) argue that all subordinate groups are constructed as problematic for the dominant society. And because they are problematic, they must be watched and controlled for the good of society. Stereotypes help to reinforce the notion of the problematic and the necessity of surveillance and control. Stereotypes also make prejudice, oppression, and even violence at the personal level more acceptable. For example, if there is a culture of oppression and homosexuality is seen by the dominant group to be perverse, deviant, and sinful, it is likely that a degree of gay-bashing on an individual level would be tolerated.

Focusing on Jews, black persons, and gay and lesbian people, Adam (1978) discusses a 'composite portrait' that the three share because of the stereotypes imposed on them, a portrait that calls for surveillance and control. First, all three groups have been placed into subhuman categories at various times throughout history. Black slaves were sold without regard for family ties because it was believed that black sexuality could not include love. Hitler wrote in *Mein Kampf* of his discovery of Jewish smell (smell is a sign of lower races and base animals in modern Western civilization) following his reading of anti-Semitic pamphlets. In the not-too-distant past, psychiatric ideologies denied the possibility of gay or lesbian love and echoed popular opinions that homosexual people are given to 'mindless animal promiscuity' (Hodges and Hutter, 1974, cited ibid.). Similarly, all three groups have historically been characterized as exhibiting 'uncivilized behaviour'—unrefined, ill-mannered, unscrupulous, unethical, unclean, and deceitful. Adam shows how all three groups have a history of being stereotyped by the dominant group as hyper-sexual, as heretics and conspirators (religious and sexual heretics; conspiracy to take over the world or our culture or our children), and as 'in-your-face' and overly visible (loud, pushy, aggressive, or offensively flamboyant).

Although it is beyond the scope of this book to present a comprehensive and detailed overview of the stereotypes associated with each form and source of oppression, a few additional examples may help to illustrate the hurtful and oppressive consequences of stereotyping. Poor persons are often presented in the mass media, cartoons, social and political commentary, and in all types of literature as a lazy, degenerate, irresponsible, unclean class of people who cheat on their welfare and breed like rabbits. This portrait leads the dominant group to believe that poor people represent a dangerous class who must be constantly watched and monitored because they cannot be trusted and they pose a threat to law, order, and the economy. Questions of need among poor people are seldom considered because they are portrayed as the architects of their own fate; indeed, because it is believed they cannot look after themselves properly, some claim that they should have no say in any form of public decision-making. They should be grateful for any meagre assistance (public or private) rendered to them and should, in return, allow themselves to be exploited by taking up low-wage, menial (or dangerous) dead-end jobs; by participating in workfare programs that do not lead to jobs; by fighting wars; by being blamed for government deficits; and by serving as examples to others of what can happen if one does not conform to the dominant group's rules and expectations.

Dominelli (1997: 96) presents an overview of racial stereotyping of black families:

Common stereotypes of the black family, particularly of African or Afro-Caribbean descent, cover the sexual prowess of black men; the lack of sexual morality amongst black women, as evidenced by a high ratio of single parenthood; the absence of a stable family tradition; the lack of family bonds between family members; and the power of strong domineering matriarchs complemented by weak black men incapable of sustaining stable relationships. (*Ebony*, 1986, and Staples, 1988, both cited in Dominelli)

This stereotype not only problematizes 'the black family' and reinforces white cultural supremacy, it arrogantly presents the notion that there is a universal black family, when, in fact, there is a rich and diverse variety of black family forms, each with its own specific set of relationships, obligations, and networks. However, it is the myth or stereotype of the black family as deviant and unstable that permeates society and is often used to establish social policy and social work practice (Ahmed, 1991; Dominelli, 1997).

Carlen and Worral (1987: 3) describe a gendered stereotype of the 'normal woman':

Being a normal woman means coping, caring, nurturing and sacrificing self-interest to the needs of others. It also means being intuitively sensitive to those needs without them being actively spelt out. It means being *more than man*, in order to support and embrace Man. On the other hand, femininity is characterised by lack of control and dependence. Being a normal woman means needing protection. . . . It means being childlike, incapable, fragile and capricious. It is being *less than man* in order to serve and defer to Man. (Cited in Thompson, 1997: 43)

This concept of normality is, of course, grounded in a patriarchy that takes for granted certain stereotypical expectations of men and women. For example, women are considered to be natural nurturers and caregivers, which makes them primarily responsible for child care (and elder care). In turn, it makes them responsible when things go wrong with respect to such care. The focus in dangerous families, where children are at risk, is on dangerous mothers (Parton and Parton, 1989), and even if the mother is not the abuser she is still held culpable because she failed to protect the child (Beagley, 1989). Consistent with this patriarchal stereotype, parenting is equated with mothering and bad parenting is equated with bad mothering (Thompson, 1997).

Cultural stereotypes, such as those outlined above, carry out several political functions for the dominant group. Included among them are the following.

- They internalize a feeling of inferiority on the part of members of subordinate groups (Adam, 1978; Young, 1990), which, in turn, reduces questioning, challenging, or resisting the dominant culture.
- They justify the surveillance, control, and exploitation of subordinate groups and rationalize inattention to their expressed and unexpressed needs.
- By characterizing members of subordinate groups as 'bad' and their cultures as 'inferior', stereotypes dialectically convince the dominant group of its

An Inadequate Mother or Oppressive Expectations?

Susie, a young married woman, had three children under school age. Her husband, Brian, worked long hours, which meant that Susie was the full-time caregiver for the children. Brian's work required them to move to another province, halfway across the country, far from friends and family. Susie found after awhile that she was not coping very well with her children, and sought help from a (male) social worker. The social worker did not question the 'woman as the natural caregiver of children' stereotype and referred Susie for help with 'parenting skills'. No consideration was given to the likelihood that the full-time care of three small children was too big a job for one person.

own identity as the 'good' and its culture as 'superior' (Adam, 1978). This occurs without any examination or analysis by the dominant group of its privilege and power. If black people did not exist, for example, then they would have to be invented by white people.

- Negative images and stereotypes deflect attention away from the structural causes of inequality, blocked opportunities, and differential treatment and focus attention onto the perceived personal deficits, liabilities, and weaknesses of those individuals who are stereotyped. In other words, stereotypes aid and abet victim blaming.

Language and Discourse as Mechanisms of Oppression (and Anti-Oppression)

Two important concepts for understanding and analyzing oppression and for developing anti-oppressive practices are language and discourse. At the most basic level culture is transmitted through language and discourse—parents speaking to children, individuals speaking to peers, educational institutions and churches communicating to their students and parishioners, messages from texts and the mass media, the reading of literature, and so on.

Language

Through language we become members of a human community (Spender, 1990). Language helps us to make sense of the world and to communicate and interact with others (Thompson, 1998). Everyone is immersed in language and no one is independent of it (Howe, 1994). However, language is never politically neutral. It does not simply describe or reflect the reality of inequality and oppression in our society; it is also used to construct and maintain oppression, and may be used to resist and challenge it.

One of the cornerstones of postmodernism is its emphasis on the relationship between language and power. Howe (1994: 522) summarizes this relationship: 'Those with power can control the language of the discourse and can therefore influence how the world is to be seen and what it will mean. Language promotes some possibilities and excludes others; it constrains what we see and what we do not see.' The postmodernists have emphasized that language does not possess the properties of absolute truth, but is historically, socially, and culturally contextualized, and largely reflects the interests and world views (including the culture) of dominant groups (Agger, 1989).

Language may be oppressive simply by the choice of words used in communication. And some words that reflect and maintain oppression are so well established that their usage is taken for granted and their oppressive connotations not recognized. For example, 'man' is often used as a prefix or suffix or a stand-alone word: chairman, manpower, man is the centre of the universe. This sexist or gendered and exclusive use of language contributes to the invisibility of women and, therefore, to a continuation of their subordination to men. 'Black' is a word often used to portray evil (e.g., it was a black day when President Kennedy was assassinated), or is contrasted with white to refer to right (white) and wrong (black) factors, which reinforces the notion of white superiority. Terms such as 'the poor' and 'the elderly' reflect a view of people that is depersonalized and dehumanized because the words used are impersonal adjectives or descriptors. It is similar to negative medical terminology, when people are categorized and referred to in terms of their particular ailments (e.g., 'the gall bladder in Room 202' or 'the head injury in Emergency') rather than in human terms. A number of words, as noted in the last chapter, constitute overt oppression (e.g., nigger, spaz, queer) because they refer to members of subordinate groups in hurtful and harmful prejudicial terms.

Even if a person using oppressive words or language does so in good faith without any intention to hurt or insult the group involved, it is still harmful and hurtful and therefore is always unacceptable. Language reflects culture, particularly the dominant culture, and if the culture is oppressive then one of the ways of changing it is to avoid words or language that reflect and/or reinforce the oppressive elements of that culture.

Discourse

Language and its relationship to oppression are much more complex than a simple list of taboo words. Language is part of a larger framework of thought, meaning, and knowledge, or what Foucault (1976, 1980) has called a 'discourse'. Leonard (1997: 2) describes discourses as 'linguistic systems of statements through which we speak of ourselves and our social world'. A 'linguistic system of statements' is not restricted only to statements, however, as a discourse also includes the unwritten rules (based mainly on ideology and culture) of what will be included and excluded in the statements. A discourse frames the knowledge that is formulated from within it and is similar to Kuhn's (1970) notion of a 'paradigm', although Foucault makes more use of ordinary language and everyday experience to establish the parameters of a discourse (Agger, 1991). Although discourse can occur between two people, it also includes other forms of cultural expression, such as advertising, academic journal articles, and the representation of women and other subordinate groups in literary and visual culture.

An Unconscious Act of Oppression

One of my colleagues at Victoria University in Melbourne, a strong advocate for Aboriginal rights, related to me a poignant experience she had. She was telling an Aboriginal friend about her recent trip to Britain. She said that after weeks of visiting ancient buildings, she felt that Australians had no history. Her Aboriginal friend pointed out that because she saw history as being mainly about buildings, she had just ignored over 40,000 years of her (Aboriginal) history and culture.

Discourses are not politically neutral, but are related to power. They are delivery systems for political assumptions about the world that largely reflect the interests of dominant groups such as white people, bourgeois males, and Christians, and that assist in the reproduction of existing class, race, gender, and other inequalities (Agger, 1989). This reproduction occurs through the promotion of ideas that support the current socio-political order, and, conversely, through the suppression and/or marginalization of ideas that seek to challenge and transform it. For example, progressive social work scholarship is frequently excluded from social work textbooks or treated in a manner that neutralizes its political impact and transformative potential under the guise that it lacks objectivity or reality (Wachholz and Mullaly, 2000). Thus, what social work students learn from textbooks is a discourse (attitudes and scholarship) that teaches personal reform and/or limited social reform rather than social transformation as the means to deal with oppression and inequality. This ensures that the structures and cultures of oppression remain relatively untouched.

The postmodernists and social constructionists have helped to move us away from the idea that there is objective, unitary, absolute, and verifiable knowledge about the human condition and the social world that can be gathered by using scientific methods and principles. There is general agreement today in the social sciences and humanities that there is usually more than one version or interpretation or explanation of an event, a social condition, and so on. A number of alternative or competing explanations are available to us through the language of alternative and competing discourses. Each of these discourses will tell a different story about the event or the condition because each has a different way of representing the world and how it operates (Burr, 1995). In Chapter 1 we examined different explanations or theories of social problems where, in fact, each social problem perspective has its foundation in a particular discourse in which some variables will be included and others excluded. For example, the social pathology explanation of social problems includes individual characteristics (e.g., deviance, personal deficiencies) and excludes structural factors (e.g., patri-archy, cultural racism).

Similar to Kuhn's (1970) version of a dominant paradigm (e.g., capitalism) existing among a number of competing paradigms (socialism, communitarian-ism), so, too, one dominant discourse always exists among a set of alternative discourses. Not surprisingly, the dominant discourse belongs to and represents the interests of the dominant social group. In order to protect its privilege and power the dominant group must present its view of the world (i.e., its discourse) in a way that subordinate groups either agree with it and endorse it or find it imperfect but the only viable alternative, and, therefore, they must live with it. For example, the dominant economic discourse today is that the '*laws* of the mar-ket' must prevail and that the demands of global capitalism require less govern-ment involvement in social, economic, human, and environmental affairs. In spite of what neo-conservative politicians, right-wing economists, mainstream journalists, and self-interested business leaders say, there are no laws in any social science, including economics. There are only theories or perspectives or discourses. But if the dominant group can convince the public that there is no viable alternative to its view, then its position of power and privilege is consoli-dated. Furthermore, because the alliance between big business and bourgeois governments controls the major means of transmitting culture (e.g., the mass media, educational institutions), they are able to present their economic mes-sages and views (i.e., their discourse) in a favourable light while ridiculing and dismissing any alternative economic discourse as unreasonable, unrealistic, and/or socialist. In other words, those with power can control the discourse, thus influencing how the world is to be seen and how it should work.

A dominant discourse is potentially much more powerful as a social control mechanism than is an army, police force, or legislation. If subordinate group members concur with the world view and social and political practices of the dominant group, there is no need for acts of resistance or strategies for social change. However, history has shown that discourses, which contain claims to reason, order, and universality, often mask the interests of those making them. Smith (1993: 31) underscores this point:

> Imperialist nations, ruling classes, males, whites, heterosexuals, doctors, psychia-trists and criminologists have all claimed that their perspective defines a universal and rational outlook. By doing so they have effectively silenced other nations, other classes, other genders, other races, those of other sexual orientation, patients, the mad and prisoners.

Dominant discourses, then, cover up and/or contradict the interests of all sub-ordinate groups: a discourse of patriarchy contributes to the oppression of women; a discourse of white supremacy contributes to the oppression of people of colour; a discourse of capitalism contributes to the oppression of working-class persons; a discourse of heterosexuality contributes to the oppression of gay, lesbian, and bisexual persons. Dominant discourses not only reflect dominant-subordinate relationships based on social divisions such as class, race, and gender, but also occupation. For example, professions, including social work, often contribute to oppression by controlling the discourses of their practices in which pathological, diagnostic, and professional vocabularies exclude and disempower the service user.

Dominant discourses also negatively affect social welfare. Peter Leonard (1997) points out that the dominant welfare discourse today is that of 'welfare dependency', which emanates from a 'culture of poverty' discourse. This discourse, which is transmitted in the mass media on almost a daily basis, pathologizes people in need of financial assistance by portraying them in *stereotypical* fashion as dependent, inadequate, moral failures. Any alternative discourse, such as viewing welfare as an aspect of 'interdependency', is covered up by the dominant ideological illusion of individual independence, in spite of *interdependency* being our inescapable experience as human beings living in association with and depending on each other.

Although dominant discourses tend to be oppressive, the notion of a discourse itself is helpful in developing anti-oppressive practice in two major ways. First, to understand discourses as contested sites of power and conflict, as Foucault does, is very important in making sense of the covert, almost invisible nature of ideology today. This allows postmodern insights and interpretive techniques (i.e., deconstructionism) to be used to unpack a discourse and bring its hidden assumptions and arguments to light (Agger, 1998). In this way, we can make more sense of the dominant culture's current hegemony. Second, deconstructing a dominant discourse and bringing its oppressive underpinnings to light makes it easier to develop a fully articulated counter-discourse, one that critiques the ruling discourse and points the way towards more egalitarian social relations, practices, and processes. Feminism and anti-racism, for example, have been powerful counter-discourses to the dominant patriarchal and white supremacist discourses. More will be said in the final chapter about incorporating counter-discourses into an anti-oppressive practice.

Social Work and Cultural Oppression

Social work is an occupation in which most of its members are university-educated, experience a similar socialization process, share a set of common values and ethics, and organize themselves along the lines of a 'professional association' model. However, it would be a mistake to assume that social work is a monolith in which all its members practise in the same way or share the same goals or hold the same explanations for the occurrence of social problems or even agree on the merits of professionalism.[4] Elsewhere, I have presented four distinct theories and practices of social work, each of which is determined by the particular ideology held (consciously or unconsciously) by the social worker (Mullaly, 1997a). It is, of course, an oversimplification to suggest that social workers fall into one or another of the four approaches outlined in my book, *Structural Social Work*, as most will operate across more than one approach. Given that social work theory and practice may take different forms, however, an important question is: How can one avoid oppressive social work practices and carry out anti-oppressive practices? To answer this question it is necessary to understand the ways that social work has operated and does operate to maintain and reinforce the dominant culture.

It is not my intention here to bash social workers for carrying out practices of oppression, social control, or victim-blaming. Most social workers I know are concerned about the horrendous living conditions that affect so many people today in both capitalist countries and non-industrialized societies, and they want to do something about them. However, social workers, like everyone else in our society, are socialized into the dominant culture and may unwittingly (or otherwise) carry out oppressive acts. As well, social agencies tend to view social problems narrowly and to define them in terms of personal deficiencies, dysfunctional families, and inferior cultures, and they expect their social work employees to treat and reform their service users (Rose and Black, 1985; Mullaly, 1997a). Some social work scholars have suggested that the 'object' (i.e., the service user) of social work was originally determined by a patriarchal bourgeois commitment to the regulation of poor people, who were considered to be the 'dangerous classes' (Leonard, 1994; Margolin, 1997). This dangerous class (or working class) needed to be reformed in order to reduce deviance, disease, and chaos and to advance civilization. Reformation attempts would include charitable devices contingent upon socialization into bourgeois culture and moral conversion into Christian culture. A voluminous literature comprising critical or radical social work, feminist social work, anti-racist social work, postmodern social work, and other forms of progressive social work attests to various oppressive thought structures, attitudes, practice forms, and approaches that permeate and underpin much social work theory and practice of yesteryear and today.

Professionalism is a contradictory and problematic concept for social work. On the one hand, as noted by Thompson (1998), social work professionalism is committed to a (progressive) set of values, to high standards of practice, to accountability, and to the development and use of a knowledge base acquired by research and reflective practice. On the other hand, professionalism has been criticized for emphasizing the technical aspects of helping (e.g., impartiality, emotional neutrality, apolitical service) when social problems are political and moral issues; for organizing into an exclusive group based on academic credentials, which divides social workers from other workers and from the persons they serve and thus creates elitist social and occupational hierarchies; for creating the illusion that the best source of help rests with the 'expert' social worker; for treating social problems as individual misfortunes, which detracts from their structural causes (and solutions); and for ignoring the experience of all older professions, which suggests that professionalism primarily benefits professionals (i.e., obtaining personal, social, economic, and political power) more than it does service users (Mullaly, 1997a). Many progressive social work writers have argued that the 'culture of professionalism' is conservative, self-interested, and oriented towards the status quo. In effect, professionalism is for professionals, not for service users (Carniol, 2000; Galper, 1980; Hardy, 1981a; Laursen, 1975; Mullaly, 1997a; Wagner and Cohen, 1978).

Professionalism contains elements of oppression not only for service users but also for the profession as a whole and for particular groups of social workers in particular. An example may help clarify this. Recall the discussion in Chapter 2 of 'powerlessness', one of Young's (1990) five faces of oppression. There it was noted that the norms of respectability in our society are associated with a professional culture—professional dress, speech, tastes, and demeanour. It was also noted that professional respectability tends to be associated with white males, who dominate the professions. The traditional professions of medicine, law, and engineering are still over-represented by white males.And it is not just a matter of domination by numbers, but also of domination in terms of those who hold the powerful positions in professions.

Social Work Reproduces Gender and Racial Oppression

Social work is a profession or semi-profession that has always had many more female members than male members. Social work is also a profession committed to such values as social equality and social justice. In spite of this, white males are still disproportionately represented in positions of power and privilege within social work, as most directors of large agencies and social work educational programs are overwhelmingly white and male. Conversely, most front-line workers caring directly for victims of oppression are women. In this way, social work is reproducing relationships and roles of oppression along gender (and racial) lines where women and people of colour remain in subordinate positions and continue to carry out their traditional roles of caring for others. White males also remain in their traditional positions of leading, directing, and dominating others.

Although social work is a profession committed to progressive values, social change, and social justice, its members are still susceptible to oppressive practices and to reproducing dominant-subordinate relations—not only with the people they serve, but also with each other along lines of gender and race (and other social divisions). This shows how difficult it is to work and practice in a way that confronts, resists, and attempts to change the larger culture. An anti-oppressive social work practice is not restricted to working with people experiencing social problems. It must include social workers working with each other in ways that: (1) do not reproduce the inequalities of the larger society; (2) challenge attitudes and agency cultures that moralize social problems and blame their victims; (3) do not ascribe all social problems to individual deficiency (Mullaly, 1997a); and (4) avoid the pursuit of a professional culture of respectability gained at the expense of others.

Conclusion

This chapter focused on oppression at the cultural level. It adopted a broad view of culture—the norms, values, beliefs, ideals that make up 'the stuff of everyday life'. Culture is pervasive in our society and is related to everything we see, hear, believe, and do. The culture of the dominant group (i.e., the dominant culture) privileges that group at the same time that it carries out cultural imperialism by suppressing and/or repressing all subordinate cultures. The dominant culture is presented and promoted as the universal cultural norm (i.e., the official culture) by the dominant group. It is continually produced and reproduced by such cultural agents as the mass media, the entertainment industry, and our social institutions.

In an effort to understand better how cultural oppression is actually carried out (as a prerequisite to developing anti-oppressive strategies) a number of critical social theories were examined. The people who developed these theories focused, for the most part, on arguably the most influential and powerful form of culture—mass or popular culture. Several functions that mass culture carries out to protect and enhance the privileged position of the dominant group were extracted from these theories.

Two other major cultural expressions of oppression examined in this chapter are stereotyping and language and discourse. Stereotypes are biased, oversimplified, universal, and essentialist depictions of social groups. Every subordinate group has, as part of the identity imposed on its members by the dominant group, at least one stereotype that defies logic, is unduly negative and hurtful, and is so ingrained as to be seldom questioned. Stereotypes fulfill several political functions for the dominant group. Similarly, language does more than simply describe or reflect social phenomena; it can also be used to construct and maintain oppression. Language and discourse are related to power in that they are both delivery systems for political assumptions about the world, and dominant discourses largely reflect the interests of dominant groups. Finally, certain oppressive features are inherent in the culture of professionalism, and the profession of social work is no exception in this regard.

Any serious attempts at formulating and/or practising anti-oppressive social work must incorporate the concept of culture, which means being informed by research and literature from cultural studies. Cultural studies has been described by the noted critical social theorist Ben Agger (1998: 122) as 'one of the most important contemporary theoretical movements' and 'one of the best examples of an interdisciplinary critical theory'. To date, social work has tended to treat culture in narrow ways in that culture is often associated with differences based on race or ethnicity, as illustrated by the literature on multicultural social work, or it is lumped in as part of the larger social environment that extends beyond individuals or families. Such conceptualizations fail to understand that culture is more than a context or a particular tradition or set of ideas. Culture is also an everyday practice where the ruling hegemony is carried out. No one in society is free from participating in everyday cultural practices—practices that support the position of the dominant group. Social workers are quick to say that the personal is political (and the political is personal). However, this stated relationship is overly simplistic because culture mediates between the personal and political. The relationship between the personal and political is not a direct relationship, but an indirect one. The dominant cultural messages invariably legitimize such political effects on individuals as conformity and oppression, and the dominant culture must be demystified and exposed for individuals to see the need for structural or political change.

Chapter Five

Oppression at the Structural Level

Introduction

In Chapter 2 oppression at the structural level was defined as the means by which oppression is institutionalized in society. It consists of the ways that social divisions, practices, and processes, along with social institutions, laws, policies, and the economic and political systems, all work together to benefit the dominant group at the expense of subordinate groups. This chapter will examine the social, economic, and political systems in terms of how each contributes to overall oppression at the structural level. Although these three spheres are looked at individually, they cannot be separated in reality. A symbiotic relationship exists among them, with each sphere constantly acting upon and influencing the other two. At the same time, each sphere is acted upon and influenced by the other two spheres.

Social Relations and Oppression

It has already been discussed how social divisions based on class, gender, race, age, and so on engender oppression. It has also been argued that most people today would not overtly subscribe to or condone acts of oppression, as evidenced by the existence of considerable legislation and policies to combat prejudice and discrimination, such as equal rights and human rights laws. Among the potential ways or policies that might be adopted to deal with negative effects brought about by social divisions or 'difference', two are particularly noteworthy—assimilation (or monoculturalism) and multiculturalism. The former, a modernist and liberal humanist approach, accords equal social status and treatment to everyone, regardless of class, gender, age, race, etc., according to the same principles, rules, and standards. The latter, a politically engaged postmodern approach, is based on the belief that people's differences are more important than their similarities. Obviously, these two approaches are diametrically opposed: assimilation tends to adopt a blind approach to difference and multiculturalism tends to adopt a blind approach to commonalities or similarities. Proponents of each claim their particular approach is best at combatting the hierarchical sets of dominant-subordinate relationships that characterize our pluralistic and heterogeneous social system.

Assimilation

Wasserton (1980) outlines three reasons for choosing assimilation as a solution to group-based oppression. First, by imagining a society in which class, race, gender, and so forth have no special social significance, one sees more clearly how these categories unnecessarily limit possibilities and opportunities for some people. Second, a clear and unambiguous standard of equality and justice for all is promised, and any group-related differentiation or discrimination would be suspect. That is, any social benefits distributed differentially according to group membership would be viewed as unjust. Third, assimilation eliminates the situation of group differences resulting in social differences. Thus, people would be free to develop themselves as individuals. In sum, assimilation promises subordinate groups a 'deal' where their identities, culture, and values are to be surrendered for the promise or opportunity of improved life chances. Submission to the social rules of the dominant group supposedly mitigates the barriers confining subordinate groups (Adam, 1978).

Many writers (e.g., Young, 1990; Adam; 1978) have criticized assimilation as an unacceptable goal for liberation politics. Today in most Western democracies, there is widespread agreement that no person should be excluded from political, economic, or social activities because of ascribed characteristics. However, group differences continue to exist, and certain groups continue to be advantaged. Although some persons from disadvantaged groups have succeeded in improving their overall life chances, the overall scheme of allocating privilege and resources has remained unchanged (Adam, 1978).

Young (1990) outlines three ways that assimilation, by ignoring group differences, has oppressive consequences. First, assimilation entails bringing formerly excluded groups into the mainstream, but this means coming into the game after the rules and standards have already been established and having to prove oneself according to these rules and standards. The privileged group defines the standards against which all will be measured. And, because their privilege involves not recognizing these standards as culturally and experientially specific, they are perceived to be the ideal of a common, universal, and neutral humanity in which all can participate regardless of differences and inherent disadvantage to some. Because these standards are in fact specific to the dominant class, they put subordinate groups at a disadvantage in trying to measure up to them. For that reason assimilation policies perpetuate their disadvantage.

Second, the notion of a universal humanity devoid of group differences allows dominant groups to overlook or not recognize their own group specificity. The assimilationist's blindness to difference perpetuates cultural imperialism because it is the subordinate groups who must surrender their respective cultures and adopt the dominant culture, which is presented as a common, universal humanity.

Third, assimilation often produces an internalized devaluation by members of subordinate groups. To participate in the assimilationist project involves accepting an identity other than one's own and being reminded by others and by oneself of one's true but now submerged identity. As result, for example, children of non-English-speaking groups are often ashamed of the accents of their parents, women seek to control their tendency to cry, and gay and lesbian couples avoid displaying affection towards each other in public.

Because it has historically operated within the liberal humanist paradigm, conventional social work has (unwittingly for the most part) supported assimilation (Wachholz and Mullaly, 2000; Potocky, 1998).[1] By developing approaches and interventions that help people cope with and adjust to the dominant culture, by emphasizing impartiality as a principle of practice (i.e., treat everyone the same), by advocating for equal rights legislation (without the legal/financial resources to utilize it), and by privileging expert knowledge and dominant Eurocentric discourses, conventional social work has contributed to the subordination and homogenization of oppressed populations to the logic of capitalism and the dominant culture (Leonard, 1994).

Multiculturalism

Multiculturalism[2] is a North American offshoot of postmodernism (Agger, 1998). It is concerned that any overarching theory of oppression may omit or de-emphasize the unique and specific expression of each oppressive construct and context (e.g., see hooks, 1990; West, 1993). Multiculturalism posits a sharp break (a great divide) between modernity and postmodernity and emphasizes a theoretical logic based initially on the trinity of class, gender, and race as separate and coequal dimensions of oppression and liberation (Agger, 1998). This trinity has been extended to include age, disability, and other forms and sources of oppression, thus embracing a politics of identity (Arnowitz, 1992), or what Wineman (1984) calls 'parallel oppressions'. Separating different forms of oppression from each other leads to a conservative brand of politics that mitigates against any notion of solidarity among groups or uniting different groups into common causes to begin to change oppressive social structures. Instead, a competition for resources, media attention, and public support among various subordinate groups occurs—a competition that obviously benefits the dominant group.

Agger (1998) presents several reasons why postmodern multiculturalism has gained popularity in the United States. (1) It does not oppose the liberal capitalist framework within which issues of monoculturalism and multiculturalism are cast (conversely, it opposes Marxism as illiberal or un-American). (2) Rather than social change, multiculturalism makes the self its primary political agenda by focusing on how individual initiative and taking advantage of social and economic opportunities can lead to fulfillment of the American dream. (3) Multiculturalists hold that people's subject positions are influenced by gender and race as much as by class, but that these variables operate independently from one another so as to fragment people into racial, gender, and class groups with unique identities and with no intersections or interweaving occurring among these three variables. In sum, Agger contends that whereas postmodernists such as Lyotard wanted to break from all grand narratives that hold a singular reading of history, much of American postmodernism, in the form of multiculturalism, breaks only with Marxism.

Multicultural Celebrations

I have had the good fortune of having lived in Toronto, Canada, and Melbourne, Australia, two cities that pride themselves on their multicultural character. However, I have been struck in both cities by the number of people who equate multiculturalism with annual ethnic celebrations where there are traditional rituals, interesting entertainment, colourful dress, and wonderful food. Although these self-proclaimed advocates of multiculturalism may enjoy these exotic festivities, many of these same people show little interest in or knowledge of the struggles, blocked opportunities, and second-class citizenship that members of these (subordinate) cultures experience on a daily basis.

Given their emphasis on individualism, liberalism, and the politics of identity, along with their rejection of social change theories, how do multiculturalists deal with oppression, which, as discussed in Chapter 2, is a group-based phenomenon? Because each form and/or source of oppression is considered to be unique by multiculturalists, they believe that each oppressed group should be encouraged to 'narrate' its *own* experience of oppression and that only members of the oppressed group can tell their story (Healey, 1995). Others from outside the group cannot understand or appreciate another's experience or know what it is like to be 'them'. The political purpose of these narratives is to allow members of oppressed groups to formulate coherent personal identities based on their membership in these groups, in other words, to remake the self aided by hearing and reading narratives of other like-group members (Agger, 1998). This process is obviously one of consciousness-raising, but unlike the consciousness-raising of critical social theory, which uses it as a means to political action, the remaking of one's identity is an end in itself. What one does with this remade identity is, of course, an individual choice.

Colin Powell, the African-American former Chief of Staff of the American Armed Forces and currently the Secretary of State in the George W. Bush government, is an example of the postmodern politics of identity. He identifies himself as an African American and in his speeches often tells stories or narratives about his own life that do not deny his identity as an African American. In fact, his narratives often express and enhance his identity, subjectivity, and personhood. To the multiculturalist, the achievement of such selfhood is effective social change. Powell has succeeded in enhancing his personal identity as a major player in the

American mosaic (a multicultural goal), rather than as a change agent against a culture and institutions that oppress African Americans (and others).

Multiculturalism does not seem to possess much potential for anti-oppressive work. It may go a step further than assimilation in that it acknowledges the importance of group identity in formulating personal selfhood, but it also produces a status quo political agenda. By simply attempting to improve the well-being of individuals within various multicultural fractions, it leaves the structures of society intact. That is, multiculturalism may attempt to make adjustments so that subordinate cultures have a place in society, but it does nothing to undo the hierarchy of dominant-subordinate (superior-inferior) cultures. It views multicultural narratives as ends in themselves rather than as springboards to radical or structural change. It also denies the possibility of entering into coalitions or alliances with other oppressed groups. In fact, joint action on the part of members of a particular oppressed group is diluted by the fact that the major concern is to produce narratives that express and enhance victims' selfhood or identity. Finally, its acceptance of individualism and liberal capitalism makes it difficult to foster a commitment to social change.

The Politics of Difference

Because a policy of assimilation leads to oppressive consequences and a policy of multiculturalism to a ghettoization of subordinate groups, something else is needed to combat oppression at the structural level. As an alternative to assimilation Barry Adam argues for collective resistance to oppression on the part of subordinated groups. He emphasizes the importance of community for developing self-identity, solidarity, and resistance to domination. Communication among members of a subordinate group over time engenders social networks and language that nurture collectivization and a new understanding of their life situation—one defined by the group itself.

> Shared experiences identify effective strategies for coping with social limitations, methods of survival and self-betterment, sources of freedom and joy. Brotherhood or sisterhood is not the simple correlate of, for example, physical resemblances; it is the mutual creation . . . of each member by the other. (Adam, 1978: 122)

Although this process of group solidarity and self-identity is crucial to maintain one's culture, it could, if unchecked, lead to a situation of ghetto-like communities of oppressed groups separated from the dominant culture and from each other. To overcome this possibility Young (1990) proposes a 'politics of difference'. She elaborates on Adam's notion of community as the means of overcoming oppression. Rather than attempting to transcend group differences, as the assimilationist approach would do, the politics of difference seeks equality among all socially and culturally differentiated groups, where mutual respect and affirmation of their differences would occur. Group differences would be considered as positive and desirable rather than as a liability or disadvantage. The positivity of group difference would be liberating and empowering in that the identity the dominant group has taught them to despise would be reclaimed, affirmed, and celebrated. This positive view of one's specific culture and experience would make it increasingly difficult for the dominant group to parade its values and norms as universal and neutral.

It might seem at this point that there is not much difference between multiculturalism and a politics of difference since both advocate that different subordinate groups establish separate organizations that exclude all other groups. However, there is a crucial difference between the two in terms of the purposes of establishing exclusionary organizations. Multiculturalists view separate organizations as an 'end' in themselves—a place where members can meet and tell their stories. Proponents of a politics of difference view them as a 'means' to an end, that is, a means to full participation and first-class (equal) citizenship in society. The politics of group difference would promote a notion of group solidarity against the individualism of liberal humanism because it is recognized that a positive view of one's specific group would require separate organizations that exclude others. However, this would not eliminate the need for coalitions among groups or the need for oppressed groups to combat other types of oppression (e.g., white people against racism or men against sexism)—an impossibility of the multicultural approach. Group autonomy is an important vehicle for empowerment and the development of a group-specific voice and perspective (Young, 1990), but it does not, by itself, eliminate practices of oppression by the dominant group.

Young (1990) notes that there is a fear by many that asserting group differences will lead to a justification of subordination. However, she contends that a politics of difference confronts this fear because it presents group difference not as essentialist, otherness, or exclusive opposition but as ambiguous, relational, and shifting, marked by specificity and variation. In this way group differences are conceived as relational rather than defined by substantive categories and attributes (Minow, 1985, 1987; Ng, 1993). A relational view of difference does not focus on the attributes of groups as the measure of difference, but on the interaction of groups with institutions (Littleton, 1987, cited in Young, 1990; Ng, 1993).

With this relational view, the meaning of difference becomes contextualized (Ng, 1993; Scott, 1988, cited in Young, 1990). Group differences are conspicuous, depending on the groups compared, the purposes of the comparison, and the point of view of those making the comparison. Such contextualized understandings of difference undermine essentialist assumptions. Young provides the following example to underscore this point. Wheelchair-bound persons are different from other people in terms of athletics, health care, and social service support, but they are not different in many other respects. At one time disabled persons were excluded and segregated from society because the differences between able-bodied and disabled persons were conceptualized as extending to all or most capacities.

A relational understanding of group difference rejects social exclusion. Differences among groups do not mean the groups or their members are different in all respects. Overlapping experiences, common goals, and shared attributes are recognized. The assumption that oppositional categorization is inherent in group differences must always be challenged. A relational and contextualized understanding of difference also undermines the notion of an essential individual identity. Persons have many different identities as they tend to be members of many affinity groups, not just one. Black persons, for example, may be poor, rich, old, or gay. These differences produce different identities as well as potential conflicts with other black people and affinities with some white people. Thus, contextualizing the meanings of difference and identity helps us to see the differences that may exist within affinity groups. Oppressed persons are seldom oppressed along one dimension only. They tend to be multiply oppressed. 'In our complex, plural society, every social group has group differences cutting across it, which are potential sources of wisdom, excitement, conflict, and oppression' (Young, 1990: 172–3). This intersectional nature or multiplicity of oppression is the subject of Chapter 7.

A politics of difference, of course, has serious implications for policy-making. A goal of social justice (and anti-oppressive social work) is social equality. As discussed in Chapter 2, social equality refers both to an equitable distribution of social goods and to full participation of everyone in society's major institutions, and this must involve the socially supported opportunity for all to develop and exercise their inherent capacities. Although formal legal equality for most groups exists in Canada, and in many other Western societies, these societies are still marked by extreme social inequality. Instead of policies that are universally formulated and thus blind to differences of class, race, gender, age, and so forth, a politics of difference would require policies that reflect the specific situations of oppressed groups. 'Groups cannot be socially equal unless their specific experience, culture, and social contributions are publicly affirmed and recognized' (ibid., 174).

A politics of difference would require a dual system of rights: a general system of rights for all, and a more specific system of group-conscious rights and policies (ibid.). We already have a precedent for such a system in the form of civil, political, and human rights for all citizens, as well as affirmative action and employment equity programs for some groups (e.g., women, people of colour) who have been historically disadvantaged in our society. To extend this dual system of rights to the point that there would be effective recognition and representation of the voices and perspectives of oppressed groups (as opposed to interest groups), Young proposes the implementation of institutional mechanisms and public resources to support the following: (1) the self-organization of subordinate groups whereby group members could achieve collective empowerment and a reflective understanding of their collective experiences and interests in the context of society; (2) group analysis and generation of policy proposals in institutionalized settings whereby decision-makers are obliged to demonstrate that their deliberations have taken relevant group perspectives into consideration; and (3) group veto power regarding specific policies and decisions that affect a group directly, such as land use for Aboriginal communities or reproductive rights for women. Such institutional mechanisms would go a long way towards combatting oppression at the structural level.

Economic Relations and Oppression

Capitalism is one of the structures that maintains hierarchical social divisions. In the previous chapter we looked at capitalism as a totalizing culture (Leonard, 1997) that produces and maintains dominant-subordinate relationships in all areas of society. And in Chapter 2 we saw that three of Young's five faces of oppression (exploitation, marginalization, and powerlessness) are related to the social divisions of work inherent in the capitalist economic system. Here we will look at how capitalism as an economic system has changed its form over the past few decades (but not its oppressive function) along with the contemporary and related discourses of capitalism and welfare.

That the face of capitalism has changed since the mid-1970s is now a matter of record. Although seldom steady and never free from tensions and conflict, post-war capitalism managed to maintain an economic boom from 1945 until 1973. This long boom raised material living standards for much of the population in advanced capitalist countries and provided a relatively stable environment for corporate profit-making. The particular set of labour control practices, consumption patterns, and configurations of political and economic power that characterized post-war capitalism depended on a series of (unwritten and tacit) compromises on the part of its key players: the corporate sector, the trade union movement, and the nation-state. In his celebrated book, *The Condition of Postmodernity* (1989), David Harvey outlines the nature of these compromises and the roles played by their major actors.

For its part, large corporate power was to assure steady increased investments and to commit itself to ongoing technological development, mass fixed capital investments in plants and equipment, and mobilization of economies of scale through standardization of products. Scientific management became the cornerstone of bureaucratic rationality, and the massing of workers in large-scale factories became the modus operandi of productive processes that, in turn, depended on hierarchical work relations and a deskilled workforce. In exchange for real wage gains and job security from employers and for social insurance and minimum-wage benefits from the state, the trade union movement undertook to control their membership and collaborate with business in plans to increase productivity. The state, for its part, was to promote a favourable environment for business through an appropriate mix of fiscal and monetary policy, and to supplement the social wage by providing programs of social insurance, health care, education, and housing.[3] This form of capitalism (with a welfare state) became (and continues to be) known as 'welfare capitalism'.

The assumption underpinning the above model of capitalism was that of infinite economic growth. The production and consumption of more and more products would be followed by more and more jobs, increased profits, higher wages, and more government revenue for an ever-expanding welfare state. Although there were already cracks appearing in the post-war capitalist economy (Harvey,

1989), the sharp recession of 1973, combined with the oil crisis of that year (which saw a quadrupling in the price of oil) and the inflationary impact of the Vietnam War, set in motion a whole set of processes that shattered the 'grand corporate-labour-state accord'. By this time capitalism was in a state of crisis and could no longer contain its inherent contradictions. These contradictions can be summarized in one word—rigidity. There were rigidities in the existing long-term and large-scale fixed capital investments in mass production systems. There were rigidities in labour markets, labour allocation, and labour contracts that seemed immovable because of working-class power. And there were rigidities in state commitments to provide statutory social programs in the face of shrinking government revenues.

The corporate sector was the first to confront these rigidities directly (and the first to break the accord with labour and the state), and thus began a process whereby a new form of capitalism has replaced the post-war model. For the past two-and-a-half decades we have been experiencing a rapid transition from a rigid form of capitalism to a more flexible (for the capitalists at least) form. For the corporate sector the crisis in capitalism meant that stable growth in consumer markets could no longer be assumed. Given the rigidities of labour allocation, labour contracts, and unusable excess capacity because of idle plants and equipment, corporations were forced to rationalize and restructure their operations and intensify their control over labour. Technological change, automation, downsizing, mergers, acceleration of capital turnover, and moves to countries with cheaper and more manageable labour became the strategies for corporate survival (ibid.).

Governments also felt the effects of the 1970s crisis in capitalism and its subsequent transformation. Faced with shrinking revenues because of economic decline and growing numbers of people in need, most governments chose to reduce expenditures rather than increase taxes and targeted the welfare state as a major area of cost containment. Survival in the global economy now takes precedence over meeting the human and social needs of people. Instead of regulating corporate power, nation-states are now competing with each other to attract businesses to their respective locations. Fisher and Karger (1997) point out that capital mobility has eroded the power of nation-states to control their own economic and social matters. Countries today appear to measure their success not by the quality of life they provide for their citizens, but by how much they cut costs to become more attractive as an investment site for business (Fisher and Karger, 1997) or by how much they will cut taxes for the wealthy in light of current budget surpluses.

These changes in capitalism have occurred in all Western advanced capitalist countries. Although given different labels—Thatcherism in Britain, Reaganomics in the US, neo-conservatism in Canada, and economic rationalism in Australia and New Zealand—the changes in the economic, social, and political environment of the new capitalism have re-emphasized the vulnerability of historically disadvantaged groups, particularly women, children, immigrants, visible minorities, poor people, and workers in less-developed countries. These changes have also weakened the trade union movement since it has lost core, full-time members in the face of the transition to a flexible (i.e., part-time, subcontracted, temporary) labour force. Trade unions have also experienced legislative curbs on their power and the relocation (and the threat of relocation) of many manufacturing businesses to underdeveloped countries. And class consciousness has been reduced because struggling against exploitation in the factory or plant is very different from struggling against smaller subcontracting businesses or against a father or uncle or other type of 'godfather' who runs a home or sweat-shop-based business.

Along with a transformed capitalist economic system comes a discourse that justifies this new global capitalism—a discourse of economic determinism. The central message of this discourse on the new economy is that global capitalism is a normal, natural, evolutionary, and inevitable process. Therefore, it should not be resisted or tampered with (especially by unions or governments), but instead it should be embraced. Any form of Keynesian intervention by the state is now dead, or so we are told by the corporate sector along with its government allies, neo-classical economists, and the mainstream press. The global economy is spoken about in terms of economic *laws* (e.g., the law of supply and demand, the laws of competition) and mystical market *forces* that presumably come from a higher source than humankind—perhaps nature or divine providence. The dominant discourse on the new economy also speaks of the joys of entrepreneurial innovation and the economic necessity of worker adjustment (Leonard, 1997). At the same time, too, it is made to appear imperative that any resistance to desired changes in the labour processes or to new forms of production must be overcome by whatever means are at hand (Head, 1996).

The discourse of globalization uses Darwinian and Hobbesian language to urge us to accept that competitive life, although nasty and brutish, is necessary for survival in the global economy (Leonard, 1997). We are told that we must accept the negative consequences of the development of globalization on employment, unemployment, wages, community, and class relations because the consequences would be even worse if we did not compete successfully in the global market. Worsening poverty is deemed unsolvable because it is the product of an 'underclass' subculture (Fisher and Karger, 1997). Economic development is part of the discourse applied to exploitation of the developing world by corporate capitalism, yet this latter world continues to provide cheap resources just as it did in the days of colonial rule. Needless to say, such a system maximizes profits for global corporations while contributing to global poverty.

A significant part of the discourse on the new economy is to present the market and social investment as a contradiction. That is, how can a lean economy that must compete in the global market support a welfare state? The predictable answer, of course, is that it cannot. Leonard (1997: 113) comments on this position:

> the old ideas which ruled the modern welfare state—universality, full employment, increasing equality—are proclaimed to be a hindrance to survival. They are

castigated as ideas which have outlived their usefulness: they are no longer appropriate to the conditions of a global capitalist economy.

Ironically, while many ideas associated with the modern welfare state are presented as irrelevant and outmoded in the discourse of the new economy, old ideas about work are given a renewed emphasis. The notion of work is that of waged work and is framed as a moral obligation (reinforced by the emphasis on the Protestant work ethic during the stages of early and middle capitalism), which, in effect, subordinates individual needs and capacities to the imperatives of accumulation, profit, and social regulation (ibid.). The social paradox this creates is that in the face of increasing poverty among both traditionally and non-traditionally poor groups there is diminished social spending as governments roll back social gains made by working populations. The caring and empowering aspects of the welfare state are reduced at the same time as its regulating and controlling functions are enhanced. 'Need' is no longer the absolute criterion for assistance, as evidenced by compulsory work-for-welfare schemes and the recent program of the Ontario provincial government in Canada of mandatory drug-testing of all welfare recipients (those who test positive must seek help for their alleged addiction or lose their welfare assistance). Those in need are vilified in the new dominant discourse as being afraid to work, dependent, immoral, and a drain on the public purse.

The final chapter addresses what can be done through an anti-oppressive framework about the discursive practices of the new global economy. At this point, however, it is worth noting that the global economy has already shown cracks and a crisis of legitimacy appears to be on the horizon. The Asian and Russian economic crises show that the global economy is not as robust as its proponents contend. The growing level of poverty and the discrepancy in material and living conditions between rich and poor cannot be tolerated indefinitely, nor can the growing number of people in need at the same time the welfare state is cut back. In addition, there is a limit to the geographical expansion of capitalism. Counter-discourses are needed to expose the myth of technological and economic determinism, which characterizes contemporary debate about the welfare state. The doctrine that unfettered capitalist development on a global scale is necessary for economic survival also must be challenged by showing that such development has occurred because of decisions and actions made by a relatively small group of people (corporate power and its government allies). What was made by people can be unmade and/or remade.

Political Relations and Oppression

Politics refers to the activities carried out through which people govern themselves—that is, how they determine what they will do collectively, how they will live together, and what they want in the future (Pitkin, 1981). This decision-making can occur on a small group level (e.g., work unit or family or interest group) or on a macro level (e.g., provincial or state or national government). The focus here is on the latter—how decisions are made in the public arena, who makes them, and who benefits from them. In Chapter 1, the consensus and conflict views of the nature of society were presented. In contrast to the consensus view, the conflict perspective holds that many groups in society have conflicting interests and that political decisions are made on the basis of economic and political power. In other words, the powerful or dominant groups are able to exercise their power at the political level to have legislation or policies enacted that protect their interests and domination, often at the expense of subordinate groups. But how does this happen in democratic societies such as the Anglo-American nations?

Politics and governance in most liberal or neo-liberal market societies today are couched within a discourse on democracy or democratic participation. However, as Peter Leonard (1997) points out, there is a contradiction between the social ideal of democracy required for the legitimation of our current political system and certain social practices, such as centralized hierarchical decision-making, that are necessary for the continuation of the system. While acknowledging that some democratic gains, historically, have been made through political struggle by a bourgeoisie in pursuit of its class and gender interests, he argues that embedded within the dominant discourse on democracy are bourgeois and patriarchal assumptions about representation, leadership, majority rule, dissent, and diversity. These assumptions underpin how our current democracy operates to protect the interests of the dominant group under the guise of a free and participatory political system.

Social work subscribes to democratic ideals such as self-determination, participation, and an equal distribution of political power. In fact, much of social work practice is directed towards individuals and groups, helping them gain or regain autonomy and control over their lives. However, there are basically two methods by which democracy can be practised: representative democracy and participatory democracy. We are all used to the representative form of democracy, as it is the model practised in most Anglo-American nations today. Let us briefly examine the dominant discourse on (representative) democracy before discussing participatory democracy.

Representative Democracy Discourse

Although there are elements of other political philosophies (e.g., conservatism and social democracy) within most Anglo-American nations, by and large, liberal values, ideals, and beliefs have formed the basis of their political systems since World War II (Marchak, 1981; Mullaly, 1997a). The fundamental political beliefs of liberalism lie in representative democracy (Marchak, 1981) and pluralism (Sills, 1968). Liberal democrats would argue that direct participation in the day-to-day business of government by the electorate is impossible. Rather, the essence of modern-day democracy rests in the popular control of elected representatives. Control is exercised through the competition of people running for office, selection by the people of representatives in periodic elections, limitations on the power elected representatives can exercise while in office, and removal of the incumbent representatives if they fail to perform to the people's satisfaction.

In sum, liberals contend that the ultimate control within a representative democracy rests with the people who elect and hold accountable a representative government.

According to the liberals universal suffrage has led to a transformation of political systems in Western democracies from institutionalized ruling-class governments of the eighteenth and nineteenth centuries to open and democratic structures, where the ordinary citizen now has direct and immediate access to his or her elected representative. However, 'modern society has become considerably more complex during the twentieth century and "political power" has become more "diffused" and more "corporate" ' (Pritchard and Taylor, 1978: 93). In other words, governments are more involved in a whole range of issues and areas, and numerous competing interest and pressure groups have emerged whose purposes are to influence the decisions of elected representatives.

The second fundamental political belief of liberals is that in a representative (liberal) democracy political power is divided among competing interest groups so that no one group dominates another, let alone dominates the government. This view of political power is called pluralism. The government acts as an independent arbitrator (umpire) of these competing interest groups, controlling their activities by a set of rules—the law—through which it acts as the guardian of the public interest and of individual rights. Thus, it is claimed, no government can fail to respond to the wishes of its citizens because the individual is heard through his or her membership in particular interest groups and at election time.

Critique of Representative Democracy

The discourse or ideal of representative democracy is very different from its actual practice. Although this model of democracy may be relatively efficient in terms of the time it takes to make decisions, its weaknesses have been well documented in the literature (e.g., Galper, 1975; Hardy, 1981b; Lees, 1972; Marchak, 1981; Pateman, 1970). (1) Political elites at times make decisions that are not responsive to the wishes of the electorate. (2) Interest groups may gain some sectional advantage at the expense of more general welfare. (3) Unorganized sections of society may be ignored or exploited by powerful, organized sections. (4) The right to vote every few years is inconsistent with the notion of democracy. (5) Such a system promotes and relies on a considerable degree of passivity in the majority of people. (6) In the absence of participatory principles, those who make decisions will be those who have been most successful in getting to the top, which is an individualistic and not an egalitarian practice. 'Though democratic in the way it is chosen, representative government has been shown to be elitist in the way that it operates' (Lees, 1972: 39).

A major concern with the pluralistic nature of representative government is that it reflects the Darwinian notion of competition that characterizes the capitalist economic system. Competition permeates not only the way the governing party assumes power (i.e., by winning an election), but how political decisions are made. Various interest groups (including dominant and subordinate groups) compete with one another to gain the attention of legislators and government officials to have their needs and interests recognized and to have legislation and policies enacted to help meet these needs and interests. And, of course, in any competition there are winners and losers. Furthermore, the dominant groups have more financial resources and political connections to help them better make their needs and interests known. Thus the system is biased in their favour. One does not win by persuading the public that one's cause is just (Young, 1990). In a system of interest-group pluralism no distinction is made between the assertion of selfish interests (e.g., a plea by the wealthy for a tax break) and normative claims to justice or rights (e.g., a plea by gay and lesbian couples for same-sex family benefits). The winner in a pluralistic political system will most likely be the group able to mount the most effective campaign, which, of course, will be largely determined by the size of the group along with the financial and political resources available to it.

To be sure, politicians and their close advisers directly decide on public policy, but who are these decision-makers in terms of their social and economic characteristics? Since the system is based on the notion that an elected government represents all the people in society, do politicians reflect the makeup of society in terms of class, gender, race, and other social variables? Addressing the Canadian situation, which does not appear to be significantly different from that of other Anglo parliamentary democracies, Wharf and Cossom (1987) make two important observations. First, the number of people making political decisions (i.e., proposing new policies and revising existing policies) in Canada at the federal and provincial levels are few in number—usually the Prime Minister (or Premier) and a few powerful cabinet ministers and their senior advisers. Second, these few decision-makers are relatively homogeneous. For the most part, they are middle-aged white men with a business or professional background who have benefited and prospered from the existing social, economic, and political arrangements. Because they are 'successful', they have little personal commitment to change in a fundamental way any aspect of Canadian society.

While the rhetoric or discourse of representative democracy is that elected representatives govern with the best interests of all people in mind, the reality is that elected officials will make decisions consistent with their world views, which in this instance have been shaped by their experiences as white, middle-aged, prosperous, and successful men. In effect, decisions that affect the quality of life and opportunities for development of members of subordinate groups are made by persons who are not members of those groups and, in many cases, have little understanding of the day-to-day realities faced by these group members. For example, poverty policy is made mostly by people who have never experienced poverty. Policies on Aboriginal issues are made by people who may never have visited an Aboriginal community. Housing policies are made by people who have never been without adequate housing, let alone no housing. And policies on race relations and human rights are made mainly by people who have never been turned down for a job or housing because of the colour of their skin. How can these people possibly represent the needs and best interests of marginalized and subordinate groups in any meaningful or constructive way—especially if it means changing society in ways that would erode their (the dominant group) own social privileges and standing?

Two Societies

Fiona, the daughter of a business executive, Jill, the daughter of a newspaper publisher, and Roger, the son of a university professor, had similar experiences growing up. All had comfortable homes in crime-free and mostly white neighbourhoods. All attended the finest schools, had extra money from their parents when they needed it, wore the latest teen fashions, and belonged to the most popular clubs and organizations for adolescents. All went on overseas vacations with their families, which broadened their horizons and provided them with a certain sense of confident worldliness. All had their university education paid by their parents and were able to make use of family connections to get good jobs after graduation. Conversely, Bill, the son of a seasonal worker in the Maritimes, Jim, one of five children in a lone-parent family, and Frances, daughter of parents in receipt of welfare, also had similar experiences growing up. They lived in neighbourhoods with inadequate housing and where heavy traffic and crime were problems. The schools they attended lacked resources, their parents could not provide extra help for them, and many of their clothes were bought at 'Sally-Ann' stores. They could not afford to join clubs or organizations for teens or go on holiday trips, and spent most of their spare time on the streets. There was always tension in their homes and a steady stream of bill collectors, police, and social services officials at their doors. There was no money for university and no family friends provided jobs. Whereas the former group saw and experienced a stable and orderly society full of opportunities, the latter saw and experienced a chaotic and crisis-ridden society with no opportunities.

A few words must be said about the theoretical incapacity of liberalism to explain certain social, economic, and political phenomena in a liberal society. Marchak (1981) provides an impressive amount of data that reveal some of the realities of Canadian society, in particular, but that could apply to any Anglo-American country. Liberalism does not explain why: there is poverty in the midst of affluence; there is evidence of interference in the political process by privately owned corporations; there are persistent divisions of the population along economic lines, which liberals refuse to recognize as class division or dominant-subordinate divisions; the decisions of large corporations more profoundly affect the lives of people than do the actions of politicians. These empirical facts of a liberal society are not accounted for within the liberal discourse.

Liberalism accounts for differences among individuals in terms of quality of life as due to individual differences in talent or effort or due to slight imperfections in a system that may not be perfect, but which the discourse claims is the best there is (and therefore should be preserved). According to liberals, the consequences of the former can be alleviated and the latter can be corrected or reformed. However, the evidence does not substantiate these beliefs but suggests, rather, that there are consistent and persistent differences among identifiable groups in Canada (and elsewhere) with respect to wealth, political power, and access to goods, services, and social institutions. The evidence also shows that these differences are attributable *not* to individual characteristics but to social characteristics such as ethnicity, gender, age, place of residence, and family of origin (Curtis et al., 1988; Marchak, 1981). In other words, dominant-subordinate relations tend to be maintained and reproduced rather than reduced or eliminated under a liberal representative democracy. The major criticism of liberalism is that it has failed to reform the system to correct the causes of different levels of living and opportunities that exist among different social groupings. Writing on the Canadian situation, Marchak (1981: 42–3) articulates this criticism:

> Regional inequalities persist in spite of equalization payments; poverty persists in spite of a welfare system; the taxation system is finally unable to redress the considerable imbalances between the rich and the poor. These are puzzles that the liberal ideology, with its emphasis on individual achievement, equality of opportunity, a market-place for competing talents, and an openness to reform, cannot explain.

Participatory Democracy

By way of contrast, participatory democracy would produce a very different world (Hardy, 1981b) from that of a liberal representative democracy. Aristotle associated citizenship with the rights of sharing in decisions (Berry, 1986). Lees (1972) and Pateman (1970) contend that a participatory democracy would permit and encourage greater popular participation in such non-governmental arenas as industry, trade unions, political parties, corporations, schools, and universities. Pateman (1970) argues that this participation is educative and that a participatory system is self-sustaining because the qualities needed to support it are generated by the very act of participation itself.

Like Pateman, Bachrach (1969) believes that participation is both political and personal, for it recognizes the self-developmental nature of human beings and enables them through participation to gain in self-esteem. In turn, this self-development will reveal to individuals their authentic identities (as opposed to the ones imposed on them by dominant groups) and what it is they really want (as opposed to manufactured wants and desires). Through participation, people may come to understand themselves as political beings capable of understanding issues that affect them and able to make decisions on these issues. This contrasts with the beliefs of such proponents of representative democracy (and critics of participatory democracy) as Joseph Schumpeter (1950) and Robert Dahl (1970) (cited in Berry, 1986).[4] A participatory democracy would delegate a larger share of public power to local communities small enough to permit effective and meaningful general participation in decision-making. Lees (1972: 41) elaborates on this point:

Participation in politics would provide individuals with opportunities to take part in making significant decisions about their everyday lives. It would build and consolidate a sense of genuine community that would serve as a solid foundation for government. The first and most important step is to recognize that personal self-development is the moral goal of democracy and that direct popular participation is the chief means of achieving it. When this is generally accepted, then society can get on with the largely technical job of thinking up new and better means for increasing popular participation.

With respect to thinking up new and better means for increasing political participation of subordinate or oppressed groups (as opposed to interest groups), the suggestions put forth by Young (1990) in her 'politics of difference' model would be good starting point. A dual system of rights, support for self-organization of subordinate groups, a political imperative of considering the perspectives of subordinate groups, and a group veto power over decisions that affect the group directly would go a long way towards reducing the 'tyranny of the minority' that often accompanies the 'rule of the majority' found in most representative democracies. Many participatory mechanisms and models found throughout the world could be considered to increase the political participation and power of oppressed groups. A first step, however, is to break free from a discourse that presents representative democracy as the only viable model of democracy.

Effects of Structural Oppression

Given the above discussions of *how* subordinate groups are excluded from or marginalized within or exploited by the three subsystems (i.e., social, economic, and political) of the structural level, this section addresses the question of *what* structural oppression means for dominated people with respect to their everyday living. What are the actual effects of maintaining group-based social hierarchy by structural means? Specifically, this section will look at the ways that social institutions, laws, policies, and practices disproportionately allocate goods and services with positive social value (e.g., good health care, decent housing, high social status) to dominant group members and disproportionately allocate goods and services with negative social value (e.g., inadequate housing, low social status, incarceration) to members of subordinate groups.

Most (but not all) structural oppression today in most Western democracies is covert. That is, unlike overt structural oppression, it does not openly and explicitly target particular social groups for differential treatment. Examples of overt structural oppression would be not allowing women or black persons to vote in elections (as existed in many Western jurisdictions in the first half of the last century) or not allowing gay and lesbian persons to marry or to have other benefits such as pension rights that heterosexual couples have (as exists today). Many writers today argue that much of the overt structural discrimination or oppression of yesterday has been replaced by its 'covert shadow' (Sidanius and Pratto, 1999: 128).

Covert oppression at the structural level is a powerful force in maintaining group-based hierarchies. First, it contradicts the spirit and intention of the civil and human rights legislation and the principles of liberty and equality that have been developed over the past hundred years to prohibit institutional discrimination and to extend citizenship status to previously excluded groups. Second, its hidden nature results in many dominant and subordinate group members not recognizing it, which, as will be seen in the next chapter, may result in subordinate group members blaming themselves for their own oppression (i.e., internalizing their oppression). Even if recognized, the hidden and subtle nature of covert oppression makes it very difficult for subordinate groups to employ collective action for change. The belief that modern Western democracies are largely free from discrimination and oppression at the structural level is not only held by the lay public, but is widespread among political commentators, public intellectuals, and a number of scholars (ibid.). However, the evidence overwhelmingly contradicts this belief. As will be seen below, rather than social equality and equal opportunity being of central importance in democratic societies, widespread institutional or structural oppression affects all the major areas of an individual's life—employment, housing, health, education, financial opportunities, and treatment by the criminal justice system. Structural oppression constitutes a total environment, or what Sidanius and Pratto (1999: 129) call a 'circle of oppression'.

Oppression as Structural Violence

Violence, as defined in Chapter 2, includes both actions that result in physical injury and threats, intimidation, harassment, and bullying. When violence is systemic, that is, when it happens to someone because he or she is a member of a particular social group, then it is a form of oppression. Gil (1998), Bulhan (1985), and Fanon (1968) have argued convincingly that oppression at the structural or institutional level is a form of violence. A definition of violence that links it to structural oppression (as well as to oppression at the personal level) is provided by Bulhan (1985: 135): 'Violence is any relation, process, or condition by which an individual or a group violates the physical, social, and/or psychological integrity of another person or group.' From this perspective Bulhan points out that violence negatively affects human growth and development, interferes with the inherent potential of individuals, limits productive living, and causes death.

Bulhan identifies five assumptions that underpin and flow from the above definition of violence. First, violence is not a simple random act but is any relation, condition, or process that negatively affects the well-being of its victim. Second, violence is not only moral or ethical, but physical, psychological, and social as well. Third, violence in any of these three areas has repercussions for the other two areas (e.g., physical violence will have psychological and social effects). Fourth, violence occurs not only between individuals, but also between groups and societies. And, finally, the intention is less important than the consequence of most forms and acts of violence. This concept of violence also includes the vast array of legitimized or socially sanctioned forms of violence that create and maintain a condition of oppression. Some of these forms are presented below.

Bulhan contends that violence at the personal level is relatively easy to detect and control as it usually involves direct action in which the act of violence and its consequences are observable. The perpetrator and the victim are normally distinguishable, and the purpose of the violence can be verified and its effects assessed. Structural violence is a much more complex and higher-order phenomenon. It is a feature of social structures and social institutions. The social processes, relations, and practices associated with social inequities often span generations. They are deeply ingrained in people and dominate everyday living. 'Structural violence involves more than the violation of fairness and justice. . . . [It] leads to hidden but lethal inequities, which can lead to the death of those who lack power or influence in the society' (ibid., 136). Rather than a quick death by state execution or a personal act of lethal violence, structural oppression in the form of such inequities as inadequate income, substandard or no housing, unemployment, and lack of health care leads to a slow, agonizing, unpunished, and premature death for countless numbers of subordinated people all over the world on a daily basis.

In *Social Dominance* (1999), Sidanius and Pratto present an impressive amount of empirical data and powerful evidence showing that covert structural oppression can be found in all the major areas of an individual's life in Western democratic nations.[5] These major areas include employment, financial opportunities, the housing and retail markets, education, health care, and the criminal justice system.

Discrimination in the Housing and Retail Markets

Although most Western nations have housing legislation and programs, broad-based and systematic yet covert housing discrimination relegates many subordinate group members to areas that are impoverished, underserviced, and dangerous. Having examined American, Swedish, and British studies on housing and retail discrimination with respect to race, Sidanius and Pratto (1999: 148) concluded that 'Housing discrimination is found at each stage of the housing search, from initial information concerning housing availability, to efforts made to conclude transactions, to the availability of financing, and to the final location of housing.'

The studies showed that agents gave people of colour much less information on available housing units for sale or rent than was given to white people. Also, people of colour did not receive from agents the same level of positive comments on prospective homes or special incentives to take a rented apartment, as was given to white persons, and they were more likely to be asked to call the agent back rather than have the transaction pursued immediately. Even when the housing agents decided to complete a transaction with members of visible minorities, they were more likely, in spite of the minority persons having adequate financial resources, to direct them to an area other than the one originally requested. The areas to which minority persons were directed tended to be those with greater minority populations, lower incomes, lower housing values, substandard schools, and higher crime rates.

As well as discrimination in the housing market, subordinate groups were found to be discriminated against in the retail market. Retail outlets located in neighbourhoods occupied by subordinate groups charged higher prices for the same goods as stores located in neighbourhoods occupied by dominant groups. Furthermore, for goods that have negotiations attached to them in terms of prices (e.g., cars), it was found that black people pay more than white people and women pay more than men for the same goods, even when the location of the retail outlet is controlled.

Discrimination in the Labour Market

Sidanius and Pratto also examined labour markets and found discrimination of subordinate groups. Studies that looked at the labour markets of 12 Western democracies showed that job discrimination occurs in all of them. Of course, work is a strong determinant of one's perceived worth, social position, and general well-being. By allocating various kinds of jobs to different social groups, societies produce and maintain group-based social dominance.

In their review of the research into labour market discrimination Sidanius and Pratto discovered widespread systematic discrimination against women and subordinate classes, races, ethnicities, religions, and nationalities in all countries studied. Subordinate group members have less chance of being hired, receive less pay for the same job, have fewer opportunities for on-the-job training, have less chance for promotion, and have greater risk of dismissal. The level of labour market discrimination is greater: (1) for jobs requiring more rather than less contact with people; (2) in the private sector over the public sector; (3) for jobs requiring fewer qualifications; (4) when for-profit employment agencies are used; (5) in jobs that are narrowly rather than broadly advertised; and (6) during times of economic recession. They also found that although most job discrimination is covert, a significant number of businesses still discriminate overtly, 'even when such discrimination is patently illegal' (ibid., 177). Finally, they found that social policies intended to address problems of discrimination in the labour market, such as affirmative action and employment equity, are the very policies that are most unpopular with the dominant group, and, therefore, may not be sustainable in the long run.

Discrimination in the Education System

Another area considered by Sidanius and Pratto was education. Again, studies in over a dozen Western and Eastern democracies indicate discrimination against subordinate groups in educational systems in all jurisdictions. Both the quantity and quality of education are lower for subordinate groups than for dominant groups. The authors identified four mechanisms of institutional discrimination that help to produce these differential outcomes: (1) differential funding—children in dominant groups receive a larger proportion of public education resources for their education; (2) differential referral—children who are poor, non-white, from disadvantaged neighbourhoods are more likely to be regarded as emotionally disturbed or mentally challenged and referred to special education or remedial classes; (3) differential tracking—students from subordinate groups are more likely to be channelled into non-academic or vocational programs and students from dominant groups are more likely to be channelled into academically enriched classes regardless of academic abilities; and (4) differential teacher expectations—students regarded and treated by teachers as dull fall below the performances of those students who teachers consider and treat as bright, and children from subordinate groups usually fall into the first category while those from the dominant group are in the second category.

Discrimination in the Health-Care System

Consistent with almost all national and international studies looking at health status with respect to dominant-subordinate groups, Sidanius and Pratto found that subordinate groups experience higher morbidity and premature mortality rates. Conversely, those at the top of the social hierarchy are generally in better physical and psychological health than those below them (Aboriginal people in all nations with Aboriginal populations rank far at the bottom). Subordinate group members are less likely to have access to the economic and social resources that promote health (i.e., plentiful and nutritionally balanced food, living and work environments that are not dangerous or stressful, and access to immediate and high-quality medical care).

In addition to lack of resources or ready access to medical care, subordinate populations are discriminated against within the health-care system, although there does not appear to be as much overt discrimination today as there was in the past. For example, in the past many countries have had forced sterilization policies for poor people, black persons, mentally challenged people, and ethnic minorities. There have been experiments on prisoners as well, which involved withholding food to see how little a person could live on, and medical treatment has been withheld from poor persons to determine the long-term effects of such diseases as syphilis (Jones, 1993, cited ibid.).

Although such overt discrimination is not common today, there is considerable covert discrimination against subordinate populations within health-care systems. Sidanius and Pratto contend that this covert discrimination takes the forms of: (1) differential treatment by health-care professionals; (2) differential dissemination of health-care information; and (3) the physiological effects of discrimination. With respect to differential treatment, they found that white persons received higher levels of medical care than black people for coronary problems, extreme kidney failure, and cancer. They also found that poor people have lower rates of immunization than affluent persons and black people have lower immunization rates than white people. Similarly, mammography rates were lower for black women than for white women and lower for poor persons than for affluent persons. Finally, disfiguring medical procedures (amputations, castrations) were higher among black people than white people.

With respect to differential dissemination of health-care information, one study (Kogan et al., 1994, cited ibid.) found that, controlling for all other factors, black women were given less prenatal information than white women on smoking cessation and alcohol use. The studies looked at by Sidanius and Pratto also suggested that the psychological experiences of racial discrimination contribute to the negative health status of subordinate groups (e.g., high blood pressure and other stress-related illnesses). Interestingly, one study (Krieger and Sidney, 1996, cited ibid.) reported lower blood pressure among black persons who said they challenged racial discrimination than among black persons who reported accepting what they regarded as unfair racial discrimination. This finding supports Frantz Fanon's (1968) thesis that resistance to oppression has positive physical and psychological effects on oppressed persons, which is important to note in developing an anti-oppressive social work practice.

Discrimination in the Criminal Justice System

The final area of institutional discrimination looked at by Sidanius and Pratto was the criminal justice system. Consistent with a critical social theory approach to oppression and with the notion that structural oppression is akin to structural violence, the authors found that the law does not function in a value-free and neutral manner, but rather acts as a mechanism to protect the rights and privileges of the dominant groups and to enforce the oppression of subordinate groups. Subordinate group members are substantially overrepresented within the criminal justice system. For example, indigenous Australians are imprisoned at a rate of more than 15 times that of non-indigenous Australians (Walker, 1994) and African Americans are incarcerated at a rate 6.8 times that of white persons (Walker et al., 1996). Almost 40 per cent of California's young African-American males are either in prison, on parole, on probation, or wanted by the police (Schiraldi et al., 1996).

According to Sidanius and Pratto, the existence of systematic and institutionalized discrimination against subordinate groups accounts for this overrepresentation of subordinate group members within the criminal justice system. Evidence for this claim is that subordinate group members face more severe sanctions than dominant group members. Data from the Netherlands (Junger and Polder, 1992), Australia (Walker, 1994), Sweden (Guillou, 1996), and Ontario, Canada (Cole and Gittens, 1995) show that after all legally relevant factors (e.g., type and seriousness of crime, criminal record) are controlled, members of subordinate groups have a higher likelihood of: being arrested, having more serious charges laid against them, having a higher amount of bail set, being convicted, and having a more severe sentence imposed. At the same time, they are less likely to receive probation or early parole.

A Canadian study showed that prison guards are more likely to subject black prisoners to harsh treatment, especially when the correctional officer has the greatest degree of interpretational discretion (Cole and Gittens, 1995). Sidanius and Pratto also found that crimes committed by subordinate group members against dominant group members were more severely punished than those committed by the latter against the former. One study (Chevigny, 1995, cited in Sidanius and Pratto, 1999) looked at police violence across the Americas and found that police brutality against subordinate group members often results in institutional rewards rather than punishment.

An examination of the living situation of almost any subordinate group anywhere in the world is likely to show it experiencing oppression in all or most of the above areas. That is, subordinate groups generally will suffer directly from lack of adequate employment, low income and poverty, inadequate housing, discrimination in the retail market, lack of educational opportunities, inferior health care, and an overrepresentation within the criminal justice system. These inequities are part of structural violence in that people who experience them, in turn, suffer from disproportionate levels and incidences of stress, anguish, frustration, alienation, exclusion, and so on that result in differential rates of mortality (i.e., lowered life expectancies), morbidity, incarceration, homicide, suicide, and infant mortality. There can be no doubt, as Bulhan (1985) argues, just as Fanon (1968) did before him, that oppression at the structural level leads to violence at the personal level (e.g., suicide and self-mutilation), at the interpersonal level (e.g., homicide and domestic violence), and at the institutional level (premature death because of social inequalities). What makes this type of violence so insidious is the fact that no known perpetrator or intention can be identified as responsible for the violence.

Bulhan presents a litany of glaring examples of racial violence in its different forms as experienced in two countries, the United States and South Africa. A brief look at the American situation is presented here. Although the days of lynching, whipping, and/or castrating African Americans may be over, structural violence has replaced much of this interpersonal violence. Bulhan cites studies showing that African Americans suffer all the inequities discussed above. As a result, relative to the dominant white group, African Americans have lower life expectancies, higher mortality rates (including infant mortality), and higher rates of heart disease (hypertensive heart disease), stroke, cancer, and homicide—all associated with social inequality. As well, African Americans suffer high levels of chronic unemployment and are more likely to be hired for dangerous job assignments (including high-risk assignments in the military). Higher rates of African Americans are incarcerated and many more are on 'death row'. They also experience more severe sentencing and more unjust arrests. There is a much higher incidence of homicide among African Americans than among white people and a higher incidence of violence within domestic and intimate contexts. Alcoholism and drug addiction are higher among African Americans than among white persons and the suicide rate has been rising faster than among white people (although white people still have a higher suicide rate). In sum, African Americans carry an inordinate amount of the burden of violence in American society.

Subordinate groups in Canada have similar experiences to those of African Americans with respect to structural violence.[6] Of all the oppressed groups in Canada, First Nations people, by all indicators, suffer most from social inequalities and, therefore, experience the most structural violence. Almost half (47.2 per cent) of First Nations families live below the poverty line (Oberle, 1993); the average life expectancy is 10 years less than that of Euro-Canadians (Health and

Welfare Canada, 1991a); and approximately 20 per cent of First Nations children are removed from their families by child welfare authorities (Clarke, 1991). First Nations families have an infant mortality rate more than double the national Canadian average and the suicide rate for adolescent girls is about seven times higher than the national rate and four times higher for male Aboriginal adolescents (Health Canada, 1994). Incarceration rates for First Nations people are much higher than for the general population. In general, alcohol and drug abuse is higher among First Nations populations than the general Canadian population (Health and Welfare Canada, 1992), with 50–80 per cent of Aboriginal youth having abused alcohol (Round Lake Treatment Centre, 1992). Chappell (1997) cites studies showing that family violence is disproportionately high among First Nations people; in fact, one study (Taylor, 1991) suggests that as many as one in three Aboriginal women in the province of Manitoba has experienced spousal abuse.

Examples of other subordinate groups in Canada experiencing structural oppression and violence are older Canadians and women. Although Canadians, on average, are living longer these days, the high rate of mental health problems among the elderly cannot all be attributed to old age. Poverty, loneliness, and a sense of uselessness contribute to depression and exacerbate other mental disorders such as Alzheimer's and related dementias (Health and Welfare Canada, 1991b). Suicide among elderly people is a major concern in Canada, with males over the age of 80 having the highest suicide rate of any age group in the nation (Health Canada, 1994). Abuse of prescription drugs is a major concern, with older Canadians consuming about 25 per cent of all prescription drugs in Canada (Health Canada, 1989).

The rate of violence against women is disturbingly high in Canada. One national study found that over 51 per cent of Canadian women have been physically or sexually assaulted since age 16 and that, out of 12,300 respondents, 29 per cent had been physically or sexually abused by a current or former partner (Statistics Canada, 1993). Immigrant women and women with disabilities are particularly vulnerable to abuse. As well, the rate of poverty among single mothers has been growing steadily, reaching 57.3 per cent in 1994 (National Council of Welfare, 1996). Discrimination against women has also been documented in the workplace with respect to wages, occupational segregation, training, and pensions (Canadian Advisory Council on the Status of Women, 1990). This discrimination is an example of structural oppression, which, of course, makes women more vulnerable to structural violence.

Conclusion

Oppression at the structural or institutional level is legally and socially sanctioned in that it is manifest in the ways our social institutions, public policies, laws, and the economic and political systems all work together to benefit the dominant group at the expense of subordinate groups. The nature of the relationship between both dominant groups and subordinate groups was discussed with respect to their location within and treatment by society's social, economic, and political institutions. Assimilation and multiculturalism have been proposed and pursued as ways of dealing with difference, but both approaches have oppressive consequences. A 'politics of difference' offers a more viable anti-oppressive policy. The transformation of capitalism from a fixed and predominantly local or national basis to a global form, along with its legitimizing discourse of 'economic determinism', has been presented by many in places of power and influence as an inevitable, normal, natural, and evolutionary process that should be embraced rather than resisted. This discourse dictates that to be successful in the global economy we must accept for subordinate groups worsening poverty, greater social inequality, diminished social investment, and worker exploitation on a global scale. Alternative economic discourses that confront, resist, and challenge this dominant discourse must be developed as one anti-oppressive strategy. With respect to people's relationship to the political system, subordinate groups are not well served by representative democracy. Most political leaders are members of the dominant group who benefit from our current sets of dominant-subordinate social, economic, and political relations, and have no commitment to change. Participatory forms of democratic structures and decision-making are seen as alternatives to representative democracy.

Finally, structural inequalities often have violent effects or outcomes. Terms such as 'social inequality' and 'structural inequality' tend to cover up the violent outcomes that many people from subordinate groups experience. Structural inequalities are much more than one person or one group having a greater quantity of or more access to social goods, rights, and opportunities. They are more than violations of philosophical notions of fairness, equity, and justice. Structural inequalities are socially sanctioned forms of physical and psychological violence, which over time will lead to hurtful discrimination and slow, agonizing, premature, and unpunished death. The term 'structural violence', I contend, more accurately reflects the realities of oppressed persons. 'Structural inequality' is a somewhat abstract, technical, bourgeois, and polite term that covers up its violent outcomes. We should call it what it is—*socially sanctioned structural violence*.

Chapter Six

Internalized Oppression and Domination

Introduction

Most writers today agree that oppression is linked to social conditions and that the environment (social, cultural, political, and economic factors) plays an important role in influencing the individual psyche (Moane, 1999). Conversely, there is broad agreement that the individual plays an active role in mediating the effects of these environmental factors. The basic dialectic of the psyche and society shaping each other is captured in many different theoretical perspectives—social constructionist, critical (social and psychological theory), interpretive, discursive, feminist, psychoanalytic. Because oppression will be experienced differently by different people, it is impossible to construct a general theory of oppression, in general, and internalized oppression, in particular. Thus, the intention in this chapter is to present a general account of the nature, causes, and effects of internalized oppression.

Psychology of Oppression

In the previous chapters the focus has been mainly on social factors as they relate to oppression. The emphasis has been on those social dimensions and social relationships (gender, race, class, and so on) that constitute social hierarchies and on the social processes and practices that produce and maintain these hierarchies. Although psychological material was presented with respect to coping mechanisms and to some of the obvious consequences of oppression for the psyche, social theories, critical social analyses, and social science literature have so far dominated. However, any discussion of oppression would be grossly incomplete if psychological factors associated with oppression were omitted. A comprehensive treatment of the psychology of oppression is well beyond the scope of this book, but a synopsis of some of this material is included in this section[1] and the ideas of some writers on the subject are included in subsequent sections.

Oppression and its associated social conditions of discrimination, powerlessness, subordination, exclusion, exploitation, scapegoating, low social status, and blocked opportunities are bound to have impact on the psyche of dominated persons. The personal is political and the political is personal. In other words, the psyche and society shape each other. The personal is influenced and shaped by the social, political, economic, and cultural context and, therefore, in order to understand the personal, one must understand the larger context.[2] This is one of the basic tenets of critical and liberation psychology and tends to separate them from more traditional individualistic schools of psychology that ignore broader social and cultural factors (see, for examples of psychological theorizing that includes social factors, Bulhan, 1985; Fox and Prilleltensky, 1997; Moane, 1999; Wilkinson, 1996). It is one of the fallacies of many models of psychology that it is possible to change the person without changing the social context (McLellan, 1995). 'Psychological development and psychological change are not privatized individualized processes which happen regardless of social context, but are intrinsically and dynamically related to the individual's specific context' (Moane, 1999: 7).

Bulhan (1985) links a psychological analysis of oppression with a systematic exploration of its links with psychological functioning in such areas as sexuality, identity, self-esteem, emotions, psychological distress, and interpersonal relationships. In a review of writers who discuss various psychological aspects of oppression derived from various oppressed groups (women, black women, colonized people, Aboriginal persons, and homosexual people), Moane notes that oppression has a profound negative impact on psychological functioning. This impact includes loss of identity, powerlessness, fear, suppression of anger, isolation, ambivalence, and sense of inferiority. These (and other) psychological problems obviously will undermine the capacity of oppressed persons to resist domination and to take action to bring about social change. Two of the psychological conditions brought about by oppression are a sense of inferiority and its correlate of internalized oppression. Internalized oppression is a theme found in writings on women, racism, colonialism, homophobia, and experiences of other forms of oppression. Moane points out that internalized oppression is associated with such psychological patterns as self-hatred, helplessness and despair, mutual distrust and hostility, feelings of inferiority, and psychological distress and madness. Internalized oppression constitutes the subject for the remainder of this chapter.

Inferiority and Internalized Oppression

In *The Mass Psychology of Fascism*, Michael Reich (1975: 53) pointed out that '[w]hat has to be explained is not the fact that the man [*sic*] who is hungry steals or the fact that the man [*sic*] who is exploited strikes, but why the majority of those who are hungry *don't* steal and why the majority of those who are exploited *don't* strike.' In the same vein, Rosen (1996) asks in his aptly titled *On Voluntary Servitude* why the majority of subordinated or oppressed people accept the rule of the minority elite, even when it is patently clear that it is against their interests to do so. Rosen makes the point that this is not a new question by referring to de la Boetie, who asked as far back as 1552 why some people accept their servitude voluntarily.

Reference has already been made in earlier chapters (especially Chapter 3) to the terms 'inferiorization' and 'internalized oppression'. Inferiorization denotes not only an acceptance of a second-class or inferior citizenship status in society by a member of an oppressed group, but a belief that he or she and all members of that group are inferior to the dominant group. It is a belief that their oppression is deserved, unique, unchangeable or temporary (Adam, 1978) and that their problems in living are due to their personal shortcomings (Shulman, 1992). It is an acceptance of the negative identity defined by the larger society and of the stereotypes assigned to them. Inferiorization describes a situation whereby oppressed persons often understand their interests in ways that reflect the interests of the dominant group (Freire, 1994).

Internalized oppression takes inferiorization a step further as it includes not only a *belief* that one's self and one's social group are inferior, but also encompasses the *behaviours* (discursive practices) that are self-harming and contribute to one's own oppression. These self-destructive behaviours on the part of some oppressed people, of course, reinforce the dominant group's view of them as inferior and lead to a rejection of them, which in turn often confirms the low image they may have of themselves (Moreau and Leonard, 1989). Shulman (1992) points out that these self-perceptions can be reinforced by social workers who focus on personal pathology and ignore external or structural factors that create and reinforce this negative self-image.

Irish psychologist Sean Ruth (1988: 435) writes that 'the key to the maintenance of oppression . . . is what we call internalized oppression or internalized control. This is where people come to believe in their own inferiority and their powerlessness to change things.' Ruth links feelings of low self-esteem, inferiority, and powerlessness on the part of oppressed persons to a mistrust in their own thinking and intelligence, with the result that they pay scant attention or respect to each other and give much weight to the views of outsiders, particularly the dominant group. Mistrust, in turn, leads to divisiveness within the group. Ruth identifies three other characteristics of oppressed people centring on power and authority that emanate from internalized oppression: (1) they learn to behave in ways that do not provoke retaliation or draw attention; (2) they have ambivalent feelings about their own leaders, expecting much but not supporting them; and (3) they often oppress other oppressed groups to feel better about themselves (creating an oppressed person's snobbery), rather than attempting to change the system.

A number of responses that oppressed people may adopt, which either reinforce or contribute to their oppression, were examined in Chapter 3, including those identified by Freire (1970)—fatalism, horizontal violence, self-depreciation, attraction towards the oppressor and his or her way of life—and those responses discussed by Adam (1978)—mimesis, escape from identity, psychological withdrawal, guilt-expiation, magical ideologies, inter-group hostility, and social withdrawal. It was also pointed out in Chapter 3 that although these responses may appear to be peculiar, unnatural, or neurotic in that they function to sustain and reproduce oppression, they are more complex than this. Some of them may be acts of resistance to oppression (Kanuha, 1999). As well, some of them function to reduce the everyday suffering of oppression experienced by those who are oppressed, which makes these responses or positions much more difficult to deal with from an anti-oppressive perspective. What follows is a more systematic exploration of some of the causes or explanations or correlates of internalized oppression as they exist in the literature with a view to developing a more inclusive and informed anti-oppressive social work practice.

The Master-Slave Paradigm

Lerner (1986) contends that the emergence of slavery is the most important development in tracing the history of domination because it provides a model for other forms of domination-subordination at both the social and psychological levels. Moane (1999) notes that slavery involves the creation of a class of human beings who are deprived of freedom and forced against their will to labour for and serve another group of human beings. It requires the explicit development and institutionalization of a set of legal and social practices and processes that mark the enslaved group as different (the Other), excludes them from participation in society, and treats them as commodities to be bought and sold and exploited for their labour. These legal and social practices were the forerunners of the unwritten and silent rules, expectations, and practices that underpin oppression today.

As well as legal and social practices, psychological components that originated with slavery characterize dominant-subordinate relations today. Lerner (1986: 100) writes of the stigma and internalized oppression associated with slavery, but she could just as well have been describing a part of the psychology of oppression as it exists in contemporary society:

> Stigma becomes a reinforcing factor which excuses and justifies the practice of enslavement in the minds of the dominant group and in the minds of the enslaved. If the stigma is fully internalized by the enslaved—a process which takes many generations and demands the intellectual isolation of the enslaved group—enslavement then becomes to be perceived as 'natural' and therefore acceptable.

Given that some of today's oppressive social and legal processes and practices and psychological conditions seem to have their origins in slavery, the 'master-slave' relationship would seem to be a useful concept in furthering our understanding of oppression. Hegel (1966 [1807]) wrote of this relationship in one of his seminal works, *The Phenomenology of Mind*, a book that has had a profound effect on many subsequent writers, including Karl Marx and Jean-Paul Sartre, both of whom found in it ideas to understand, critique, and attempt to transform European society (Bulhan, 1985). Hegel's discussion of the 'master and slave' dialectic, contained in this seminal work, has since informed intellectual discourse on oppression, particularly the psychology of oppression.

Hegel's philosophical argument was that the individual becomes conscious of him or herself only through recognition *by* the Other. In order to achieve such recognition, a struggle or conflict occurs between two individuals. The winner becomes the master and attains recognition by the Other. The loser becomes the slave and does not attain recognition by the master. In addition to gaining recognition, the master also reduces the slave to an instrument of his or her will—to labour for and fulfill the needs of the master. (However, Hegel believed that the advantages accruing to the master actually compromised him or her and thwarted his or her self-actualization, and thus the slave in the end became the real victor.)

Kojeve (1969) was able to extract deep and rich psychological meaning from Hegel's 'master-slave' dialectic that helps to enhance our understanding of oppression. Kojeve's lectures on Hegel in the 1930s to the intellectual elite of Europe directly influenced the works of such intellectuals as the existentialist, Jean-Paul Sartre, and the postmodern psychoanalyst, Jacques Lacan, and indirectly influenced Frantz Fanon, the revolutionary black psychiatrist who fought against colonialism in Algeria (Bulhan, 1985). Essentially, Kojeve (1969, as cited in Bulhan, 1985) argues that Hegel's 'master-slave' dialectic presupposes that people are fundamentally social, since recognition is possible only in the presence of and confrontation with the Other. The 'desire' for recognition leads to a search that involves a perilous struggle between two adversaries who attempt to force recognition one from the other, without reciprocating. The winner becomes the master and gains recognition by the Other (i.e., the slave), which confirms the master's self-worth, identity, and humanity. And because the master does not reciprocate a recognition of the slave, then the latter loses self-worth, identity, and humanity. The master is elevated to human life and the slave is reduced to animal life. The former becomes autonomous and self-determining; the latter becomes dependent and determined. The master consumes and enjoys what the slave produces because the slave is only an extension of the master's will and body. This, according to Kojeve, is the foundation of human oppression.[3]

In his book, *Frantz Fanon and the Psychology of Oppression* (1985), the African-American writer Hussein Bulhan traces the use of the concept of the master-slave dialectic in developing a psychology of oppression. He initially looks at and critiques Hegel's original notion of the concept along with Kojeve's interpretation and extension of Hegel's work. He then analyzes the use of the 'master-slave' relationship in French psychoanalyst Mannoni's (1962) explanation of the origin and dynamics of colonialism. And finally, he reviews Fanon's development of Hegel's master-slave paradigm and the way he used it to analyze the relationship between contemporary white and black people. Bulhan notes that whereas Hegel and Mannoni directed most of their attention to the *whys* of oppression, Fanon (himself a descendant of slaves) explained *how* oppression dehumanizes all involved. Fanon reformulated and extended the abstract master-slave paradigm of Hegel and Mannoni so that he could apply it to concrete, lived experiences under slavery and colonialism.

Bulhan's book makes for fascinating reading on psychoanalytical and psychological interpretations of the minds of both oppressors/colonizers and oppressed/colonized people. Some of his conclusions about internalized oppression developed within the framework of the master-slave dialectic (particularly Fanon's version) are presented below.

- For a system of oppression to be effective, various forms of social control must pervade the life of the oppressed. These may include acts and the threat of physical harm, a narrow circle of tame ideas (ideological hegemony), infiltration of family and community to limit the capacity for bonding and trust, an obliteration of the subordinate group's history and culture, and a system of rewards and punishment based on loyalty to the oppressor to foster competition among the oppressed.

- In situations of prolonged oppression, the oppressed group will internalize the oppressor 'without' by adopting the dominant group's guidelines and prohibitions and assimilating its image and social behaviours (see also Adam, 1978). In this way, the oppressed group becomes the agent of its own oppression—an oppressor 'within'. Internalized oppression is highly resistant to change since it would require a battle on two fronts: the oppressor within and the oppressor without.

- Patterson (1982) notes that a distinctive characteristic of the slave or oppressed person is his or her generalized condition of dishonour. In the oppressed person's eyes (and those of others), the person and status of the slave lack integrity, worth, and autonomy—all necessary characteristics for one to battle the master or oppressor group.

- The well-known inferiority complex of oppressed groups originates in the process of internalization, and the attendant but repressed rage will cause some oppressed persons to act out, on each other, the very physical and/or psychological violence imposed on them. When oppressed persons engage in self-destructive behaviour, injuring themselves, their loved ones, or their neighbours, they often experience confounding ambivalence and guilt, which reinforce their sense of inferiority. Paulo Freire (1994) refers to this type of violence as 'horizontal violence' (see below).

- There are two sets of contrasting attitudes and behaviours between a member of the oppressor group and a member of the oppressed group whenever they encounter each other. The former acts as a majority, demands more space and privilege, and exudes confidence and a sense of entitlement. The latter acts as a minority of one, settles for less, and displays self-doubt and a readiness to compromise. The dominant ideas, values, and rules of conduct serve the former and entrap the latter.

- Oppressed persons find everyday living to be a challenge. Being confined to another's rules, culture, expectations, and so on requires a marked degree of personal versatility and repression. Of this, Bulhan (1985: 123) says, 'The oppressed learn to wear many masks for different occasions; they develop skills to detect moods and wishes of those in authority, and learn to present acceptable public behaviours while repressing many incongruent personal feelings. . . . This pattern of adaptation no doubt entails a personal toll, an excessive use of energy, and a higher vulnerability for psychopathology.' It is not surprising, then, that morbidity, mortality, incarceration, and psychiatric hospitalization rates are higher for oppressed groups than for oppressor groups.

The works of Fanon and Bulhan, in particular, give some important insights into the psyche of the oppressed person (i.e., the slave). The search for peace and harmony in conditions of oppression, the desire for personal safety and security in circumstances of social violence, and the wish for individual success at the expense of collective aspirations require few risks on the part of the oppressed person because such efforts accept the status quo. Emancipation, on the other hand, requires courage, vision, and a commitment full of risk. The dehumanizing master 'without' must be killed, at least psychologically, and the slave 'within' must be cast out. Both require organized action and both risk a psychological crisis and even physical death (Bulhan, 1985). However, none of us will escape physical death. There is also psychological, social, economic, and political death—all of which hasten physical death. Within the master-slave paradigm, this presents the oppressed person with a paradox. Out of fear of physical death, the slave will submit to the superiority of the master, but in so doing will suffer the other slower, tortuous, and agonizing deaths and likely will die at an earlier age.

27 Million Slaves

The master-slave relationship is not just a philosophical concept or an artifact of the past. Today, 150 years after the world's slave trade was abolished, as many as 27 million people (approximately the population of Canada) are living as slaves. Between 1.5 and 2 million children are bought and sold into lives of sexual slavery and exploitation. Up to 10 million children are believed to be working in bondage in India, including 300,000 in rug factories. In Pakistan, about 7.5 million of the country's estimated 20 million bonded labourers are said to be children. On cocoa farms in Ivory Coast, 15,000–20,000 children have been driven by hunger into working as slaves. Thousands of women have been trafficked by organized crime groups from the former Soviet Union to the streets of Central and Western Europe as prostitutes. Tens of millions of people are held in bonded labour, working up to 18 hours a day as domestic servants and farm and factory workers. One spokesperson for an American anti-slavery group remarked that 'Our global economy creates demand for cheap goods, and there is no cheaper labor than slave labor.' A correspondent writing for *The Age*, Melbourne's premier daily newspaper, refers to the slave trade as 'the dark underbelly of globalisation'. He comments further, 'While the world looks away, human lives are routinely being bought and sold for less than the price of a pair of shoes' (Riley, 2001: 1, 13).

False Consciousness

In Chapter 1, it was pointed out that a key concept of critical social theory is 'false consciousness'. Marx originally used false consciousness as an explanation of why a numerically superior working class seemed to accept capitalism as an economic system when clearly it exploited and alienated them by assigning them to a lifetime of horrendous working and living conditions. Simply defined, false consciousness is 'the holding of false or inaccurate beliefs that are contrary to one's own social interest and which thereby contribute to the maintenance of the disadvantaged position of the self or the group' (Jost, 1995: 14). Eyerman (1981: 33) views false consciousness as 'the acceptance of an un-reflected notion of the world as given, as it appears: as truth without mediation or interpretation, and thinking that this world cannot or is not shaped through human action'.

False consciousness is a form of internalized oppression. It is associated with the concept of ideology (a consistent set of social, economic, and political beliefs) in that ideas, values, and beliefs of the dominant ideology may be internalized by subordinate group members because they are presented in ways that are consistent with reason, inevitability, and normalcy. False consciousness, however, is not just a simple matter of ideological indoctrination (or brainwashing) or the subjective realization of ideology. Rather than a passive assimilation of ideas and ideology from various organized sources, such as the mass media and the school system, the individual actually participates in developing his or her world view and place in the world through everyday activities and interactions. To make sense of social conditions, social relations, and social interactions, they must be mediated through some theoretical framework. In the absence of a critical perspective, the interpretation and framework are usually that of the dominant group (ibid.). An individual not only sees him or herself through the eyes of the dominant group and judges him or herself on its values, but adopts them as his or her own even when the interpretation serves other interests at the expense of the individual.

As discussed in Chapter 4, there are two primary means of maintaining dominance over subordinate groups: the threat or actual use of physical force and the control of ideas or what is known as 'ideological hegemony'. It was pointed out that the latter method is much more effective than the former because there is no perceived injustice or exploitation occurring that could be the catalyst for acts of resistance or insurgency. Subordinate groups are integrated into the established order through a process of socialization (or indoctrination) and ideological manipulation. False consciousness is one outcome of this process and is manifest when both dominant and subordinate groups are convinced of the purported fairness, justice, desirability, or inevitability of particular hierarchically organized social relations and the discourses that underpin them (Sidanius and Pratto, 1999). Coercion is probably not enough to sustain oppression for any length of time. Also needed to reproduce unequal societies and exploitative social relations is some degree of false consciousness.

A number of theories of how the dominant culture is reinforced and reproduced through popular or mass culture were presented in Chapter 4. These theories of cultural hegemony attempt to explain how and why subordinate group members accept as their own the ideas, messages, and representations transmitted through mass culture that mainly serve the interests of the dominant group, often at the expense of themselves. Such concepts as Marx's ideology, Lukac's reification, Gramsci's hegemony, and the Frankfurt School's culture industry were discussed in terms of their attempts to explain how people exploited by such systems as capitalism, racism, and patriarchy come to accept, reproduce, and actually defend these systems that oppress them. Accepting, believing, or supporting any ideas or discourses associated with oppression is a form of false consciousness.

One example of a false conscious belief is that of 'fatalism', the belief that nothing can be done to improve social conditions or one's lot in life. This belief is cultivated by the dominant ideology when it presents the status quo as normal, natural, inevitable, and, consequently, that which ought to be accepted. A force or deity greater than humankind is often suggested as responsible for the way things are and no one should tamper with them. Fatalism is often related to such religious beliefs as 'it (oppression) is God's will'. However, accepting or believing that a hierarchical society based on oppression for any reason—religious, political, philosophical—is the way that it is or has to be and that nothing can be done about it is a form of false consciousness in general and fatalism in particular.

'Life would be a whole lot simpler'

Lest anyone minimize the impact or pervasiveness of 'fatalism' as a powerful mechanism of social control, one need only to look at the profession of social work. Paradoxically, although much is written and said by social workers (including most social work academics) about the need for and approaches to social change, I have been told by many of these same people throughout my career that my (and others') ideas about social change and my (and others') approaches to social work and social problems are unrealistic. Furthermore, my life, I have been told, would be a whole lot simpler if I would just accept the way things are or, at least, diminish my 'extreme' views and goals. In many ways, my life would be simpler and easier. Teaching a critical or political approach to social work is difficult work and being labelled (i.e., defamed and marginalized) as an interesting but 'out-of-touch lefty radical' is often hurtful. This position, held and sometimes espoused by mainstream social workers, is, in my view, an example of fatalism and false consciousness. It does not recognize that the nature and form of the society we have today are the result of conscious decisions made by elite groups of people, and that what has been made can be unmade and remade if we (social workers and others) can first shed some of our false beliefs.

Sidanius and Pratto (1999) report on the results of a 1997 public opinion study on race relations in the United States that contains another example of false consciousness. A large number of black and white people were asked whether or not they believed that both groups had the same chances to get any kind of a job, education, and housing. In spite of all the evidence to the contrary, the majority of both groups indicated their belief that there is equal opportunity between them in these three domains (although the belief was higher within the white group than within the black group—over 80 per cent as opposed to 56 per cent). Obviously, there will be little potential for or commitment to fundamental social change when *both* the dominant and subordinate groups believe that no socio-economic advantage or disadvantage exists between them on account of race.

In his celebrated book, *Pedagogy of the Oppressed* (1970, 1994), Paulo Freire offers an explanation of why some members of oppressed groups commit violent acts against other members of their own group that is based, in part, on a false consciousness. Such acts of violence are referred to as 'horizontal violence' by Freire and 'lateral violence' by the North American Native activist and writer Lee Maracle (1996). Freire (1994: 44) says that 'the oppressed feel an irresistible attraction towards the oppressor and his way of life. Sharing this way of life becomes an overpowering aspiration. In their alienation, the oppressed want at any cost to resemble the oppressors, to imitate them, to follow them.' This creates a dual (and false) consciousness within the oppressed person. On the one hand, he/she views the oppressor as omnipotent and invulnerable and would do anything to be like the oppressor, even to the point of acting like an oppressor. 'Their ideal is to be men; but for them, to be men is to be oppressors. This is their model of humanity' (ibid., 27). On the other hand, they see themselves as their oppressors see them—ignorant, unproductive, and lazy. Given this dual consciousness, Freire says of them:

> the oppressed cannot perceive clearly the 'order' which serves the interests of the oppressors whose image they have internalized. Chafing under the restrictions of this order, they often manifest a type of *horizontal violence*, striking at their own comrades for the pettiest reasons. . . . Because the oppressor exists within their oppressed comrades, when they attack those comrades they are indirectly attacking the oppressor as well. (Ibid., 44; emphasis added)

Similarly, Frantz Fanon (1968) speaks of horizontal violence among colonized people (particularly black people in North Africa) in *The Wretched of the Earth*, and Lee Maracle (1996) speaks of lateral violence among North American First Nations people and how it invades their intimate relationships and family life.

Agger (1998) contends that false consciousness today is promoted by positivist social sciences such as economics and quantitative schools of sociology that depict society as governed by intractable laws (e.g., law of supply and demand, any social change must be incremental and slow, collectivism is a threat to individual liberties). This depiction of society suggests that people ought to adjust to these allegedly fixed social, economic, and political patterns. Critical social theory and anti-oppressive social work attempt to pierce this kind of false consciousness by emphasizing the power of agency, both personal and collective, to transform society. Similarly, progressive or critical or liberation psychologists have criticized the fundamental individualism of psychology with its emphasis on adjustment and its neglect of powerlessness, inequality, and other social conditions as contributing factors to both external and internalized oppression (Bulhan, 1985; Moane, 1999; Starhawk, 1987).

The notion of false consciousness is certainly not without its critics. Many interpretive theorists[4] (e.g., symbolic interactionists, ethnomethodologists, social phenomenologists, social constructionists, some schools of feminism) argue that it is arrogant and presumptuous on the part of social theorists and analysts to suppose that people have a false consciousness about their lives. Agger (1998) observes that rather than unduly claiming the right to decide whether or not someone's consciousness is true or false, interpretive theorists treat all narratives as having truth value since they represent people's attempts to describe and make sense out of their lives. In other words, to the interpretive theorist, one's consciousness is true for that person and that is all that matters.

In comparing and contrasting interpretive and critical social theories, Agger makes several other observations about how each views and/or treats false consciousness. First, although postmodern critical theorists and many feminists reject the polarity of true and false consciousness as presented by Marx, they do not accept the sheer relativism of many interpretive theorists, who simply accept what people say about their own lives as true. Instead, postmodernists and feminists analyze the discourses (e.g., advertising, anti-welfare sentiments, free market imperative) of people's everyday lives as sources of power and control that people confront as inescapable structures of culture and consciousness. Foucault (1977), for example, did not adopt Marx's notion of false consciousness, but understood certain discourses of criminality and sexuality to be agents of discipline and punishment that constrained people by restricting their views and experience of what is possible. In other words, people's narratives about their lives will reflect, to some extent, the definitions and discourses of reality that are given to them. And these definitions and discourses of reality are usually reflective and supportive of the interests of dominant groups.

Consciousness is not mechanically manipulated, as some structural Marxists believe, nor does it become established free from the influences of ideology and hegemony, as many interpretive theorists suggest. It 'develops in a dialectical interplay between experience and language that borrows from prevailing conceptions of reality and yet reflects people's own free imaginations' (Agger, 1998: 33). An example of someone who builds on this dialectic is Norman Denzin (1991), who deals with people's narratives but in ways that show them to be simultaneously true and false. Their narratives about their lives reveal both how they have been socialized into accepting reality as defined for them by dominant ideologies and institutions, and the ways in which they resist and transform these definitions (Agger, 1998). Another example cited by Agger is the feminist theorist Patricia Clough (1994), who stresses that women tell important stories about their lives that contain both falsehood and truth, reflecting both their socialization and their feminist imagination.

Psychologists Jim Sidanius and Felicia Pratto also take exception to the true-false dichotomy implied in the concept of false consciousness. To them the truth or falsity of legitimizing beliefs is not only difficult to ascertain, but has nothing to do with their power to legitimize inequality. What, in part, gives power to beliefs that justify inequality is not their truth value, 'but rather the degree to which people accept these beliefs as true, right, or just. The more firmly myths (beliefs) are tied to the basic values and points of view of their culture, the more difficult they will be to change' (Sidanius and Pratto, 1999: 104).

Although capitalism has changed since Marx presented the notion of false consciousness, an understanding of the concept is still required to disabuse people of the belief that this is the best of all worlds in spite of its many imperfections. Ideology has not gone away, but is found in venues not anticipated by Marx (e.g., the culture industry, the World Wide Web). It is much more pervasive and total than when Marx wrote. It is so tied into cultural discourses, practices, and representations that people often confuse what is real and what is illusory. Although the pervasiveness of ideology has increased since Marx's time, Agger (1998) contends that it conceals its representation of the world in order to increase its efficacy as 'silent argument'. That is, ideologies that appear polemical, doctrinal, or adversarial are viewed as old-fashioned by many and, thus, not to be taken seriously. This view, of course, serves by default to maintain the dominant ideology and discourse as unquestioned reality (i.e., a reality of hierarchy and oppression). This view is also a prime example of false consciousness—a consciousness that must be pierced, exposed for its oppressive functions, resisted, and deconstructed so that liberating alternatives can be developed.

Other Perspectives on Internalized Oppression

Many writers have addressed 'internalized oppression' from a number of different perspectives, but probably not as comprehensively as that contained in the master-slave dialectic or in the theory of false consciousness. It was mentioned at the beginning of this chapter that, given different people's different experiences of and responses to oppression, it is impossible to develop a general theory of internalized oppression with universal applicability. Thus, the remainder of this chapter will present some observations and insights made by an array of writers from different disciplines who have addressed the phenomenon of internalized oppression. Although I present some of these observations and insights separately below, it is important to note that in reality many of them intersect with one another.

Internalized Labels

Albert Memmi (1963, 1967, 1968, 1973) has written extensively on his experiences both as a Jew and as a person living in Tunisia, a country colonized by the French. He (1968) identified several characteristics that the colonizer/oppressor tends to assign to colonized/oppressed people—lazy, stupid, backward, irresponsible, evil, brutish, cowardly, indulgent, uncivilized, unreliable, extravagant, unpredictable, mysterious, impulsive, and undisciplined. Moane (1999) identifies three consequences that this labelling process has for colonized people: (1) it stereotypes them as inferior in contrast to the colonizer, who is intelligent, brave, responsible, civilized, industrious, and so on; (2) it depersonalizes the colonized people, who are viewed as an undifferentiated mass; and (3) it objectifies colonized people in that their behaviour is attributed to their perceived negative characteristics rather than to social conditions. Of course, this labelling and its internalization justify the colonizer's privileged position and the dependent and inferior position of those who have been colonized.

Memmi (1963: 321–2) argues that oppressed persons come to accept the stereotypes imposed on them over time, and tend to behave in ways that reinforce these stereotypes: 'The longer the oppression lasts, the more it profoundly affects him [i.e., the oppressed]. It ends by becoming so familiar to him that he believes it is part of his own constitution, that he accepts it, and could not imagine his recovery from it. *This acceptance is the crowning point of oppression*' (emphasis added). The only areas of autonomous action open to oppressed persons is their own community and family, and here feelings of rebellion, resentment, anger, and frustration are often acted out in forms of horizontal or lateral violence.

Socialization of Internalized Oppression

In Chapter 4 some of the ways in which the dominant culture is transmitted through various social institutions and becomes internalized by both dominant and subordinate group members were presented. A similar process occurs whereby individuals in a society learn the dominant ideas, rules, expectations, norms, culture, practices, and ideology of that society. The process of socialization is carried out by social institutions and authority figures and is learned in a variety of ways—through teaching, modelling, observation, experience, and identifying with and imitating role models and idealized persons. Not only do individuals learn these social phenomena, they internalize them as well—they become part of the self of the individual. Oppression is a learned and internalized social phenomenon. Although a number of writers allude or refer to internalized oppressive thoughts, attitudes, and behaviours being learned, two who discuss the socialization of internalized oppression are Gil (1998) and Bishop (1994). In a brief historical overview of oppression Gil (1998: 44) contends that throughout history 'dominant social groups succeeded in coercing and inducing dominated groups to internalize and accept as valid those social values which served the perceived needs and interests of the dominant groups, but affected adversely the needs and interests of dominated groups.' He points out that this internalization of social values was achieved initially by coercive means, but today coercion has been complemented, and often replaced, by socialization and social control rooted in such systems of ideas as ideology, mythology, and organized religion. For example, organized religion[5] has often taught that nonconformity to established values (e.g., women to honour their husbands; avoidance of masturbation, premarital sex, and birth control; perform an honest day's work, even if exploited) would be severely punished, including eternal damnation. Anne Bishop (1994: 35) talks about the consequences of internalized oppression for herself (a lesbian and a woman) and others: 'To a certain extent we do keep ourselves and each other down. We reproduce the social, economic, and political system that formed us, again and again, by playing out our internalized oppression against ourselves and each other.' Bishop believes that internalized oppression begins with childhood, as children suffer pain and powerlessness when they encounter racism, poverty, sexism, and discrimination based on language, geographic location, religion, and the like. This oppression, along with feelings of powerlessness to do anything about it, often results in fear, low self-esteem, and strategies for self-protection that are carried into adulthood.

Bishop contends that children learn to be afraid, distrustful, watchful, and to differentiate clearly between 'us' and 'them', between safe and dangerous. They learn that they are part of a hierarchy based on deception and force, and they learn to judge the situation and make a decision (that faces all oppressed people) whether to go along with it or resist it. When children decide to resist or fight back, they learn to take every opportunity to grab a little power for themselves and to use that power to its limit. They develop a large repertoire of methods for manipulating, controlling, and disempowering others. On the other hand, when they decide to go along with the situation, they obey, conform, and remain silent. Bishop (ibid., 50) elaborates on this point:

> Children learn to cozy up to those who can hurt them, say what the adults want them to say, please and protect adults, act on their behalf, disguise their own intelligence and power, and pretend to take pleasure in their own abuse. They learn to be afraid of what power they do have; they learn to deny it and see themselves as even more powerless than they really are. They also blame themselves for the situation and thereby reduce their self-esteem.

Bishop's argument then is that people learn in childhood to behave in ways that contribute to their own oppression. And, of course, the longer those behaviour patterns are employed, the more difficult it is to confront them, especially when they have been developed for survival. Survival also requires the suppression of feelings because emotions can make a person with little power even more vulnerable. Miller (1980, cited in Bishop, 1994) claims that the denial of feelings makes people obedient and adaptable, and thus capable of being used for anything. At the same time, however, oppressed persons often misuse or abuse power because they have learned that we live in a hierarchical society and that power is something that must be exercised over another. Indeed, many oppressed people believe that if they can control the situation they must do so, even if this involves the oppression of those less powerful, but if control is not possible they must protect themselves by placating and obeying more powerful people. In other words, they have learned (from childhood) about hierarchy and their place in it. Bishop (ibid., 55) sums it up well: 'We carry within us a blueprint of the culture's oppressive patterns to be reproduced wherever we have influence. The name for this is "internalized oppression".'

The Abject Other

Because of ideological and cultural hegemony, all people in society tend to identify with the subject view of the dominant group. In the modern West, Young contends that there is only one view or position—that of the unified, disembodied reason identified with the white bourgeois male. From this supposedly neutral subject position all subordinate (inferior and deviant) groups are viewed and experienced as the abject Other. Thus, because members of subordinate groups tend to perceive the world through the lens of the dominant group, they will see themselves as inferior, deviant, lazy, irresponsible, and so on. In other words, they will see themselves as the abject Other and will 'often exhibit symptoms of fear, aversion, or devaluation toward members of their own groups and other oppressed groups' (Young, 1990: 147). Some women will hold sexist views. Working poor people will often resent non-working (i.e., not attached to the labour force) poor people who, in their view (consistent with the dominant view), are getting a 'free ride' in society with the help of 'generous' welfare benefits. Some light-skinned black people will avoid contact with dark-skinned black people. Gay and lesbian people will sometimes exhibit homophobic behaviour. More common than intra-group oppression (i.e., oppression by members of the same oppressed group) is inter-group oppression, whereby members of one oppressed group fear, despise, and oppress members of other oppressed groups. Some black people, for example, are hostile towards Asian people or towards gay, lesbian, and bisexual people. Some poor people hold sexist and racist views.

'I made it without help. Why can't they?'

At a community meeting a discussion ensued about allocating some of the community's resources to recently arrived families of refugees. A few residents, who had arrived from the same country a generation ago, argued strongly that refugee groups should not be assisted. One woman exclaimed, 'No one helped my family when we arrived. I had to work hard for my right to be here. They should do the same.'

Writing in the post-colonial East Indian context, Ashis Nandy presents a view similar to Young's 'abject Other' being the basis for internalized oppression. He sees the relationship between colonizer/oppressor and colonized/oppressed as complex and one in which a polarization (culture, lifestyle, status, power, etc.) between the two groups occurs. The colonized group internalizes the colonizer's culture, not vice versa. A splitting of the self occurs whereby part of the self, which relates positively to the dominant group and its culture in terms of acceptance of, desire for, and participation in, is acknowledged and accepted. Conversely, that part of the self that relates to the subordinate group and its culture is rejected (as is Young's 'abject Other'). Thus, Nandy (1983: 100, cited in Moane, 1999) observes that colonized people survive by 'overstressing those aspects of the self which they share with the powerful, and by protecting in the corner of their heart a secret defiance'. In this way colonized people often reinforce colonial stereotypes of themselves, but resistance to colonialism always comes from their secret defiance (Gandhi, 1998)—a defiance based on cunning and passivity (Moane, 1999). This defiance provides some potential for anti-oppressive practice.

Service-to-Others Orientation

In her seminal work, *Toward a New Psychology of Women* (1986), Jean Baker Miller talks about the interrelationship between particular social roles and psychological patterns of women that contribute to their subordination. Although focusing specifically on women, Miller contends that her observations and insights could apply to any person in a subordinate position or role, for 'anyone in a subordinate position must learn to be attuned to the vicissitudes of mood, pleasure and displeasure of the dominant group' (Miller, 1986: 39). Subordinate persons may be more attuned to persons in the dominant group than they are to themselves, to the extent that they are unaware of their own needs. Consequently, they may act (and are expected to act) in ways that serve the interests of the dominant group but that negate their own interests.

Miller (1986, cited in Moane, 1999) argues that the lack of self-knowledge that comes from a 'service-to-others orientation' means that subordinate persons will tend to value themselves in terms of what they give or do for the dominant group and obtain self-worth on the basis of how well they satisfy the needs of others. The 'self-sacrificing homemaker' is a common social role carried out by women even in contemporary society. Reinforcing this subordination (with its feelings of inferiority) is the fact that many of the activities of subordinate people (e.g., especially women's 'unpaid labour') are not valued by society and, therefore, they are often seen as not doing anything. Caring for others and fostering the advancement or careers of others, along with the emotional work that goes with it, is not seen as a work activity, because it is done (usually) for love and not money. It is invisible.

Miller identifies two other patterns of internalized oppression. First, subordinate persons will often avoid direct action to serve their own interests because such actions may result in social ostracism, financial hardship, and even violence. Instead, they are forced to act in subtle and indirect ways, which are often perceived by dominant group members as manipulative (e.g., the conniving woman). This, of course, reinforces the negative image that those in the dominant group often hold of subordinate group persons. The second pattern of internalized oppression identified by Miller is that although subordinate persons are constantly in positions that elicit anger, they are not allowed to exhibit this emotion for fear of retaliation. Ideology makes it appear that subordinate people have no reason to be angry at the dominant group (only at themselves), and in the case of women it is against their nature (gentle, feminine) and ascribed social role (caring, nurturing). Consequently, the anger of subordinate persons (in Miller's work, particularly women) becomes transformed into depression, ambivalence, or hysteria.

Nietzsche's Socratism

One final explanation of internalized oppression to be mentioned here, which could be interpreted as a form of false consciousness but, in my view, deserves separate mention, is what Nietzsche (1967, 1969) called 'Socratism'. By Socratism, Nietzsche means that there is a reason for everything, including suffering. He explains it in the following sentence: 'Man, the bravest of animals and the one most accustomed to suffering, does not repudiate suffering as such; he desires it, he even seeks it out, provided he is shown a meaning for it, a purpose of suffering' (1967: 162, cited in Rosen, 1996). Although part of a much larger and more complex philosophical treatise, basically Socratism is part of the attempt to make the world acceptable by making it intelligible. Suffering from oppression, then, must have a larger purpose. For Christians the larger or higher reason for suffering was so that after death one could enter the Kingdom of God, where there would be no suffering. The more one suffered in life and lived according to certain (conforming) principles, the greater the likelihood of escaping eternal damnation and entering heaven.

Socratism is a search for justification about the nature of reality, a way of giving meaning to the world and of accommodating oneself within it intellectually (Rosen, 1996). Obviously, this belief in a higher purpose of suffering has no limits with respect to applying non-rational beliefs as justification for suffering, whatever form that suffering may take—dispossessed groups suffering on earth for the reward of heaven; university students putting up with a non-democratic, one-sided, authoritarian education for the prospect of a good job; small children accommodating all kinds of silly rules and wishes of adults so Santa Claus will come with presents at Christmas.

In sum, the above theories of internalized oppression shed light on a major aspect of oppression. It helps those of us who are concerned with developing anti-oppressive forms of social work practice to go beyond the notion that oppression is simply what one group does to another. It shows us why and how oppressed persons contribute to their own oppression. Internalized oppression has received increased attention in recent years, as evidenced by its inclusion into a psychology of liberation.

Psychology of Liberation

Many people within and outside social work view psychological approaches to social problems as, at best, unrealistic and, at worst, as contributing to the maintenance of social problems. Progressive social work has a long history of criticizing and accusing clinical or counselling social workers, psychologists, psychiatrists, and other helping professionals of: selling out to the status quo by controlling and managing the 'dangerous (i.e., oppressed) classes'; attempting to cajole or coerce victims of social problems to adjust to the very systems that victimized them in the first place; diverting attention away from the real source of problems (i.e., an oppressive society); attempting to humanize an inhumane society; and promoting personal development through 12-step and other programs.

Kitzinger and Perkins represent those who reject psychology and psychiatry altogether. Concerned with women in general and lesbian women in particular, they criticize psychology for its obsessive preoccupation with the self and the quest for finding the real or inner self, which locks women into a perpetual cycle of self-discovery. Too often, they argue, have women entered therapy for depression, alienation, and exhaustion because of oppression only to focus on their childhood and endless analysis of their feelings. Psychotherapy and personal development have become substitutes for political action. According to Kitzinger and Perkins (1993: 198), American and British lesbians do not need psychology: 'Psychology is, and always will be, destructive of the lesbian/feminist enterprise.'

Such a radical position not only overlooks the obvious psychological consequences of oppression, but also the psychology of both the oppressor and the oppressed, including the psychological process of internalized oppression. It is just as unacceptable to omit psychological phenomena as it is to omit social phenomena when analyzing oppression (or any other social or psychological phenomenon). In reality, one cannot separate the psychological (or the personal) from the social (or the political)—they constitute a symbiotic and dialectical relationship, with each acting upon and being acted upon by the other. The position of Kitzinger and Perkins tends to homogenize psychology and overlook those schools mentioned at the beginning of this chapter—critical and liberation psychologies, which also criticize mainstream psychology for its inattention to social variables. These schools of psychology start with the premise that psychological patterns can only be understood by analyzing the social context in which individuals live their lives.

Moane represents the critical and liberation schools of psychological thought. In *Gender and Colonialism: A Psychological Analysis of Oppression and Liberation* she seeks 'to develop a political explanation of psychological phenomena, and to harness psychological insights for the purposes of political activism' (Moane, 1999: 20). Along with the obstacles to political activism inherent in social, economic, cultural, and political forces, Moane includes internalized oppression. Her book outlines many psychological patterns associated with internalized oppression and presents a number of themes or elements of psychological processes for breaking out of internalized oppression and bringing about social change. She refers to this as a 'psychology of liberation'. This psychological approach is consistent with the anti-oppressive approach that is a major concern of this book, and many of Moane's ideas on the process(es) of liberation are presented in the section on 'anti-oppressive social work practice at the personal level' in Chapter 8. As Moane (1999: 182) says, 'Breaking out of oppression, whether at the psychological level or at the political level, requires changes in both psychological and social patterns.' Not attending to the need for social change means that social conditions associated with oppression continue to impinge on individuals and shape psychological functioning in oppressive ways. Not attending to the need for psychological change means that the attempt will be undermined by the negative psychological patterns (such as internalized oppression) associated with oppression.

Internalized Domination

Thus far, this chapter has presented the concept of internalized oppression, a concept that presents enormous challenges to the anti-oppressive social worker. It is not enough to understand that social conditions and forces will lead to the oppression of many people; one must also understand how these oppressive forces affect subordinate persons both materially (i.e., socially, politically, culturally, and economically) and psychologically. To have a fuller understanding of domination and oppression, however, it is probably also important to be cognizant of the psyche of the oppressor and the dynamics of internalized domination.

It has already been mentioned in Chapter 2 that much of oppression today is unintentional, non-conspiratorial, and covert, and that the major reason it occurs is because it protects a privileged kind of citizenship for dominant group members. Members of the dominant group rationalize their monopoly on privilege as their earned right, which subordinate group members do not have because they are incompetent and lazy (Freire, 1994). Several myths, which are part of a larger ideology of oppression, were also presented in Chapter 2 (e.g., myths of scarcity and equal opportunity) and it was argued that these myths help to reinforce the dominant group's positive image of themselves and negative image of subordinate group members. All the evidence indicates that dominant-subordinate relations and oppressive behaviour are very difficult to change once they are established. We can begin to understand the persistence and tenacity of oppressive behaviour by dominant groups by examining the phenomenon of 'internalized domination'.

Just as a number of complementary and competing sets of theories or theoretical positions seek to explain internalized oppression, so, too, are there a number of explanations for internalized domination. Some theories attempt to explain both internalized domination and oppression. For example, socialization or social learning theory holds that both dominant group and oppressed group members are subject to the same dominant culture, messages, and so on. Thus, both groups will, to a large extent, internalize the dominant culture because from early childhood, members of both groups have been socialized to feel and behave in certain ways. For dominant group members, the primary reason they exhibit hostile, discriminatory, and exploitative behaviours towards subordinate group members is because of socialization. Those oppressive behaviours and attitudes towards others that are deemed appropriate are rewarded, while those considered inappropriate are punished and eventually disappear from the person's inventory. This theory of internalized oppression and domination may have some validity, but it does not explain the existence of variation in attitudes and behaviours of people (whether oppressors or oppressed) who grow up in the same society and are exposed to the same socialization process.

Albert Memmi (1967) has constructed a portrait of both the colonized (see above) and the colonizer. The colonizer experiences guilt and ambivalence over the colonization experience and it does not matter whether or not the colonizer supports or criticizes the colonial regime. The critics of the colonial project find themselves estranged from both the colonizers and the colonized. They are seen as traitors by the former and can never become members of the colonized group even if they become revolutionaries—a situation full of ambivalence. The colonizer who supports the colonial regime develops rationalizations and justifications for colonization and becomes blind to poverty, misery, and injustice. Absolute faith is accorded to the system and inordinate self-confidence is developed within the colonizer, along with a glorification of power, especially the power of the colonizing nation.

The fundamental illegitimacy of the above position produces what Memmi labels the 'Nero Complex'—an obsession with denying the extent of colonization and with establishing legitimacy for it. This is carried out in ongoing demonstrations of the colonizer's merits and the colonized's demerits. The illegitimacy and inhumanity of the colonization act engender guilt within the colonizer, which increases hostility towards the colonized—almost to the point of wishing to destroy them. This cannot occur, however, because of the colonizer's dependency on the colonized, a situation that brings about more conservatism and discrimination, and more violence on the part of the colonizer towards the colonized. Guilt and denial are ever-present. Although Memmi developed his ideas based on his experiences as a colonized person, they can obviously be applied to the situation of any oppressed group. However, similar to socialization, Memmi's ideas represent only a partial explanation of internalized domination—a social and psychological phenomenon that is too complex to be explained by any one universal or monolithic theory.

Paulo Freire has also constructed a portrait of the oppressor. Freire asserts that acts of exploitation of another and interference with another's pursuit of self-affirmation as a responsible person are situations of oppression. Even when sweetened by generosity or benevolence, such a situation constitutes violence because it interferes with the subordinate or oppressed person's ontological vocation of becoming more fully human. 'With the establishment of oppression, violence has already begun. . . . Violence is initiated by those who oppress, who exploit, who fail to recognize others as persons—not by those who are oppressed, exploited, and unrecognized. It is not the unloved who initiate disaffection, but those who cannot love because they love only themselves' (Freire, 1994: 37). Paradoxically, the oppressed always are said to be violent, savage, deviant, or barbaric when they react to the violence of their oppressors. Consequently, the oppressed are seen as constituting the dangerous classes and, therefore, they must be monitored, managed, and regulated so that they do not become violent against the dominant group.

Freire argued that for the oppressors, 'human beings' refers only to themselves and that all other people are 'things'. Oppressors have one primary right—their right to live in peace. However, they do concede (but not necessarily recognize) the right of oppressed persons to survive—but only because their existence is necessary for the existence of the oppressors. Any restriction on the oppressors' way of life is a profound violation of their individual rights, although they may have no respect for the pain, sorrow, misery, and despair of oppressed persons.

This way of understanding the world and their oppressive behaviour is explained by their experience as a dominant class. A climate of violence, both physical and structural, is perpetuated from generation to generation of oppressors. This climate creates in the oppressor a well-developed possessive consciousness, which, in turn, tends to turn everything around it into an object of possession and/or domination. Freire (ibid., 40) says of this situation, 'For the oppressors, what is worthwhile is to have more—always more—even at the cost of the oppressed having less or having nothing.'

Even 'humanity' is a thing to be possessed by the oppressor as an exclusive right. The pursuit of their full humanity by subordinate persons, including the pursuit of freedom, is viewed by the oppressor as subversion. And the more that oppressors control oppressed people, the more they change them into inanimate objects or possessions. Freire and Fromm (1966) contend that this tendency on the part of the oppressor to transform all things and all persons into inanimate possessions corresponds with a tendency towards sadism. By this they mean that as the oppressor blocks the oppressed person from pursuing full humanity and freedom, this 'kills' the creative energy and power, which characterize life. 'The oppressed as objects, as "things," have no purposes except those their oppressors prescribe for them' (Freire, 1994: 42).

With respect to internalized domination, Freire presents an issue that is extremely relevant to anti-oppressive social work practice. Some members of the dominant or oppressor class inevitably join with a subordinate group in their struggle for liberation or emancipation. Freire argues that throughout the history of social struggle, those oppressors who move to the side of the exploited always bring with them the markers of their internalized domination, that is, their prejudices, their stereotypes, and their lack of confidence in the ability of subordinate people to think, to organize, to strategize, and to mobilize. They often exhibit a type of generosity nourished by the unjust order, which must be preserved to justify that generosity. Accordingly, these dominant group members who sincerely wish to transform the unjust social order run the risk of becoming as paternalistic as the oppressors because they believe that they must be the executors of the transformation. Such a position, of course, is not liberating at all. Freire (ibid.) says of this benevolent and paternalistic oppressor group that seeks to lead the struggle for social transformation: 'They talk about the people, but they do not trust them; and *trusting the people is the indispensable precondition for revolutionary change*' (emphasis added). More will be said about this theme in the final chapter.

Frantz Fanon (1968) developed a theory of internalized domination based on his experiences in French-colonized Algeria, where he witnessed and experienced the military and police violence that was necessary for the colonial domination of that country.[6] Central to Fanon's theory is the idea that a Manichean psychology underpins oppression and violence in all its forms (Bulhan, 1985). A Manichean viewpoint is one that divides the world into compartments or categories and people into different species. This division is based on irreconcilable opposites or binary categories of 'either/or' such as 'good versus bad', 'intelligent versus stupid', 'beautiful versus ugly', 'white versus black', 'us versus them', and 'rich versus poor'. Although each of these categories constitutes a duality rather than a dialectic where one of the terms is considered undesirable or unacceptable, in fact, each duality of opposites is interdependent. This is so because each is defined in terms of its opposite, derives its identity from its opposite, and would have no meaning without its opposite. In spite of each half of the duality being dependent on the other half, clear lines of division are necessary or else the Manichean psychology collapses. Oppression and violence create and require a Manichean psychology because such a view legitimates the favoured part of the duality to carry out any kind of action it deems necessary to keep the unfavoured part in check. And, as has been argued throughout this book, the dominant group defines what is good and bad, beautiful and ugly, desirable and undesirable, and so on. That these definitions favour and privilege the dominant group while discriminating against and dehumanizing subordinate groups should be no surprise.

In oppressive situations, the Manichean psychology permeates the everyday lives of people. It is reflected in the living environment of people and how they are treated by social institutions. Bulhan presents an example in the form of the polarity of living conditions between dominant and subordinate groups. In the part of town where the oppressor resides, the houses are spacious and grand, the streets are tree-lined and well-lit at night, there is little litter, the residents are well-fed and well-dressed and friendly towards each other, and the police are both cordial to them and at their service. In the ghetto on the other side of town, people live in crowded and dilapidated buildings on streets that are ill-lit at night and have no trees, where garbage collection is sporadic and litter prevails. The residents are poorly clothed, not healthy-looking, and are friendly only to the few people they know and trust. The police are often suspicious and hostile towards them. In effect, two different species are living in different environments, one enjoying the good life and the other trying to survive while living on the edge.

The Manichean psychology is also reflected in the prevailing or dominant values and beliefs of society. The oppressor or dominant group identifies itself in terms of goodness and beauty while portraying the subordinate group as ugly and evil. Members of the former group see themselves as the epitome of civilization and high values, and skin colour, habits, class, and all other markers of identification signify their superiority. Conversely, those characteristics of the oppressed or subordinate groups are despised because they personify filth, irresponsibility, and evil as opposed to ethical, civilized values. The duality here is that the dominant group puts itself beyond human attributes and reduces the subordinate group to subhuman status. Bulhan (1985: 142) speaks about the tenacity of the Manichean psychology:

> The Manichean psychology is hard to counteract once it takes root in people, the environment, and the culture. Those who live it rely on it for their individual and collective identity. On the surface, the oppressor benefits in the continuation of the Manichean psychology. His identity is more secure; his self-respect is maintained;

his confidence seems firm; and he enjoys a relatively harmonious bond with his own kind. He has a sense of history, a measure of control over his destiny. All this is founded on the wreckage of and dehumanization of the other. Thus, the oppressed is full of self-doubt; he is made to feel inferior; his self-worth is undermined; his confidence and bond with others are weakened; his history is obliterated; he cannot control what happens to him; he feels victorious if he escapes an ever-present peril.

The concept of 'Other', which is part of the Manichean psychology, has become a key concept in writings on post-colonialism to refer to colonized people, in some forms of feminism to refer to women, and in postmodernism to refer to all excluded groups. Both Fanon (1968) and Simone de Beauvoir (1961) used the idea of the Other to show how characteristics of the dominant group (men for Beauvoir, white colonizers for Fanon) become the norms while areas of weakness and vulnerability are imposed on women or colonized people. Beauvoir (1961: xvi, cited in Moane, 1999: 28) says that woman is 'defined and differentiated with reference to man and not he with reference to her; she is the incidental, the inessential as opposed to the essential. He is the Subject, he is the Absolute—she is the Other.'

'Black Is Beautiful'

A key to understanding the psychology of domination or internalized domination is the notion of the 'Other'. All oppressed groups are defined in oppositional terms (i.e., as evil, ugly, subhuman, etc.) to the dominant group. This concept not only helps us to understand unjust and often violent acts of oppression, it also shows us an area where anti-oppressive practice might occur. African Americans in the late 1960s and early 1970s built a whole social movement on the slogan 'Black is beautiful.' This slogan was developed to resist and overcome the dominant view of African Americans (i.e., the Other) as ugly, inferior, dangerous. 'Black is beautiful' not only helped African Americans reclaim part of their identity, it also started a cultural revolution where, in addition to skin colour, such cultural artifacts as black clothing, art, food, and hair texture became sources of pride to the black community rather than of shame and inferiority. This is an important lesson in attempting to identify areas and strategies for overcoming oppression.

Conclusion

The basic question addressed in this chapter has been: 'Why do significant numbers of oppressed individuals comply with, participate in, and contribute to their own oppression?' To help answer this question two concepts associated with the psychology of oppression—inferiorization and internalized oppression—are useful. A number of theories attempt to explain the existence and causes of these psychological states. The converse of internalized oppression—internalized domination—helps to explain why significant numbers of people from the dominant group seem to hold oppressive thoughts and exhibit oppressive behaviour, but do not consider themselves to be oppressive.

The material in this chapter will assist the anti-oppressive worker to better understand the thoughts, attitudes, and behaviour of those persons who have internalized their oppression and who, as a result, are behaving in ways that are destructful to themselves, to members of their own subordinate group, and to members of other subordinate groups. Similarly, the psyche of the oppressor must be better understood before anti-oppressive practice can succeed, for any strategy of anti-oppression must take into consideration not only internalized oppression but internalized domination as well. The implications of the material in this chapter for anti-oppressive social work practice will be outlined in Chapter 8 of this book.

Chapter Seven

The Multiplicity and Heterogeneity of Oppression

Introduction

In Chapter 3 we saw that a person's identity is associated with physical, psychological, social, and cultural variables such as appearance, personality, social status or class, social roles, and race or ethnicity. One's identity is seldom, if ever, determined solely by one characteristic, although one characteristic may be a major marker of an individual or more prominent in most situations or contexts than others (e.g., one's gender or skin colour). These characteristics are termed 'contents' of identity by some writers, 'sub-identities' by others, and 'identities' by still others. Although the terms vary, they all have the same meaning in that they refer to those conditions or features that mark or characterize or identify an individual. The term used in this chapter is 'identity'. The individual does not possess a single identity, but multiple identities that may shift and change over time and/or with changed contexts. This concept of identity is consistent with that of most post-structural, postmodern, and post-colonial writers.

The concept of multiple identities contains much potential for the development of anti-oppressive social work theory and practice. There has been the tendency in social work to focus on the specifics of particular oppressed groups (Langan and Day, 1992) as they make their presence and needs known. Originally concerned with poverty and its victims, social work eventually turned its attention to issues of gender oppression and then racial oppression. Today, social work is concerned with many oppressed groups, but still has the tendency to separate them for purposes of study, analysis, and intervention. With few exceptions (e.g., Day, 1992; Baines, 2001), even those writers who point out that oppression seldom occurs along a single line do not pursue this issue beyond saying that multiple oppression is more complex than a simple, singular form of oppression. Much more work is needed in this area. A typical example of multiple oppression found in the social work literature is that of a black woman (sometimes mentioned as poor) who, it is pointed out, will experience sexism differently from a white woman. An explanation or analysis of this difference, however, is not pursued in any detail or depth in the literature.

Given the call for more research in the area of multiple oppression (e.g., Thompson, 1997) and the lament by Bishop (1994) that no critical analysis of multiple oppression currently exists, this chapter will explore some of the complexities of the multiplicity of oppression and the heterogeneity that is part of every oppressed group or category. Guided by the notions of multiple identities and multiple oppression, I will: (1) argue that multiple identities are a major influence on the production, persistence, and complexity of oppression; (2) present a tentative model of multiple oppressions; (3) analyze the concept of interacting or intersecting oppressions; and (4) present a brief overview of some selected forms and sources of oppression and domination with respect to the heterogeneity that exists within each of them.

Multiple Identities and the Persistence of Domination and Oppression

Given the array of forms and sources of domination and oppression, most people obviously belong to more than one category. In fact, as stated by Anne Bishop (1994: 61), 'we are oppressors in some parts of our identity, and oppressed in others.' She suggests it would be much easier to fight oppression if a line could be drawn between oppressors on one side and oppressed people on the other side, but there are probably only a few who would fall almost entirely on one side or the other. This position is also taken by Gil (1998: 11), who says that 'people . . . tend to be oppressed in some relations and oppressors in others, while some relations may involve mutual oppression.'[1] This means that most oppressed persons also have access to some form of superiority or domination. As such, the experience of either superiority/domination or inferiority/subordination on any one form of oppression can induce people to seek or maintain positions of superiority or domination on other forms of oppression.

Because many people have at least one form of domination as part of their identity, it becomes very difficult to wage a campaign to extinguish oppression. Once oppression is integrated into people's consciousness and into society's culture and structural order, oppressive tendencies become a central part of almost all relations (ibid.). Individuals will likely want to maximize and enhance their life chances and opportunities, but this may come at the expense of others (Moane, 1999). So, although an individual may want to see the end of oppression with respect to those parts of his or her identity that are subordinate (e.g., old age, gay), he or she may be unwilling to surrender the power and privilege that come with that part of the personal identity that is dominant (e.g., affluent, white). And, of course, this unwillingness is reinforced by the larger oppressive tendencies that permeate a society characterized by inequality and by competition. In other words, people may agree to combat oppression as long as it does not affect their particular forms or sources of privilege and domination. For example, low-income working-class males often exhibit overt and extreme racism, sexism, and homophobia even though they are victims of similar attitudes and treatment by dominant groups.

Life chances and opportunities are not the only reasons for clinging to one's particular source of domination. Oppression also may bring to the oppressor certain psychological value. As discussed in the previous chapter, oppressed persons often experience feelings of inferiority, powerlessness, uselessness, alienation, self-doubt, and self-hatred. One negative and counter-productive way of coping with these feelings is to take comfort in the belief that some people are even worse off. For example, poor working-class white men may support and participate in racist and sexist actions to compensate for their poverty and oppression (i.e., to feel better about themselves). Furthermore, they may believe that those who are worse off really deserve their fate and second-class treatment because they are lazy, deviant, irresponsible, and so on. In this way, worse-off groups receive the same value judgments from other oppressed groups that they receive from the dominant group. This phenomenon of oppression against one subordinate group by another subordinate group is known as a 'poor person's snobbery' in that the former believe themselves to be at some higher level than the latter in a perceived hierarchy of oppressed groups.

The net effect of protecting those parts of our identity that accord us relatively favourable treatment from society, as well as participating in and contributing to the oppression of others, is to keep the whole system of oppression and dominant-subordinate relations in place. As long as separation, competition, and hierarchy among subordinate groups exist, there is no potential for solidarity and collaborative action on the part of oppressed groups, which leaves the status quo preserved and protected. Only a complete and complex understanding of our own contradictory roles as oppressors and oppressed will allow us to recognize our shared interests and to resist rather than collude with oppression (Bishop, 1994).

A Model of Multiple Oppressions

Although the social work and anti-oppressive literature generally acknowledges that oppression is usually multi-faceted, no satisfactory conceptual representation or model depicts the multifarious nature of oppression. Donna Baines (2000: 6) argues that even those critical theorists who have sought to expose the bases of dominant-subordinate relations in society have failed 'to explicate the interrelations between and within the totality of oppressive relations', and that 'no one model exists which reveals how multi-oppressions continuously interact with, contest, and reinforce each other.' Other feminist and anti-racist writers (e.g., Anthias and Yuval-Davis, 1992; Day, 1992; George, 2000) have argued in a similar vein and contend that existing theories and analyses of the complex relationships among class, race, gender, sexuality, and other forms of difference are still inconclusive. This section will discuss the intersections of oppression and present a modified version of Steven Wineman's (1984) 'intersectionist model' of multiple oppression.

Single-Strand Model

The simplest model of oppression is the 'single-strand' model, which depicts one form or source of oppression as being fundamental to all others. For example, orthodox Marxists identify classism or exploitation of the working class as the primary source of all oppression and believe that all others are derived from and secondary to it. While recognizing sexism, racism, and other forms of oppression, conventional Marxists contend that these are secondary oppressions and that because these groups are more susceptible than others to oppression in a capitalist economy they are oppressed, not because they may be women or non-white, and so on. In other words, they are oppressed because they are workers and their gender or race only exacerbates rather than causes their oppression. Eliminate classism and you eliminate the root cause of all secondary oppressions. Early forms of radical or progressive social work were colour- and gender-blind and focused on class oppression only (e.g., Bailey and Brake, 1975).

Other groups have argued against the centrality of class oppression, but on the basis that some other form of oppression is primary. For example, some radical feminists have insisted that patriarchy or the exercise of male power is the central organizing category of oppression and that the basic class difference is between the sexes (Hartmann, 1981). Similar positions have been adopted with respect to race. Black radicals and nationalists from different countries, such as Stokely Carmichael, Malcolm X, Louis Farrakhan, and Frantz Fanon, have all argued that racism is the oldest and most fundamental source of oppression. Even one of the foremost progressive social work writers today, Lena Dominelli, seems to argue from a single-strand position in *Anti-Racist Social Work* when she asserts that 'class and gender inequality will be included in the transformation resulting from the struggle against racism' (Dominelli, 1997: 167).

Although single-strand models may contain a comforting sense of simplicity, they are also overly reductionist and simplistic. Complex social phenomena such as domination and subordination cannot be adequately understood on the basis of a solitary (no matter how fundamental) variable or category. The single-strand model does not account for the interconnections and intersections of oppression that exist. For example, women of colour experience racism and sexism together (George, 2000) and not separately, as one form of oppression is continuously mediated by the other(s) (Day, 1992). Nor can the single-strand model account for the dynamic ways in which social relations complement and contradict or reinforce and undermine each other at different historical moments and in different contexts (Baines, 2001).

In addition to its conceptual and explanatory limitations, the single-strand model holds little potential for social solidarity and joint action by oppressed individuals and groups. Wineman (1984: 163) states that 'it [a single fundamental source of oppression] at once fails to create a basis for unity which respects the dignity and felt experience of all the oppressed individuals and groups who are supposed to become unified, and it fails to generate a practical strategy and process which can . . . effectively challenge all forms of oppression.' Furthermore, a single-strand view does little to overcome the existing divisions and fragmentation that presently exist among oppressed groups. In fact, it may generate resentment as some groups are asked to submerge their 'secondary' interests and less-favoured forms of oppression until the 'root cause' of all oppression has been eliminated (ibid.).

Parallel Model

A more pluralistic model of oppression, originally outlined by Wineman (1984) and used by many early progressive social workers, such as the originator of structural social work in Canada, Maurice Moreau (1979, Moreau and Leonard, 1989, cited in Carniol, 1992), is the parallel-tracks depiction of oppression. Rather than adopting a model positing a single primary source of oppression, the parallel model depicts all forms and sources of oppression running alongside each other in a non-hierarchical, parallel fashion. Figure 7.1 presents a somewhat modified version of Wineman's 'parallel-tracks' perspective of multiple oppression. According to this perspective, different forms and sources of oppression all involve similar dynamics of dominant-subordinate relations, but each is caused and maintained by an autonomous set or configuration of social, economic, cultural, political, and historical factors. In addition, each form of oppression affects only a single distinct group of oppressed people (Wineman, 1984). For example, sexism only oppresses women; class exploitation only oppresses working and poor people; homophobia only oppresses gay, lesbian, and bisexual persons; and racism only oppresses people of colour.

An obvious limitation of the parallel model is that it does not account for people who experience two or more sources of oppression, that is, it does not address how oppressions are relational and interact with each other. As noted above, Usha George (2000) makes the point that women of colour experience

Figure 7.1 Parallel Model of Oppression

Class   Gender   Race   Age

sexism and racism simultaneously, not as single or parallel strands of oppression. Wineman identifies another limitation to the parallel model. Although it does not claim that a separate solution to one form of oppression is the key to eliminating all forms of oppression (i.e., the single-strand belief), the parallel model offers little potential for solidarity and joint social action among oppressed groups. Because the causes, interests, and experiences associated with each form of oppression are seen to be distinct, requiring separate solutions, there may be occasions for ad hoc joint actions where one oppressed group supports another, but the emphasis is still on the 'single issue' of each group. In other words, the form of oppression experienced by a particular group is given particular emphasis by that group because it affects its members most deeply; in fact, the oppression is often used to promote internal solidarity and to strengthen group members psychologically and politically (Wineman, 1984).

Intersectional Model

A model of oppression proposed by Wineman that does account for intersecting, interlocking, and/or interacting oppressions is the intersectional model (Figure 7.2). Wineman asserts that although the different forms of oppression may be distinct in some ways, they are not unrelated. 'Different oppressions intersect at innumerable points in everyday life and are mutually reinforcing, creating a *total system* of oppression in which one continuum of stratification cannot be addressed in isolation from all the others' (ibid., 169). This model accounts for multiple identities in that an intersection is the location where a person's race, for example, will meet his or her class, age, or any other component of the person's identity. Figure 7.2 is a modified version of Wineman's intersectional perspective of multiple oppression. It shows that although there may be distinct *categories* of oppression, there is no oppression that creates a distinct *group* of oppressed people who are unaffected, one way or the other, by other forms of oppression. Oppressed groups overlap with each other—an important fact conceptually both for understanding the nature of oppression and for seeking alliances and coalitions of oppressed groups (the latter to be discussed in Chapter 8).

Figure 7.2 Intersectional Model of Oppression

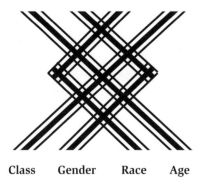

Class   Gender   Race   Age

The intersectional model does not argue for hierarchies of oppression (i.e., 'my oppression is greater than yours). This does not mean, however, that all oppressions are considered to be of equal severity or that they affect all oppressed persons in the same way. Similarly, as pointed out by Baines (2000), the model does not attempt to predict or define how different forms of oppression reinforce, contest, or complicate each other in different contexts. It must be remembered that the intersectional model is a model and not a theory or analysis. Models usually do not contain explanatory or predictive features. That is the job of analysis and theory. Models may identify or depict certain social realities, but they do not explain them. For example, general systems theory or an ecological model may be used to depict a family in its social context and identify the relationships among family members, but it does not account for power relationships within the family, nor does it explain conflict. It is a pictorial representation of the various subsystems that have a connection with a particular family (or other social system). It does not explain the nature of the family, problems being experienced by the family, the nature of the relationships pictured in the model, the extent of influence of various subsystems, and so on.

No model (or theory) can account for or explain how individuals will experience oppression because each experience is different; nor can it account for the ways in which different forms of oppression constantly change in relation to each other or how they vary in different contexts. The best we might hope for is to understand that the different forms, sources, and relations of oppression are continuous, contentious, dynamic, and mutually reinforcing social processes (Baines, 2001). The contribution of the intersectional model of oppression is that it highlights the multiplicity of oppression. It reveals the complexity and multiple or intersecting nature of oppression. It also indicates areas for further analysis in our attempts to understand the multiplicity of oppression. Two of these areas, which will be explored below, are the nature of an intersection or interaction of oppression and the heterogeneity that exists within each category or form of oppression.

Intersections of Oppression: An Analysis

Most of the recent social work literature on anti-oppression emphasizes the importance of examining how various forms of oppression intersect or interact. The majority of radical, feminist, and anti-racist social work writers today go beyond the discrete, single-strand analysis of oppression, although they tend to restrict themselves to the trinity or triumvirate of race, class, and gender forms (e.g., Baines, 2000; Day, 1992; George and Ramkissoon, 1998). They recognize, for example, that oppression based on patriarchy is not experienced the same by all women, as it will be mediated in some way by a woman's class position, race, sexuality, etc. As well, one's oppression in one particular area will be mediated not only by other experienced forms of oppression, but also by forms of domination (e.g., male, white) attached to an individual and by his or her psychological characteristics (e.g., sense of self, personality). In addition, the particular historical moment in which the oppression occurs and the surrounding social conditions or context in which it occurs will also affect the experience of oppression.

Multiple oppression is a very complex phenomenon. To understand its full effects would require a separate analysis of all the permutations and combinations of factors connected with each individual case of oppression. Such specificity would, of course, mitigate against any possibility for generalization or commonality (Nicholson, 1990). This, in turn, would undermine identity, solidarity, and the capacity for political action (Brodribb, 1992, cited in Moane, 1999). Conversely, an overemphasis on commonality can lead to universalizing tendencies that ignore local conditions and impose inappropriate frameworks and patterns on particular oppressed groups or individuals. Making links between oppressions, therefore, will require the recognition of both commonalities and specificities across different forms and experiences of oppression (Moane, 1999).

As was argued in previous chapters, much can be learned about the nature, dynamics, and processes of oppression without going into a case-by-case analysis of each instance of oppression. With respect to the multiplicity of oppression, one important area that is underdeveloped in the literature is the nature of an intersection of oppression. What does it mean when it is said that two forms of oppression intersect with each other? Or, what does it mean when two intersecting forms of oppression mediate each other? Is it only forms of oppression that intersect? Or do forms of domination also intersect with forms of oppression and with other forms of domination as well?

Several writers (e.g., Moane, 1999; Young, 1990) make the point that multiple oppressions are not simply cumulative or additive. For example, the oppression experienced by a black woman goes beyond a simple summing of race and gender oppressions. Something else happens at the intersection of race and gender. In the language of statistics, a new variable is created. Not only does the black woman experience oppression as a woman and as a black person, but she also experiences oppression as a black woman. Her colour interacts with her gender. Interactive effects have long been recognized in social science research. In fact, the interactive effects of bringing two or more variables together are often measured statistically using multivariate analyses. This does not mean that oppression can be measured statistically in any meaningful way. Because much of oppression is qualitative in nature and presently not well understood, we do not have the conceptual knowledge or methodological tools to measure oppression quantitatively. Rather than positivist, the point I am making is conceptual. Whenever two or more independent social variables are combined (such as race and gender), the result is an effect on the dependent variable (such as oppression) that goes beyond a simple addition of the effect of each variable. The combinations (i.e., interactions) of variables will also have an effect on the dependent variable. An analogy from chemistry may help. When sodium and chloride are combined, a chemical reaction or interaction occurs producing a different substance—common table salt. Salt may result from combining two elements, but the result goes beyond simple additive effects in that salt is an autonomous substance with different properties and effects than either sodium or chloride.

Let us look at a couple of examples in an effort to clarify this discussion of interactions. In the first example, we will consider two sources of oppression, race and gender. In Equation 1 the letter 'a' is assigned to race and the letter 'b' to gender. Their combined effects on oppression may be represented as:

Equation 1: oppression = a + b + (ab)

[i.e., oppression = race + gender + (race x gender)]

Thus, a black woman will experience the oppressive effects of patriarchy, a term that refers to the system of social structures and practices that subordinate women, as will a white woman. However, patriarchy is not a simple concept whereby all men dominate all women equally. Women will experience patriarchy differently based on their class, race, sexuality, age, etc. (Collins, 1990; Emberley, 1993; Maracle, 1996; Moane, 1999). In other words, a black woman will experience patriarchy differently from a white woman because it will be mediated (affected, influenced) by her racial identification or skin colour. All other things being equal, a black woman will likely experience a more complicated and potent form of oppression emanating from sexism and patriarchy than will a white woman. Just attempting to sort out whether particular incidents of abuse or certain obstacles to development and progress that a black woman experiences are the result of her gender or her race or both is a question and struggle that the white woman does not experience. This additional and complex effect of oppression is reflected in the interaction component in Equation 1. The interaction of race and gender is not a part of the gender component of oppression or the race component. Like the example of common table salt, it is a separate factor in itself and contains oppressive effects separate from either gender or race.

What Is It about Me?

Nancy, a black woman, is a member of the Department of Social Work at a university. Six months ago she had been appointed head of the department. One of her new duties was to attend meetings of the Academic Senate, the senior academic committee in the university, comprised of deans, department heads, and other senior academics. Most of the members of Senate were white men who had been at the university for years. During the first few meetings that Nancy attended she noticed that whenever she spoke, she received polite attention but then the discussions would proceed as if she had not said anything. As time went on, the polite attention disappeared. Other Senate members would interrupt her and act as if she were invisible. In discussions with some of her female colleagues about what was happening, she was told that it was a gender issue and that she should raise it at a Senate meeting. In conversations with some of her family and black friends, she was told it was a race issue and that she should raise it at a Senate meeting. This is probably a situation where Nancy is experiencing sexism and racism simultaneously. Obviously, it is a delicate issue for Nancy. How should she approach Senate?

Just as a black woman will experience sexism differently from a white woman, so, too, will she experience racism differently from a black male. Both will experience racism, but only the black woman will also experience patriarchy as a form of oppression, and patriarchy will mediate how she experiences racism. This exacerbates the level and severity of racial oppression she experiences, and thus makes the black woman's racial oppression more complex or multi-dimensional than racial oppression experienced by a black male (all other things being equal). The black woman, as mentioned above, may be subject to a constant dilemma of wondering whether it is her race or her gender that accounts for some of her negative experiences and, therefore, what her target for remedying the treatment ought to be.

The above scenario of an interaction between two forms or sources of oppression is relatively simple (conceptually at least) compared to situations where more than two forms of oppression interact with each other. Let us look at an example of multiple oppression where there are three forms or sources of oppression (e.g., race, gender, and class). As above, let us assign letters to each of these forms of oppression: a = race; b = gender; and c = class. Their combined effects on oppression are reflected in the following equation:

Equation 2: oppression = a + b + c + (ab) + (ac) + (bc) + (abc)
[i.e., oppression = race + gender + class + (race x gender) +
(race x class) + (gender x class) + (race x gender x class)]

In this example, the black woman, who experiences a more complex form of racial oppression than a black male because of her gender and who also experiences a more complex form of gender oppression than a white woman because of her colour, will have these two forms of oppression mediated by her class position. If she is poor, she will be oppressed by class, which, in turn, will exacerbate her experiences with the other two forms of oppression with which she may be struggling. And, in turn, her class oppression may become more intense, severe, and pervasive because of her gender and race oppressions. Equation 2 shows four interactive effects associated with three forms of oppression compared to one interactive effect associated with two forms of oppression only. Obviously, the interactive effects of multiple oppression increase exponentially with the addition of more forms of oppression.

The above equations illustrate the complexity of multiple oppressions. As different forms of oppression are added to an already oppressive situation, the interactions increase exponentially, which, in turn, increase the complexity (and perhaps the severity) of oppression on a person. The equations do not reveal anything about the nature of an interaction or how much an interaction contributes to oppression, but it is unrealistic to attempt to measure interactions as they will vary in different contexts at different times with different individuals. The point of the above exercise is to show what an interaction or intersection is, how they contribute to the complexity of oppression, and to highlight the interactional nature and effects of oppression.

Multiple oppression becomes even more complex when forms of domination are factored into the situation. It was suggested earlier that the identities of most people contain both dominant and subordinate characteristics. Just as different forms of oppression will interact with one another, so, too, will different forms of domination interact with other forms of domination as well as with different forms of oppression. If the black woman in the examples above is affluent instead of poor, her experiences with oppression would be affected in the following ways. First, she obviously would not be oppressed along the lines of being an exploited worker or poor. Second, her other forms of oppression (race and gender) would not be made worse by her class position. Finally, her class position would mediate or alleviate some of the negative effects of being black and a woman. For example, she would be able to purchase such services as health care, live in a decent house in a relatively crime-free neighbourhood, send her children to decent, well-equipped schools, and pay for legal services to fight instances of gender or race discrimination. The black woman's privileged class position would not eliminate her experiences with gender and race oppression, but unlike her black sisters living in poverty, this position would mediate or alleviate some of the severity, harshness, and pervasiveness of the oppression she did experience.

A caution should be noted here. The above analysis does not mean that a hierarchy of oppressions can be created simply by summing the number of different forms of oppression a person may be experiencing and subtracting the number of different forms of domination one occupies from the sum total. Oppression is irreducibly a qualitative and not a quantitative experience (Wineman, 1984). One form of oppression may be experienced as more severe than a combination of two other forms of oppression because there is enormous individual variation within any particular oppressed group (to be discussed below). For example, a white working-class older woman (oppressed by class, gender, and age) is not necessarily more oppressed than a black working-class male (oppressed by class and race). Nor is it true that every black woman is more oppressed than every black male, as she may have material and/or personal resources that he does not.

The intersectional nature of oppression holds significant implications for an anti-oppressive social work practice. It helps the social worker see that oppression seldom comes in a single form. It also helps us to understand that it is not simply a case of identifying and summing the different oppressions that one may be experiencing in an effort to obtain an appreciation of the oppressed person's total situation. Social workers should also be aware of the ways that different forms of oppression intersect with each other and how these intersections contain oppressive effects themselves. They will recognize that not all members of a particular oppressed group will experience oppression in the same way or with the same severity or intensity. Just as there is heterogeneity between groups of oppressed people there is also heterogeneity within each oppressed group, as suggested in the above discussion of the mediating effects of different forms of oppression and domination. We now need to examine this concept of heterogeneity in more detail.

Heterogeneity within Oppressed Groups

When we consider different forms and sources of oppression and different groups of oppressed people, there is a danger of viewing and treating everyone within a particular group as the same. As suggested in the discussion on intersecting oppressions, and as Lyotard (1988) argues, any homogenization of people over-simplifies the complexities and varieties of social reality by not acknowledging the incredible diversity inherent within people's various gender, class, race, age, sexuality, and other social positions. So, for example, although all people of colour may be oppressed as non-white people, there is great diversity among people of colour that will result in more or less oppression.

Wineman argues that our contemporary socio-economic-political system has an inherent capacity for creating and maintaining deep divisions both among oppressed groups and within each oppressed group. These divisions among oppressed groups serve the interests of the dominant group in that the competition among subordinate groups for some resources and recognition is a major obstacle to their recognizing common interests and issues and organizing and mobilizing around them. Making matters even worse for subordinate groups is the fact that the fragmentation and segmentation of oppression occur not only among oppressed groups, but within each oppressed group as well. There are gradations or hierarchies of privilege and advantage within each oppressed group. In a society marked by oppression, inequality, and competition, these gradations tend to motivate people who hold relative advantages to defend their positions and to support the status quo. This often causes resentment on the part of those who are relatively disadvantaged towards those who rank immediately above them (Wineman, 1984). And just as deep divisions among different oppressed groups inhibit notions and actions of solidarity among them, so do divisions within oppressed groups inhibit solidarity on the part of members of each group.

Various forms and sources of oppression, along with divisions or hierarchies within each oppressed group, are presented below. The purpose is not to offer a complete or well-developed overview of each form of oppression addressed— other social work texts do this (e.g., Thompson, 1997). Rather, the intention is to present a succinct version of the nature of several selected forms of oppression and to highlight the divisions that exist within each oppressed group. Although I focus on several forms of oppression individually in order to show the heterogeneity within each, it should be remembered that oppression tends to be a multiple phenomenon. I isolate different forms in this section for analytical purposes only.

Classism

Class is not the simple concept today that it might have been when Karl Marx was writing in the mid-nineteenth century about the exploitation of workers by capitalists. Marx divided society into two major classes: the bourgeoisie or capitalist class, who own the means of production (factories, equipment), and the proletariat or working class, who have to sell their labour to the capitalists to survive. Marx devoted his entire intellectual life to writing about the evils of capitalism, which included the exploitation and oppression of workers by the economically and politically powerful capitalist or ruling class. Thus, classism has come to mean the form of exploitation and oppression emanating from the social divisions of class. Of course, society (including social class) has changed significantly since Marx's time so that his original analysis is no longer applicable to the current form of capitalism. However, many developments in Marxist thought attempt to update the basic tenets of his analysis and apply them to today's situation (e.g., Agger, 1998; Giddens, 1995; Habermas, 1975).

Class today is a complex phenomenon comprising different social, economic, and political theoretical conceptualizations (Thompson, 1998). The working class today is not the relatively homogeneous social group with common interests that Marx wrote about. Rather, it is a highly stratified and multi-layered hierarchy of people characterized almost as much by conflicting interests as by common interests. A typical representation of the stratified class divisions may be seen in Figure 7.3.

Figure 7.3

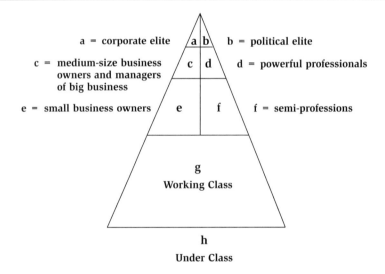

The dominant groups at the top of the hierarchy consist of two subgroups: (1) those people who exert corporate power and domination through their ownership and/or control of major industrial, commercial, and financial firms; and (2) persons who exert state power through their positions as elected leaders and cabinet ministers within national and state governments.[2] The former subgroup controls the means of production and historically has been known (by Marxists) as the capitalist class.

In most Western democracies, elected leaders have a much closer relationship with the corporate elite than they do with the job-dependent working class. Marxists have referred to political leaders as 'business class allies', and many elected leaders come from or aspire to the corporate sector while the job-dependent working class is grossly under-represented in government. Given the corporate sector's economic power and its influence over and close relationship with the political sector, it should be no surprise that government decisions, on the whole, tend to favour capital accumulation at the expense of the working class (e.g., favourable tax provisions for corporations, anti-union legislation).

The two groups just below the corporate and political leaders in Figure 7.3 consist of the owners of medium-size businesses and key managers in the corporate sector, in one group, and self-employed members of powerful professional groups, such as law, medicine, engineering, and academe, in the other. These people probably have more in common with those above them than they do with the job-dependent working class or the underclass. In fact, they are often referred to (in Marxist terms) as the 'bourgeoisie'. Even though the bourgeoisie must work for a living, this group is the aristocracy of the working class—members enjoy certain privileges, such as high social status, prestige, and high incomes relative to other occupational groups. The organizational preference of the professional subgroup is that of a professional association rather than a union. Collectively, the bourgeoisie is able to exert significant influence on the political sector and frequently does so to advance its own interests, often at the expense of workers (e.g., the privatization of medical care). Given their privileged position in society, it is not likely that the bourgeoisie will align themselves with poor people and job-dependent workers to eliminate classism. The bourgeoisie is numerically greater than the capitalists and their allies, but not as powerful. However, by any measurement, members of the bourgeoisie are part of the dominant class.

Below the bourgeoisie is another layer in the class hierarchy comprising two groups that together constitute the petite (or petty) bourgeoisie. One group consists of small business owners (e.g., small factories or workshops), and the other is made up of members of semi-professions, such as social workers, nurses, schoolteachers, and journalists. Arguably, they form the bulk of the middle class, with other sectors of the middle class being in the bottom rungs of the bourgeoisie and the upper rungs of the job-dependent working class. The term 'middle class' is ambiguous and somewhat mythical. It has been my experience in North America and Australia that most people (including most social work students), when asked which class they belong to, are likely to say 'middle class', especially if they do not possess a class analysis. In any event, both groups in this social positioning aspire to climb up the socio-economic ladder, with small business owners dreaming of becoming owners of large businesses and the semi-professions copying and/or adopting the cultures and organizational frameworks of the established professions. Given their lack of economic and political power, as well as their upwardly mobile aspirations, they are a relatively malleable group that often carries out the bidding of the dominant group. They do this by providing employment (small businesses account for most jobs) and by caring for and controlling the job-dependent working class and the poverty-stricken underclass. Most people in this class division are able to obtain a decent or at least adequate level of living and may not see or believe the need for fundamental social change as key to addressing the social problems and conditions experienced by those in class rungs beneath them.

The vast majority (two-thirds to three-quarters) of people in advanced capitalist societies belong to the working class or proletariat. This group consists of industrial, construction, farm, clerical, distributive, and service workers; skilled, semi-skilled, and unskilled workers; young and old workers; male and female workers; blue-collar labourers and pink-collar workers; migrants, the unemployed, and underemployed workers; full-time, casual, part-time, and seasonal workers. In other words, the working class consists of all those people whose main (and usually only) source of income is the sale of their labour power and/or transfer payments from the state. Recessions hit this group harder than any other group and unemployment is higher within this group than any other group except the underclass. This group makes less money, owns less, owes more, and has less education, less access to societal goods, fewer opportunities, less respect or status, and less political power than any other group in society except the underclass. It carries out most of the necessary but menial and dangerous jobs for the dominant groups and purchases the same products that they make, with a profit going to the capitalists or bourgeoisie. They depend on and pay for the services of professionals. They pay their taxes and have fewer tax breaks than the groups above them, which effectively means that they subsidize the incomes and operating costs of the people above them on the hierarchy. Those occupying a higher tier on the class scale oppress the working class at every level and in multiple ways.

The underclass is the final group on the class hierarchy. It represents a growing group of people who have no attachment to the labour market. Members of this group are permanently trapped outside the traditional divisions of class because such divisions are based on the type of work that one does. This group is different from the working poor or the temporarily unemployed, as members have either never worked in the past or will never work again. They comprise homeless persons, mentally ill people, long-term unemployed individuals, and sick and disabled persons. In the United States members of the underclass are typically black, Hispanic, or marginalized and excluded poor white people. In Australia and Canada they are typically Aboriginal or people of colour (often refugees) or marginalized and excluded poor white people. They have little in the way of social services and their poverty and their acts of survival (i.e., their attempts to obtain food, clothing, and shelter) are often criminalized. It is left to the police to control and manage them by what Wachholz and Mullaly (1993) call covering up and mopping up after the shortcomings of society and its welfare state. In the absence of adequate social, economic, and psychiatric supports, the police will use criminal statutes to charge members of the underclass with such crimes as vagrancy, panhandling, prostitution, sleeping (and urinating) in a public place, and petty theft when someone tries to maintain some level of subsistence. Instead of the conditions of homelessness and poverty being criminalized, it is the acts of survival of the underclass that are criminalized (Wachholz and Mullaly, 1993). The underclass is despised, feared, pitied, and rejected by members of all other class divisions. They are society's disposable or throwaway population. They are at the bottom of the bottom of our class system and have little hope of ever leaving it.

This brief overview of class illustrates its divisions and some of the conflicts of interest that exist among these divisions. Workers or the working class are by no means a homogeneous group of people. Not only do conflicting interests, mistrust, suspicion, and resentment exist among categories or divisions of class, they also exist within each class division. For example, there is significant resentment and animosity on the part of the working poor towards the non-working poor. The former have inculcated many of the myths and stereotypes about people on welfare. They see themselves working hard to eke out a basic living and perceive people in receipt of welfare to be living the 'life of Riley' while laughing up their sleeves at those who work. Both groups may be poor, but society has driven a deep wedge between them that mitigates against any notion of or attempt at solidarity. It is not uncommon to have political leaders play these two groups off against each other. Thus, when welfare rates are criticized by poor people and their allies for being too low, politicians will often respond by stating that an increase in welfare benefits would give recipients more money than the working poor receive in wages and would have to be paid for by the working poor. The outrage from the working poor who are struggling on a daily basis to make ends meet is almost immediate.

A Despicable Political Response

A number of years ago in the Canadian province of New Brunswick, a campaign by anti-poverty groups and their allies sought to increase the welfare rates, especially for children's school supplies and for winter fuel. The Minister of Social Services finally responded to this request. She rhetorically, but publicly, said that she wondered how the 'working poor' would feel about such an increase, since it would be paid by the working poor and probably put welfare rates on a par with or even above their hard-earned income (which it would not). There was an immediate expression of outrage from the working poor (letters, radio phone-in shows, etc.) against such an increase, and the movement for higher rates died.

In sum, class is a complex sociological, political, economic, and cultural concept that has significant implications with respect to social inequality and life chances. Members of particular class divisions are oppressed not only by those in higher positions on the class hierarchy, but also by persons occupying the same class division. The same can be said about race.

Racism

Racism is the belief that human abilities are determined by race, that one race is inherently superior to all others and, therefore, has the right to dominate all other races. Underpinning racism is the assumption that racial classification is based on biological evidence. Skin colour, for example, is thought to be associated with other biological characteristics such as intelligence. Essentialism is also part of racism in that there is a belief that everybody classified as belonging to a particular racial group possesses the same characteristics (Thompson, 1997). There is no biological validation for many of the popular ideas concerning racial classification (Banton and Harwood, 1975, cited in Thompson, 1998). Rather, racial classifications are social constructs or ways to make sense of the social world rather than biological types. In spite of the lack of scientific validation, racial categorization remains a fixed concept because it carries out certain ideological and political functions for the racially (white) dominant group. The categories of race are not value-neutral, but constitute a hierarchy of racial groups in which white groups are dominant because of their socially constructed superiority (Ahmad, 1990). And as Thompson (1998) argues, this socially constructed superiority lies at the basis of racism.

Although race as a biological category is questionable,[3] racism is not. Through the assumption of racial superiority, racism has had profound negative effects on people of colour within most Eurocentric societies and the countries they colonized. As discussed in previous chapters, people of colour are subject to disparaging stereotypes and are oppressed and discriminated against at the personal, cultural, and structural levels of society. All non-white people are subject to racism, but they do not constitute a homogeneous group as there are colour and cultural differences among non-white people. In fact, these differences constitute a hierarchy of racism experienced by people of colour that is constructed and imposed by the dominant white group. Wineman's (1984: 172) description of the racial hierarchy in the United States is similar to that of most other Eurocentric nations: 'social distinctions are made, more or less subtly, between Latino/as [Hispanics], Asians, Native Americans, and Blacks (and between lighter and darker skinned Blacks)—as well as between people of colour who adopt white speech patterns and cultural trappings, and those who don't; as a rule, the lighter you are, physically and culturally, the "better".' However, success on white terms usually requires people of colour both to recant their culture and to accept with grace a permanent position of marginal inferiority (ibid.).

The system of stratification imposed on people of colour by the white society, based on shadings of skin colour and conformity to the dominant culture on its terms, is often internalized by people of colour. This reinforces the stratified divisions imposed by the dominant group both among the various groups of non-white people and within each group. Stratification based on shades of skin colour evokes a profound internalization of racist oppression, which may result in people of colour adopting racist attitudes and behaviours towards each other. Divisions are created and sustained among black persons, Aboriginal people, Asian groups, and Hispanic people.

Just as stratification creates and sustains divisions among various groups of people of colour, it also nurtures divisions *within* each group based on skin colour, class, and lifestyle (ibid.). People of colour are not only divided along class, gender, sexual orientation, age, and other lines of social division, but in terms of their relationship with the dominant white group as well. Those individuals who are 'whiter' (physically and culturally) often dissociate themselves for a variety of psychological and sociological reasons from others in their identity group who are not as 'white'. Conversely, those at lower levels on their respective racial hierarchies often resent those above them and view them as traitors to their own 'race'. For example, First Nations people in North America who appear to other First Nations people to have been co-opted by white society are often referred to in a derogatory manner as 'apples'—red on the outside, but white on the inside. Similarly, Australian Aborigines will refer to those among them who appear to have adopted white lifestyles and culture as coconuts—brown on the outside, but white on the inside. The term 'Uncle Tom' has long been used by many African Americans to refer to other African Americans who have ingratiated themselves to white people in attempts to assimilate into white middle-class culture.

In sum, race is a complex social construction that has significant implications for people with respect to equality and life chances. However, the social and psychological degradations attached to racism go well beyond employment, income, housing, or welfare. Wineman says it best: 'Racism attacks the core of people's sense of their own value, and it ultimately attacks their right to exist. . . . When you are taught from birth that you are inherently inferior, you are taught in the same breath that you are inherently powerless' (ibid., 128). The divisions within each category of people of colour guarantee this powerlessness.

Sexism

Although defined in different ways in the feminist literature (e.g., biological, materialist, social constructionist[4]), 'patriarchy' (literally interpreted as the law of the father) refers to a system of social structures and practices that subordinate women to men. A closely related term is 'sexism', which refers to a set of social, economic, political, and cultural beliefs, attitudes, and practices that oppress women (Bishop, 1994). Patriarchy and sexism reinforce each other. Together they produce a situation where women earn less, have greater obstacles to advancement, and are harassed more in the workplace than men; carry out a much greater load of domestic labour and are subject to the 'double shift' more than men; experience domestic and sexual violence more than men; suffer from social, economic, and political inequalities more than men (Thompson, 1997, 1998). An extreme form of oppression based on sexism is 'misogyny', which refers to the hatred, fear, and mistreatment of women by individual men (Bishop, 1994).

Sexism is similar to racism in that each is based on notions of biological determinism and essentialism. Whereas racism involves a biological difference (i.e., non-white) being associated with such socially constructed characteristics (differences) as inferior intelligence, fear of working, untrustworthiness, and undependability, sexism involves a biological difference (i.e., female) being associated with such socially constructed characteristics (differences) as passivity, emotionality, natural caregiving, irrationality, and weakness. Racism and sexism also comprise essentialist beliefs in that all people of colour have the above socially constructed characteristics associated with people of colour and all women have the above socially constructed characteristics associated with women. And, of course, these negative essentialist characteristics are used by the dominant groups to rationalize the subordination of people of colour and women.

Women, like all oppressed groups, do not constitute a homogeneous group in regard to their oppression. Although all women are oppressed by patriarchy, not every woman is oppressed to the same degree or experiences oppression in the same way. As noted above, a woman's oppression will be mediated by her class, race, and other social characteristics. In addition to differences that emanate from various combinations of intersecting forms of oppression, women are also differentiated along other lines that affect the level or extent of oppression they experience. For example, women are often ranked by both men and women according to the social status of their husbands or male partners. For the most part, if the social status of a particular woman's male partner is high, she is accorded a higher degree of status, respect, treatment, and privilege than the female partner of a man who does not have high social status. This is cause for resentment from some women, who often perceive the higher social status as not being deserved and the female recipient as a manipulative opportunist. Conversely, the woman who attains high status by her association with a privileged male has more in common with other women (and men) in her social class than with those who are not. Usually, this means that she will have less commitment to changing the system that has facilitated her relatively privileged position. Wineman (1984) identifies another group of women accorded some degree of status by many men and some women in that they are ranked according to conventional standards of beauty or appearance and sexuality. The closer a woman is to these ideals of beauty and sexuality, the more respect, admiration, opportunities, and privileges are available to her. Conversely, the further women are removed from these beauty standards, the less status they are likely to be accorded (by men and women). Sex objectification is part of sexism and, like social status, is a source of division among women.

Another source of division among women as an oppressed group is the internalization on the part of some women of their oppression. Thus, some women believe that gender equality is not only unattainable but also undesirable. They believe in the traditional family unit (headed by a man), traditional family values (woman is the domestic worker in the family), and biological determinism (because the woman gives birth, therefore she is the natural caregiver). They also subscribe to the idealized notion that a woman will be protected, provided for, and put on a pedestal by her man if she properly looks after *him, his* home, and *his* children. Such women resent 'feminists' who criticize this type of arrangement and, in turn, are resented by many women who believe that such notions and actions of servitude to men only reinforce the subordination of women.

Heterosexism

Heterosexism is a form of oppression whereby heterosexuality is considered to be the only acceptable and viable life option (Blumenfeld and Raymond, 1988). Heterosexism oppresses gay, lesbian, and bisexual people, and some writers (e.g., Bishop, 1994) argue that it also oppresses anyone who does not fit the traditional one-man, one-woman monogamous marriage with children. 'Homophobia' is an irrational fear or hatred or discomfort of homosexual people or homosexuality that is often manifest in individual violence or structural discrimination. Only recently has homosexuality been removed as a psychiatric disorder from the *DSM-III* manual (*Diagnostic and Statistical Manual of Mental Disorders*, 3rd edition) in the United States. And until relatively recently it was illegal in Britain. There continue to be anti-gay campaigns to deny gay, lesbian, and bisexual persons certain basic rights, such as same-sex pension benefits, and many churches (particularly fundamentalist churches) continue to teach that homosexuality is an abominable sin.

One of the unique aspects of oppression towards homosexuality is its lack of visibility. Unless one states that he or she is gay or lesbian or bisexual, there is usually nothing to indicate that this is so. This invisibility is an impediment to organizing as a group since it is not known what the size of the group is and members do not know who other members are. It is also an impediment to receiving support from other homosexual persons (Bishop, 1994). And, as with people of colour and women, divisions within the gay, lesbian, and bisexual community maintain its fragmentation and lack of solidarity and inhibit organizing efforts against heterosexism. Wineman (1984) presents some examples of these divisions—there are people who are 'closeted' and those who are 'out', along with a range of individuals who are out in some situations and closeted in others. And even among those who are out, there are divisions between those who appear more and less straight and those who flaunt their difference. There are divisions between 'good gays and lesbians' (with relatively conventional lifestyles) and 'bad gays and lesbians' (with so-called outrageous lifestyles). The former often resent the latter because, in their eyes, they believe the outrageous behaviour plays into some of the negative stereotypes that the heterosexual community has of homosexual people. Conversely, the 'bad gays and lesbians' resent the 'good gays and lesbians' because the latter do not appreciate or approve of the 'in your face' political statements that the outrageous behaviour symbolizes. As with other oppressed groups, gay, lesbian, and bisexual persons may form an oppressed community, but it is a diverse and divided community as well.

Ageism

Thompson (1997) makes the point that age is not just a matter of biological maturation. It is also a social division or a dimension of the social structure wherein power, privilege, and opportunities are allocated to some and powerlessness, social exclusion, lack of respect, and alienation are allocated to others. The basis of such allocation is age, and the two groups affected mainly in a negative way are children and older people, although most of the literature on ageism focuses on the latter group. Bishop (1994) assigns children to a separate form or category of oppression that she terms 'adultism'. Generally, the term 'ageism' refers to oppression (at all levels) of a group of people solely on the basis of their age.

At one time older members of many societies were accorded great respect because of their endurance in the face of death and the knowledge, experiences, and wisdom they had accumulated throughout their lives. Even today there are societies where the elderly are highly regarded and venerated. In Aboriginal communities in Australia and North America, for example, tribal elders officiate at many community ceremonies and have an active leadership role in most decision-making bodies. For the most part, however, where older citizens were often revered for their endurance and wisdom, they are now often associated with degeneracy, death, senility, incontinence, frailty, and madness (Cole, 1986). Furthermore, because of their exclusion (voluntary or enforced) from the labour market, they are no longer perceived by many to be making a contribution to the economy. And in a capitalist system where one's merit or worth is measured primarily not by one's qualities as a person but by the position one occupies in the economy, both the young and the old tend to be devalued because they have no value at the altar of capitalism. The elderly, in particular, are seen as useless and even a drain on the resources of society. Young people escape these judgments because of their potential for contributing to the economy in the future, but the elderly are often regarded as having outlived their usefulness. Thompson (1997) outlines a number of other assumptions and stereotypes about elderly people that reflect and reinforce ageism. They are often considered to be and treated as childlike, ill (including hard of hearing), lonely, asexual, poor, unintelligent (and unaware of current events), and inhuman. This list could be extended to include other assumptions, such as forgetful, meddling, and needy.

As suggested by the above assumptions attached to old age, this group of oppressed people (as with all other oppressed groups) tends to be perceived as homogeneous. Elderly persons, however, are divided along lines of class, gender, race, and other social dimensions. As well, they are divided along lines of age (the young-old—60–4, the middle-old—65–74, and the old-old—75 and older), wellness (healthy, active, frail, ambulatory), independence (living independently in own home, living in a care facility), political involvement, and so on. Like other oppressions, the stereotypes of ageism can be internalized by older people (Marshall, 1990), resulting in negative self-images, low morale, lack of confidence, and higher morbidity. It can also lead to older persons avoiding other older persons because they do not want to be associated with or be around a group of senile, incontinent, and morbid old people. Thus, there is a 'we-they' dynamic whereby some members of an oppressed group will dissociate themselves from it on the basis of stereotypes imposed on the group, and some older persons will denigrate other older persons by use of ageist stereotypes.

Ableism

Ableism, sometimes referred to as 'disableism' (e.g., Thompson, 1997, 1998), is the systematic oppression of a group of people with disabilities. This form of oppression is manifest in the combination of personal prejudices, cultural expressions and values, and social forces that marginalize people with disabilities and portray them in a negative light, thus oppressing them. The disability, which can be either physical or mental (or both), is such that it prevents a person from carrying out particular activities (e.g., walking, caring for one's self, working, learning, participating in community activities). It may be temporary, indefinite, or permanent (Barker, 1987). Bishop (1994) refers to people with disabilities as 'physically or mentally challenged persons' and cautions against using the label 'disabled people' as it suggests that 'people with disabilities' (the term preferred by persons oppressed by ableism) are not complete as people.

Traditionally, the attention has been on the medical aspects of disability—treating and compensating for the impairment and attempting to make the disabled person more comfortable. This narrow view overlooks disability as a social construction (Black, 1995) and as a social division. A whole group of people are separated and systematically excluded from full participation in the mainstream of society because of the existence of a disability. Their barriers to participation are ideological as well as physical or mental (Thompson, 1997). The disability itself has been socially constructed as a form of dependency in that disabled persons have been portrayed as helpless, dependent, needy, asexual, and not able to contribute to society. As well, disabled persons suffer the same treatment as elderly people in a capitalist society—if you have no value in the economy, you have no value as a person.

Within recent years a powerful 'disabled people's movement' has challenged the medicalization and individualization of people with disabilities and the view of them as tragic (pitiable) victims. It has also emphasized a social model of health and promoted the 'rights' of people with disabilities and denounced the view of them as 'charity cases'. Many jurisdictions now have legislation that prevents discrimination on the basis of disability in such areas as employment, housing, and access to public buildings and transportation. However, people with disabilities continue to be oppressed on the personal level (revulsion, discomfort, charity cases), cultural level (cruel jokes and stereotypes, omitted from advertising and popular culture), and structurally (discrimination, exclusion, and inequality).

Although people with different physical and mental difficulties all share the powerful bond of disability, they are still among the most divided and fragmented of all oppressed groups. Not only are there divisions among persons with disabilities based on class, gender, race, and age, which exist within all other oppressed groups, but many different types of disability serve to divide this group of oppressed persons. Persons with mental disabilities face different forms of discrimination than do persons with physical disabilities. Those who move with the aid of wheelchairs or those who are deaf face different challenges from those who suffer chronic pain or those who have incurred serious head injuries or those who are blind.

Six different forms or sources of oppression have been outlined here, and it is clear that heterogeneity is characteristic of each. There are, of course, other forms of oppression (e.g., religion, geographical region, language). However, it is believed that the major forms of oppression with which social work is currently involved are classism, racism, sexism, heterosexism, ageism, and ableism. A danger in reading about different forms of oppression is to assume that any particular oppressed group is united and that every member shares the same experiences and is affected in the same way. The divisions within any oppressed group present an obstacle for members in organizing and mobilizing against their oppression.

Conclusion

In this chapter I have focused on the concepts of multiple oppression and intragroup heterogeneity. To date, social work has tended to treat oppression as if it comprised a number or collection of singular forms or sources of oppression. Some writers have paid lip service to the fact that oppression seldom occurs in a simple, singular form, but have not gone much beyond this recognition. As well, there is a tendency to totalize each oppressed group, overlooking the considerable variation and heterogeneity within each oppressed group.

A major purpose of this chapter was to contribute to an understanding of multiple oppression. Wineman's (1984) rudimentary intersectional model of oppression illustrates how the various oppressions within the individual identity interact beyond a simple additive or cumulative notion (such as the single-strand or parallel models). This intersectional model, along with the recognition that intersecting oppressions are both complex and potentially volatile, provides social workers with more informed insights into the complex lived realities of the people with whom they work. However, much more theoretical development is needed in this area. A host of challenging and unresolved conceptual issues remain. Such concepts and dynamics as multiple identities, the fluidity of group membership, contextual variables (e.g., specific sites of political engagement), individual or psychological variables (e.g., self-esteem), status within an oppressed group, and individual variations in experiences of oppression obviously affect relationships of domination and subordination. Although they are part of the phenomenon of multiple and intersecting oppressions, no model shows how they reinforce, complicate, contest, or modify either each other individually or oppression in general. It seems that the best we can do at this point as anti-oppressive social workers is to be aware that oppression is a multiple and intersecting social phenomenon and that these concepts and dynamics are essential parts of how oppression operates (Baines, 2000).

This chapter also discussed the incredible diversity (i.e., heterogeneity) that exists within all forms of oppression. Oppression not only occurs between the dominant group and subordinate groups and between various subordinate groups; it also occurs within groups. Every so-called identity group contains a hierarchy of privilege that serves to fragment group solidarity and often results in those holding higher status or privilege oppressing others in the group in order to retain their privileged position. The heterogeneity that exists within subordinate groups also adds to the complexity of intersecting oppressions. For example, two black people living in poverty may have different qualitative experiences of oppression if one is much lighter in colour than the other. Again, much more conceptual and empirical work is needed in this area. In the meantime, the material in this chapter should help social workers to resist overly simplistic or reductionist explanations of oppression.

Chapter Eight

Anti-Oppressive Social Work Practice at the Personal and Cultural Levels

Introduction

A major aim of this book has been to present oppression as the explanatory cause of most social problems. This view contrasts with that whereby social problems are attributed to some presumed weakness or deficiency on the part of the individual (the conservative view) or to a few limited imperfections of an otherwise equitable and just society (the liberal view). These final two chapters present a broad outline for anti-oppressive social work rather than offering detailed techniques and tactics for such work. This, in my view, is a necessary prerequisite for developing emancipatory or liberating strategies that confront, resist, challenge, and undermine oppression in all its forms and wherever it exists.

Most writers in the area of anti-oppression (e.g., Bulhan, 1985; Gil, 1998; Leonard, 1997; Moane, 1999; Thompson, 1998) agree that anti-oppressive interventions are limited when they focus on only the individual level or the structural level. Bulhan outlines the pitfalls of using either approach to the exclusion of the other. The former, which focuses on the immediate and private problems of individuals, loses sight of their shared victimization and the need for social transformation. 'The result is usually either a minimalist view of change or, worse, a conservative outlook that blames the victim' (Bulhan, 1985: 269). The latter, which works towards community and social transformation, overlooks the fact that people are the subjects of history and tends to disengage the very persons on whose behalf the change is ostensibly sought. 'The result is at best an imposition of change from the "top", a paternalistic attitude toward the oppressed and a veiled tyranny in practice' (ibid.). Both approaches fail to adopt a dialectical perspective whereby interventions at both the individual and community or societal levels are carried out simultaneously, with each informing and influencing the other.

The above caution of not adopting a binary either/or approach to anti-oppressive interventions is a reflection of the 'personal is political' feminist principle or dialectic that has been incorporated into much of contemporary social work theory and practice. It is also a reflection of the need to avoid emphasizing either 'human agency' only or 'social structures' only in anti-oppressive practice and to accept that the two constitute a dialectic.[1] This dialectical view of the individual/agency and the political/structural tends to include 'culture' as a part of the political or structural level. However, as explained previously (especially in Chapters 2 and 4), my approach is to treat 'culture' as separate from (although related to) the political or structural realm. This three-pronged conceptualization of oppression occurring at the personal, cultural, and structural levels is consistent with the conceptual frameworks of such recent writers as Dominelli (1997), Galtung (1990), and Thompson (1997, 1998).

As argued throughout this book, oppressive conditions, processes, and practices exist at the personal, cultural, and structural levels. Challenges to bringing about change in oppressive situations are created by the psychological and interpersonal difficulties associated with oppression, by the mystification and hegemony of the dominant culture, and by the material and political conditions of oppression. An anti-oppressive social work practice is further challenged by the fact that much of oppression and domination at all three levels is internalized both by oppressor and oppressed groups; and also by the multiple or intersecting nature of oppression and domination.

This chapter offers an overview of anti-oppressive social work practice informed by and based on the conceptualization and analysis of oppression and domination carried out in the previous chapters. Specifically, this chapter considers some perspectives, priorities, and issues involved with anti-oppressive social work practice at the personal and cultural levels. Anti-oppressive social work practice at the structural level—along with some of the themes, principles, and prerequisites of anti-oppressive social work practice—is presented in the final chapter.

Anti-Oppressive Practice at the Personal Level

Having just made the argument that anti-oppressive social work must avoid non-dialectical approaches in which the social worker would focus on the individual or the cultural or the social context to the exclusion of the others, I may appear to be contradicting myself by dividing anti-oppressive social work practice into categorical forms or levels of personal, cultural, and structural practice. An impression may be created that these levels are mutually exclusive and that social workers ought to attend to one or another level only. This certainly is not my intention. Anti-oppressive social work practice requires modes of interventions that bridge the separation of existential freedom and socio-political liberty. It is true that much of anti-oppressive social work practice will involve activities of social care, where the victims of unemployment, inadequate housing, and lack of opportunities are consoled or partially compensated to make their situation a little more palatable. These activities, however, will be carried out in such a way that links are made between personal problems and their structural causes, between therapeutic insights and conscious deeds that enable oppressed persons to change themselves and their social conditions, and between the frustration of being denied basic individual rights and the collective action needed to attain these rights. Anti-oppressive work at any level in any area is dialectical work.

The personal level of anti-oppressive social work practice includes intrapsychic and interpersonal processes. Both of these processes involve interaction with other individuals, are interrelated with each other, and involve changes at the personal or individual level. Social work in the intrapsychic area will involve counteracting the damaging psychological effects of oppression discussed in Chapter 3 and building personal intrapsychic strengths to take action against oppression. Social work in the interpersonal area will involve building relationships with others on a one-to-one or group basis to analyze oppressive conditions, to reclaim group identity, and to change social and psychological patterns associated with oppression. An overview of anti-oppressive social work in each of these personal areas is presented below.

Intrapsychic Area

In Chapter 3 we saw that studies reviewed by Moane (1999) revealed that oppression leads to a loss of personal identity, a sense of inferiority or low self-esteem, fear, powerlessness, suppression of anger, alienation, isolation, and guilt or ambivalence. The main aims of anti-oppressive social work at the intrapsychic level are to counteract the personal intrapsychic damages associated with oppression, to build strengths in the individual for developing solidarity and community with others and for taking action (individual and collective) against oppression. Individual work, group work, or community work may be used separately or in some combination to achieve these aims.

Sometimes an individual may require some individual counselling before she or he is emotionally ready to participate in a group. This can take the form of introspective counselling or behavioural therapy or any other type of individual work that will help to stabilize a victim of oppression, relieve some pain and torment, change symptoms and behaviours, and build some strengths. Physical challenges can be used as a starting point for the reconstruction of self (Herman, 1992), and spirituality in its broadest sense is recommended by several writers (hooks, 1993; Maracle, 1996; Starhawk, 1987) to aid in undoing the damage caused by oppression. The important point for anti-oppressive practice is that, regardless of what individual approach is used, it should not decontextualize human activity or treat it in a desocialized or ahistorical way (Bulhan, 1985). Otherwise, personal changes may actually be concessions to the prevailing social order in that the person has been helped to adjust to it rather than change it. The source and situation of oppression must be central in any individual work. As well, individual work is not an end in itself, but the means to connecting or reconnecting with other persons similarly oppressed so that they might together reflect on their situation and engage in collective actions to change it.

There is a need early in the process of building strengths to acknowledge and express the many negative feelings associated with oppression, such as shame, guilt, anger, self-hatred, fear, and frustration. Often these emotions, especially anger (Daly, 1984), are suppressed, causing psychological or physical harm to the one suppressing them, or misdirected (Thompson, 1998; Wilson, 1993) at family members, loved ones, and others who are similarly oppressed (i.e., horizontal hostility). These feelings are frequently difficult to identify, let alone express, because their causes or sources are mystified through the explanations provided by the dominant group in the form of victim-blaming myths, stereotypes, and ideologies. Feminist writers, including Daly (1984) and Herman (1992), argue that the oppressed person must understand her oppression and be able to name the agents of oppression before repressed or unexpressed feelings can be acknowledged, understood, and expressed. Critical analysis and the development of awareness or consciousness-raising regarding oppression are seen by most writers as key in the process of building strengths (e.g., Gil, 1998; Dominelli, 1997; Freire, 1994; Moane, 1999; Mullaly, 1997a; Thompson, 1997, 1998; Young, 1990). As awareness of injustice and oppression grows, oppressed people are more able to identify the social causes of their oppressed situation and less likely to blame themselves (Longres, 1986; Midgely, 1982). Moane (1999) found that developing awareness of the structural causes of one's oppression and building strengths reinforce each other. As awareness of injustice and oppression grows, oppressed people are less likely to blame themselves for their oppression and are more able to identify the social causes of their negative emotions and experiences. These insights, in turn, help them to develop their analyses of their oppression as well as to build confidence and the capacity for seeking social changes.

Although a certain amount of consciousness-raising may occur in one-to-one counselling sessions (e.g., providing the oppressed individual with statistics or factual information on some aspect of his or her oppression), the most effective mode of consciousness-raising occurs in groups of individuals who share the same oppressive situation (Longres and McLeod, 1980; Mullaly, 1997a; Young, 1990). However, as suggested above, a common experience of oppressed persons upon joining a group is to feel overwhelmed and not have the confidence to speak out. Many people will feel the need for some kind of personal development to build up self-esteem and confidence before participating in a group. Personal development can occur through individual counselling or by taking a personal development course, such as assertiveness training or leadership development. Mulvey (1994, cited in Moane, 1999) found that such courses do increase people's confidence and assertiveness. However, she also found that without a social analysis, such courses may reinforce and perpetuate a 'blame the victim' ideology in that they overemphasize human agency by cultivating the belief that problems in living can be solved through personal change only (Kitzinger and Perkins, 1993; Mulvey, 1994). Thus, although it would seem that personal development is often a necessary first step in an ongoing process of change and empowerment, personal development programs and courses should be framed within a social or critical analysis of oppression and social injustice.

Other topics that may be brought into the process of restoring intrapsychic strengths are the importance of creating a sense of self by self-defining one's identity as a response to the definitions (including stereotypes) imposed by the dominant group, reconceptualizing power and self-determination to advance oneself and to limit or destroy the power of others (Miller, 1986), and 'recovering historical memory' (Martin-Baro, 1994) as a means of fostering identity and a sense of culture and community. These liberating processes are discussed below in the context of social work practice in the interpersonal or intra-group area. Although they may be carried out on a one-to-one basis with a social worker, they are part of the larger processes of recovery, normalization, and reconnecting with others, and, therefore, are most effective in a group context (Herman, 1992; Longres and McLeod, 1980; Mullaly, 1997a).

Before looking at anti-oppressive social work practice at the interpersonal level, a few words must be said about the potentially oppressive 'social worker/service user' relationship, which, although it is inherent in any kind of social work at any level, is most relevant at the one-to-one intrapsychic level. Bulhan (1985: 271) states the dilemma of therapeutic intervention best: '[F]or how can an intervention liberate the patient from the social oppression when the "therapist-patient" relationship itself is suffused with the inequities, nonreciprocity, elitism, and sado-masochism of the oppressive social order?' Bulhan is referring to such inequities as the power of the professional and the powerlessness of the oppressed service user, the comfort of the professional's office (often alien to the service user), the professional's values (often foreign to the service user), and the discourse of the professional that differentiates helper from helpee, expert from layperson, and professional from client. Given this power imbalance, Bulhan asks:

> By what conjurer's tricks could one effect fundamental changes in the personality, relation with others, and social conditions of the oppressed when presumably the 'healing' relation itself is a microcosm of the *status quo* of oppression? Is it therefore surprising that the oppressed have not come in droves to seek help from mental health professionals and, if a few of them turn to 'therapy' as a last resort, that they soon drop out and return to their old travails? (Ibid.)

To avoid reproducing oppressive patterns and relations while working with oppressed persons two vital themes of anti-oppressive practice must be kept in mind at all times. The first is the assumption that oppressed persons must be the agents of their own change, whether it is individual, cultural, or social change. Moane (1999: 183) emphasizes the importance of this control when she says, 'Change is a process which individuals undergo in their own social context and through their own processes. It is fundamental that this process of change is experienced by individuals as one in which they are in control, rather than as a re-enactment of patterns of domination. . . . Developing agency is itself a central part of the liberation process.'

The second theme or principle that should help to avoid the reproduction of oppression while attempting to carry out anti-oppressive social work practice is to ensure that one's practice is critically reflective. Thompson (1998) states that reflective practice, which has its roots in the work of Donald Schon (1983, 1987), integrates theory and practice through a process of 'reflection-in-action'. It takes the form of the practitioner engaging in a reflective conversation with the situation and, as Thompson (1998: 204) argues, 'can be used to promote an ethos in which equality issues [including the relationship between the social worker and the service user] are openly and explicitly on the agenda.' Thompson further argues that the reflection must be critical in the sense of not taking existing social arrangements for granted. Otherwise, the reflection becomes another routine, uncritical form of practice that may legitimate existing relations of inequality and oppression. Critical self-reflection is discussed in more detail in the next chapter.

Interpersonal Area

Just as there is a good deal of agreement in the literature that consciousness-raising is a critical element in the process of liberation, there is also widespread agreement that to become part of a group process with other persons who are similarly oppressed is the most effective way for oppressed persons to: (1) develop political awareness; (2) self-define a more genuine identity than the one imposed on them by their oppressors; (3) develop the confidence to 'come out' and assert their more authentic identity; and (4) establish solidarity in order to take action against their oppression (Adam; 1978; Bishop, 1994; Freire, 1994; Herman, 1992; hooks, 1993; Leonard, 1984; Mullaly, 1997a; Pharr, 1988; Withorn, 1984). However, as mentioned above, some persons will need individual counselling before they are ready for a group experience.

Adam (1978) argues that as members of particular oppressed groups enter into communication with other members, they become acquainted with their identity as defined by their own group. As oppressed persons share their experiences of frustration, unhappiness, anxiety, hurt, and blocked opportunities, they find common patterns of oppression structuring these personal stories. Young notes that what were originally experienced as private, personal problems are now seen in terms of their political dimensions. She writes of this consciousness-raising process:

> Aspects of social life that appear as given and natural come into question and appear as social constructions and therefore as changeable. The process by which an oppressed group comes to define and articulate the social conditions of its oppression, and to politicize culture by confronting the cultural imperialism that has denigrated or silenced its specific group experience, is a necessary and crucial step in confronting and reducing oppression. (Young, 1990: 153–4)

Paulo Freire also talks about the importance in the liberation process of oppressed people coming together and engaging in dialogue in order to self-define their identity. Freire calls this process of dialogue and consciousness-raising 'conscientizacao' or 'conscientization'. It lies behind his 'pedagogy' or political education of oppressed persons. He contends that once oppressed people begin to engage in dialogue, perceptions of themselves, their oppressors, and social conditions often change, and they begin to remove the blinkers of their 'banking education' (i.e., the traditional one-way mode of education where, instead of dialogue, a teacher issues communiqués and makes deposits that a students receives, memorizes, and repeats). Contradictions are discovered, which lead to more dialogue and an exploration of previously unseen possibilities with respect to non-oppressive conditions and actions for liberation. 'It is only when the oppressed find the oppressor out and become involved in the organized struggle for their liberation that they begin to believe in themselves' (Freire, 1994: 47).

One activity that can assist an oppressed group in becoming more aware about all aspects of its oppression and in self-defining its identity is to carry out what liberation theologist Martin-Baro (1994: 30) calls 'the recovery of historical memory'. This activity undermines and challenges the ahistorical propaganda that the situation of oppression is a natural reality, and fosters a sense of solidarity and identity among oppressed persons (Moane, 1999). Martin-Baro (1994: 218) says of the 'recovery of historical memory':

> Only insofar as people and groups become aware of their historical roots, especially those events and conditions which have shaped their situation, can they gain the perspective they need to take the measure of their own identity. Knowing who you are means knowing where you came from and on whom you depend. There is no true self-knowledge that is not acknowledgement of one's origins, one's community identity, and one's history.

Lee Maracle (1996: 40), the Aboriginal and feminist activist, also emphasizes the importance of knowing one's history for asserting the reality of oppression and the wish for self-determination:

> Before I can understand what independence is, I must break the chains that imprison me in the present, impede my understanding of the past, and blind me to the future. Without a firm understanding of what our history was before the settlers came to this land, I cannot understand how we are to regain our birthright as care-takers of the land and continue our history into the future.

Developing a sense of history has been an area of considerable activity with a number of oppressed groups, particularly within the women's movement, black liberation movements, decolonization movements, and Aboriginal or First Nations movements for self-government and self-determination. The loss of culture of these groups involved the erasure of subordinate groups from historical writings and records and/or distortions of their role and place in history. This leaves subordinate groups with 'a lack of awareness of their own lives, their contribution to culture and society, and their accomplishments and achievements. A sense of identity and of pride is thus undermined, and the oppressed are deprived of a sense of their own situation as historically constructed and as changing over time' (Moane, 1999: 130). Anyone who has been involved in teaching the history of a particular oppressed group to members of that group or in learning one's history as an oppressed person will be aware of the profound changes in consciousness that students experience.

Adam (1978) argues that when members of an oppressed group come together to discuss their oppressive situation a dialectical movement towards integration occurs whereby group members discover each other and, in the process, discover themselves. He points out that for this to occur, a certain withdrawal on the part of the subordinate group from an inhospitable social environment controlled by the dominant group is necessary. However, he cautions that this social withdrawal could lead to a ghetto-type situation, which may provide a safe haven from the dominant group, on the one hand, but is stifling and confining for the oppressed individual, on the other. Thompson (1998) also argues that some degree of withdrawal or separation is to be expected because greater progress can often be made if members of the dominant group are not present or involved with meetings and planning of subordinate groups. He gives as his examples some women's groups and some groups of black people who deliberately exclude men and white persons, respectively, from meetings. He echoes Adam's concern with ghettoization, which some women's groups (e.g., radical feminists) and some groups of black persons advocate, by expressing his concern that separatism can become an end rather than a means to an end. Other writers, such as Peter Leonard, have also noted that 'some' degree of segregation is a necessary element for emancipation and symbolic community identity. Leonard points out that some groups have developed their own social services, which are more relevant than mainstream services to their needs, but they still participate in the wider social services network. Speaking specifically of cultural, racial, and ethnic minority groups, he notes that 'they want or accept the maintenance of difference but without the hierarchy which is rooted in colonialism' (Leonard, 1997: 70).

The importance of segregated groups in the liberation process should not be interpreted as social workers not having any involvement with groups of oppressed persons. The significance of the above discussion for social workers is twofold. First, social workers who have had some prior involvement with some group members should not feel rejected if they are not invited to or are excluded from such groups. Letting members of the group know that you are available to them on an individual or group basis may be all that you can do at this time. Second, knowing the importance of the liberating functions carried out by segregated groups, the anti-oppressive social worker should encourage the formation of such groups and support them in every way possible. There will still be plenty of opportunities to work with oppressed persons on a group basis, as evidenced in the discussion that follows.

Groups of or for oppressed persons can have a number of purposes and functions. They can be therapy groups in which the members attempt to acknowledge and express negative emotions, find a voice for self-expression, identify personal strengths, and alter destructive relationship patterns (Moane, 1999). They can be consciousness-raising groups in which members are involved in social analysis in attempts to relinquish their victim or survivor[2] identity and to develop a sense of commonality with the shared difficulties of oppressive conditions and dynamics. They can be social or political action groups in which members strategize and plan campaigns to take action that will bring about social changes to counteract oppressive conditions, processes, and practices. Groups may focus on

Don't Take It Personally

I have been struck by the number of times some of my progressive social-work colleagues have expressed hurt or anger or a sense of unfairness or lack of appreciation when they have been rejected or rebuked by members of subordinate groups—especially when they (my colleagues) have actually defended, supported, and fought for the interests of these groups. Such experiences show how difficult anti-oppressive practice really is and how necessary it is to understand the dynamics of liberation, which includes periods of segregation on the part of subordinate groups, and the release and expression of suppressed anger when confronting members of the oppressor group (even sympathetic members). I remember the days when early second-wave feminism entered the university sector and how hurtful it was to be treated like some kind of enemy by many of my female colleagues when, in my view, I was on their side. I often felt like saying, 'Jeez, how are you going to make any progress or win anything if you treat your allies like this?' I also remember some of my Aboriginal students in the early phases of our relationships lumping me in with the colonizer group, including white racists. I often felt like saying, 'Can't you see all the things I've done to give you a voice in this university and the number of times I've taken crap from white people because I've tried to defend your interests?' As well, there have been a good number of times when I have worked with 'anti-poverty groups' and was treated in a hostile manner because I had a 'cushy' job and didn't have to wonder how I was going to feed my family. My initial impulse was to launch into some kind of diatribe about my background not exactly being a privileged one, and that they should be happy they had someone like me as an ally. We are all human, which means that we all feel some hurt when something is said to or about us that we believe to be unfair. However, to react in the ways suggested above would be counter-productive to working with oppressed groups. Knowing the dynamics of liberation and knowing that members of oppressed groups will often see a member of the dominant group as representative of the whole group should help us to avoid personalizing rejection when we are carrying out anti-oppressive practice.

emotional or cognitive content. They may be highly structured or informal. They may be long-term or short-term. Membership may be open or closed. Members may share feelings or emphasize tasks. Groups are usually dynamic, change over time, and may shift from one focus or purpose to another. For example, Freire argues that oppressed groups seeking liberation must engage in critical reflection on their common situation of oppression in order to understand it. However, this cannot be an intellectual process only, as action will be required to change the situation of oppression. But this action must also be reflected on. In this way action will lead to increased awareness, which in turn will lead to more action—'only then will it be a praxis (i.e., reflection on reality and action to change reality)' (Freire, 1994: 47). Given the obvious importance and necessity of the group experience for oppressed individuals, the anti-oppressive social worker must be familiar with group work theory, structures, processes, and dynamics.

A key concept of anti-oppressive social work practice is 'empowerment'. Unfortunately, it is a concept that has many meanings and one that has been appropriated by neo-conservatives. For example, many conservative politicians have pledged that they would 'empower people' to look after themselves by reducing the scope and benefits of the welfare state. This is quite a different meaning of 'empowerment' than that used by progressive social workers, who view it as a process through which oppressed people reduce their alienation and sense of powerlessness and gain greater control over all aspects of their lives and their social environment. There is by now a substantial literature testifying to the empowering effects that the above-mentioned consciousness-raising activities engender among oppressed people (e.g., Adam; 1978; Bishop, 1994; Butler and Wintram, 1991; Freire, 1994; Herman, 1992; hooks, 1993; Pharr, 1988). By becoming aware of existing oppressive social patterns and non-exploitative and egalitarian alternatives, by self-defining their own identity, by recovering their history, and by establishing solidarity with each other, members of oppressed groups gain a sense of confidence that enables or empowers them to attempt to overcome their situation of oppression.

Anti-oppressive social work practice necessitates a reconceptualization of power[3] and self-determination. Traditionally viewed as something that the dominant group possessed and subordinate groups lacked, postmodern thought (see Foucault, 1988, for example) has helped us to see that power is not an absolute entity concentrated among a powerful few. This latter view was a tenet of structural Marxists such as Althusser (1969), who rejected human agency as a factor in social theory. Foucault (1988) argued that power is a much broader and complex phenomenon in that it is not an absolute possession of the ruling class but a result of the interactions between individuals, groups, organizations, and institutions. It is ubiquitous to all social relations, a factor that is fluid and open to influence and change. Everyone is able to exercise power, albeit some can exercise more than others, because every decision and every action is an act of power. It is both enabling and confining (Rojek et al., 1988). It allows one individual or group to dominate others through discursive practices—the powerful ideas and assumptions of particular discourses—but power also is manifest in 'resistance'—the ability of an individual or group to struggle against oppression (Thompson, 1998). The notion of 'resistance' provides oppressed people and anti-oppressive social workers with a powerful tool of empowerment for confronting and challenging oppression. Resistance is discussed more fully in the next section of this chapter.

Much has already been said here about consciousness-raising and its importance to anti-oppressive practice. Elsewhere (Mullaly, 1997a) I have discussed several elements of progressive social work practice that separate it from conventional social work practice. Four of these elements—'the personal is polit-ical', normalization, reframing, and dialogical communication—also have rele-vance for carrying out anti-oppressive social work practice in groups (or at other levels of intervention) and are especially integral to consciousness-raising. A brief and updated overview of each is presented below. It must be noted that although these elements are presented separately, in reality they cannot be sepa-rated so easily, for they are all interrelated, functionally intertwined, and mutu-ally reinforcing.

One element in anti-oppressive social work at any level of practice is linking the personal with the political. This is a method of analysis developed and refined by feminists for 'gleaning political insights from an analysis of personal experience—in particular, female experience' (Collins, 1986: 215). The 'personal is political' analysis forces the social worker beyond carrying out mere psychoso-cial manipulations, which in effect pathologize people. This type of analysis has relevance and utility for understanding all forms and sources of oppression in our society. It can be used to understand better the nature and extent of racism in our society and how it contributes to the oppression of visible minority groups. It can be used to understand better the nature of colonialism and how it contributes to the oppression of Aboriginal persons in our society and to the oppression of developing countries by the developed societies. It can be used, as well, to under-stand better oppression based on classism, ageism, physical disability, mental disability, heterosexism, and so on. What conventional social workers treat as private problems belonging to isolated individuals, anti-oppressive social workers would treat as public problems belonging to a society characterized by oppres-sion along such lines as classism, sexism, ageism, heterosexism, and racism. The 'personal is political' analysis is a recognition that the social environment is criti-cal in shaping who we are in terms of our personality and intrapsychic formation and what we are in terms of our personal situation (Mullaly and Keating, 1991). In every case, the anti-oppressive social worker would link the individual's per-sonal situation to larger social dynamics such as class, race, and sexism. For example, the worker would not define a resource-poor person (or let the person define him or herself) as simply someone living in poverty, but instead would define the person as someone who is oppressed by class. The first definition has the potential to blame the person, whereas the second clearly places the blame on social oppression. This type of analysis, of course, puts the onus on the social worker to have some knowledge about classism, sexism, patriarchy, racism, and other forms of oppression. This does not preclude intervention at the individual or family level, for example, but instead of dealing with each level by itself the connection between private troubles and the structural source of these troubles is made in every case.

A second element that assists the consciousness-raising process is 'normaliza-tion'. The purpose of normalization[4] is to dispel any notion that any particular difficulty an oppressed individual may be experiencing is unique and idiosyn-cratic to that person only, when in fact the difficulty is a logical outcome of oppression being experienced by many members of that subordinate group. As discussed in Chapter 6, many oppressed persons will internalize guilt, shame, and blame for their oppressive living conditions because they have accepted the dominant messages that they are responsible for causing the social problems they are experiencing. The anti-oppressive social worker can assist in the normalization process in one of two ways: (1) by giving factual information to the individual or individuals who are blaming themselves for their oppressed condition (e.g., an unemployed person is blaming him or herself for being unemployed in a context where the unemployment rate is high); or (2) by encouraging members of a subordinate group to share the problems they have experienced and by assisting them to analyze critically their experiences in terms of the larger social dynamic of oppression. The emphasis is not on the uniqueness or individuality of a person's situation but on the sameness and common ground of the oppressed persons. Normalization moves away from the traditional 'personal inadequacy' mindset that ascribes all social problems to personality defects or dysfunctional families or inferior cultures by locating them in their proper social context.

Redefining or reframing is a consciousness-raising activity in which personal troubles are redefined in social or political terms, thus providing an alternative explanation. The troubles may be experienced at the personal level, but they come from a particular social and historical context. Redefining social problems identifies this context. Rose and Black (1985) argue that the traditional 'personalist' definition of social problems has several oppressive effects on persons who use social services. (1) It invalidates the service user by validating the larger system. (2) It decontextualizes the service user by separating his or her subjectivity from the materialist context that frames and influences all social life. (3) It shapes people's behaviour to correspond to the given social reality and the more one deviates from this 'proper and appropriate' behaviour, the more severe is society's treatment. (4) It saturates service users with a new language, a language of pathology and deviance that contains such concepts as diagnosis, treatment, symptoms, acting-out behaviour, resistance, and so on. (5) It forces service users to accept the problem definition imposed on them, in other words, to accept an alien reality. If one were seeking an operational definition of oppression, these five effects on service users of the prevailing definition of problems would be a good starting point. Redefining involves the social worker and oppressed persons in a process of deconstruction and reconstruction. In every instance explanations of problems that are self-blaming are challenged, deconstructed and examined in terms of the oppressed individual's specific situation, and reconstructed or redefined in terms of their connection with the larger socio-economic-political system. The task, rather than working on personal change and accommodation to society, is to engage people as producers and participants in comprehending and acting on their contextual environment.

The recovery of historical memory, the personal is political, normalization, and redefining techniques are some of the means of carrying out consciousness-raising. The medium within which these activities are carried out is dialogue, between the social worker and oppressed persons and among oppressed persons.

Dialogue is the vehicle for uncovering people's subjective reality and opening it to critical reflection.

> Dialogue cannot be professional interviewing, application of therapeutic technology, instructions for improved functioning or casual conversation. It is purposive in both process and focus. It directs itself to validation of the oppressed as persons, attempting to demonstrate their capacity to inform you, and it struggles to direct the content towards depiction and analysis of the objective situation. . . . To unveil oppressive reality is to be willing to enter it more fully, to encourage the elaboration of expression, to support the expression of experiences, to initiate the early steps in critical reflection. (Rose and Black, 1985: 45)

To be able to engage in meaningful dialogue the anti-oppressive social worker must develop a dialogical relationship with service users—a relationship based on horizontal exchange rather than vertical imposition (Freire, 1994). A dialogical relationship is one wherein all participants in the dialogue are equals, each learning from the other and each teaching the other. Of course, the social worker will have some skills and insights that the service user does not have, but the service user has experiences and insights that the worker lacks. The anti-oppressive social worker must make conscious efforts to dispel any myths of expert technical solutions to fundamental political problems. Wisdom, experience, and expertise are accepted and validated 'from below' as well as 'from above' (Ife, 1996). The worker may 'problem-pose' but not 'problem-solve', as this latter activity must be shared between worker and oppressed individuals or groups. Both work together so that they can ask the questions as well as think about the answers. As a result, both will come to a better understanding of the issue, both will learn, and both will act (ibid.). Criticism of conventional social work practice has often centred on an elitist, impersonal, and overly technical approach. As anti-oppressive social workers we do not want to reproduce the kinds of social relations that have oppressed people in the first place. 'In essence, a dialogical relationship is exchanging, comparing and communicating, rather than indoctrinating, proselytizing and generally issuing a "communiqué" ' (Moreau, 1979: 89).

An important component of working with oppressed persons is the process of liberation. Most process models of change or development comprise a number of stages or sequential steps that an individual, group, or community passes through. When considering 'process', however, one must be cautious about using developmental stages to understand human behaviour and social change because they invite linear and reductionist ways of thinking. Process models of liberation can often be interpreted as going from a situation of oppression through a series of discrete and linear stages that, if each is carried out successfully, will lead to the next stage in the forward path to liberation. Social change and human behaviour do not usually operate in this kind of linear fashion. They are more fluid and complex than this. A danger in assuming a linear or stages of progress model of change is that the oppressed person or the anti-oppressive social worker may become disillusioned or frustrated because the stages are not occurring as prescribed or expected and give up on the process. Instead of stages of progress towards liberation, Bishop (1994: 83) argues that the liberation process is more like a spiral. She claims that this 'spiral of human liberation' has been well documented and outlines its path.

> It begins with breaking the silence [about one's oppression], ending the shame, and sharing our concerns and feelings. Story-telling leads to analysis where we figure out together what is happening to us and why, and who benefits. Analysis leads to strategy, when we decide what to do about it. Strategy leads to action, together, to change the injustices we suffer. Action leads to another round: reflection, analysis, strategy, action. This is the process of liberation.

Even the notion of the spiral is problematic in that it may suggest to some that progress occurs in an onward and upward direction. However, the spiral concept is an improvement over most developmental models because it does not suggest that social change and changes in human behaviour are linear processes. It accommodates the postmodern insight that people often shift back and forth from one role or identity to another (consistent with the notion of multiple identities) rather than dropping a particular role or identity altogether (e.g., victim role or identity), as is implied in a linear process model. Also, the idea of liberation as a spiral does not suggest that social change will never be blocked or even reversed at various times throughout the liberation process, as do most linear, developmental process models. This is not to say that developmental models are useless. They may provide a general direction for liberation and may alert us to certain shifts in roles or identities that, along with other changes, could occur in the process. A major contribution of postmodern thinking is to alert us to the fact that changes in social conditions and/or human behaviour do not occur in identifiable, discrete, linear stages of progress.

When working with groups of oppressed people, it is important to keep the above limitations of linear developmental models of change in mind. This is not meant to suggest, however, that such models have no utility for anti-oppressive social work. They may be helpful in providing a general direction for liberation and in alerting us to certain shifts in roles and identities and changing dynamics and relationships that might occur as oppressed people attempt to liberate themselves from their oppression. For example, Sean Ruth (1988) presents a model consisting of three stages that he believes reflect the process of liberation. Although there can be no ideal type or universal model of liberation, Ruth's model appears to follow the general direction of anti-oppression or liberation that writers such as Bishop (1994) and Freire (1994) suggest. Using Ruth's model as a rough guide rather than a definitive map, we can gain an overview of these three stages.

The first stage occurs when the subordinate group first becomes aware that what it took for granted as necessary or natural is in fact a reflection of a systemic process of prejudice, discrimination, and oppression against its members. Becoming aware of the existence of oppression and themselves as oppressed persons often leads to an initial reaction of anger and rebellion. A polarization may occur at this point within the subordinate group. Some members may become

militant and demand, sometimes violently, that their grief and anger be acknowledged and that their mistreatment be redressed in some way by the dominant
group. Other members will attempt to pacify and appease the dominant group,
not wanting to upset them, by acting 'reasonably' (unlike their radical cohorts),
diluting their demands, and actually colluding with the dominant group to sup-
press other viewpoints. This may contribute to divisions that already exist within
the oppressed group (as discussed in Chapter 7).

The second stage in the liberation process occurs when the focus on the dominant group and the oppressive situation is de-emphasized and members of the
oppressed group begin to develop a sense of identity, pride, and self-respect
based on their own assessment rather than that of the dominant group. Dominant discourses, notions of a universal culture, and imposed inferior identities
and stereotypes have much less currency in the lives of the oppressed group at
this stage. And no longer do they act in the subservient ways they once did.[5]
These changes challenge the dominant group to examine themselves along with
their perceptions of and relationship with the oppressed group. There may be
acceptance of a new and more egalitarian relationship or there may be a backlash
by the dominant group concerned with, for example, putting those 'uppity
blacks'[6] back in their (inferior and subservient) place. An example of an extreme
backlash occurred at L'Ecole Polytechnique in Montreal on 6 December 1989
when 14 female engineering students were massacred by a man who shouted
anti-feminist vitriol while he gunned down the young women.

Ruth argues that the final stages of liberation cannot occur until the dominant
group changes itself. This is not to say that the liberation process stops at this
point, however. The history of most social movements and significant social
change efforts shows that the experiences of subordinate groups dealing with
resistance and backlash is the norm rather than the exception. Ruth's model of
the liberation process would be more complete if it accorded more attention to
issues of backlash by the dominant group against groups that are attempting to
have their legitimate needs and rights recognized and respected. And, of course,
it would be more realistic if it did not suggest that the stages of development are
linear and discrete.

The final stage in the process of liberation occurs when both dominant and
subordinate groups acknowledge that people are taught, through conditioning
and socialization, to act in oppressive and subordinate ways. Ruth argues, further, that all types of oppression are linked with each other and that it is more
effective to understand how oppressive systems operate and to change these
dynamics rather than attack members of oppressor groups because they are also
victims of socialization. The final stage of liberation will only occur when all
groups recognize the interconnections of different oppressions and participate in
the process of liberation.

Obviously, much more could be said about anti-oppressive social work practice at the personal level. The intention here is to outline the major components
of such practice. It is assumed that social work practitioners and students will
possess the core conventional micro skills of social work practice, such as

relationship-building, active listening, assessment, interviewing, engagement, etc., that are necessary for any kind of social work practice. As well, much of anti-oppressive social work practice at the cultural and structural levels is related to and overlaps with anti-oppressive practice at the personal level. Anti-oppressive social workers may carry out the bulk of their practice at one level or another, but they will also be involved at the other levels as well. This will become clearer as we move into a discussion of anti-oppressive social work practice at the cultural and structural levels.

Anti-Oppressive Practice at the Cultural Level

In Chapter 4 we examined the concept and some of the makeup of the dominant culture and discussed how the dominant group maintains and reproduces its hegemony. You will recall from that earlier discussion that the dominant culture oppresses subordinate groups through such means as the mass media, the use of stereotypes, and dominant discourses, and that professions such as social work sometimes contribute to cultural oppression. Here we consider some anti-oppressive practices that social workers and/or groups of oppressed persons might employ in attempts to undermine cultural imperialism and other oppressive actions and processes at the cultural level. Specifically, we will look at the following: counter or alternative cultures, acts of resistance, confronting stereotypes, language and counter-discourses, using the media, and minimizing the oppressive effects of professionalism.

In Chapter 4 we saw how culture is a major site of domination. However, as Agger (1992, 1998), Hall (1988), Hall et al. (1978), and Leonard (1997) argue, culture can also be a site of resistance to domination. In contrast to the notion of a 'cultural essentialism' where the dominant culture is presented as homogeneous and authentic, postmodern critique suggests that culture is always partial, contested, and changing (Leonard, 1997). Hobsbawm and Ranger (1993) argue that culture is not static, but is continually being socially constructed and is always in a state of flux. Therefore, culture is always open to the development of new practices. Seidman likens culture to a text in that both are made up of words or signs that contain meanings. However, meanings are not free-floating but are attached to social interests, power relations, and material life—'they are created by real living, struggling individuals whose lives are enmeshed in social institutions and unequal social relations' (Seidman, 1998: 202). Members of the Birmingham School of Cultural Studies contend that only by relating cultural meanings to social conditions can we understand their ideological role in, for example, promoting or challenging social privilege. Agger (1998: 8) argues that 'culture can be remade, even where it is controlled at the epicenter of global capitalism's global village.' He points out that culture is not simply laid on people from above, but is a transaction between producers or distributors of culture and consumers of culture. Consumers participate in the constitution of cultural meanings, and the meanings they make of the cultural messages may be different from what the producers intended. This insight is potentially empowering for consumers (including oppressed persons) of culture.

In *Cultural Studies as Critical Theory*, Agger (1992) presents the notion of 'cultural politics' as an important complement to traditional 'class politics'. He points out that although there may be a single dominant culture, many other cultures often intersect with one another—cultures of class, gender, race, and nation, among others. Culture does not serve to integrate society, but is instead a realm of conflict over meanings. Mainstream (dominant) culture tends to ignore cultural meanings and alternatives that fall outside its dominant discourse, practices, and hegemony. Agger calls for a decentring and decanonizing of culture, which he views as a political act that will contribute significantly to the decentring of wealth and power. The decentring of the dominant culture is a fundamental challenge to the dominant order. One major way of contributing to this is to engage in cultural conflict and politics by denouncing all forms of cultural oppression along with supporting, developing, bringing to light, and celebrating alternative cultures that have been suppressed by the dominant culture.

Alternative Cultures

Many groups have politicized culture by using alternative culture as the basis of a social movement. Young (1990) differentiates a libertarian insistence that people be allowed to do their own thing, no matter how unconventional, from cultural politics. Although cultural politics may often celebrate suppressed practices and novel expressions when they arise from and speak for oppressed groups, its critical function allows it to identify those aspects of culture that contribute to domination and to call for collective transformation of them. The feminist movement carried out (and continues to carry out, albeit with reduced solidarity and overall commitment) one of the most far-reaching movements of cultural politics. Guided by its 'personal is political' slogan, it reflected on, criticized, and offered alternatives to all aspects of everyday male culture—gender-exclusive language, stereotypical jokes, sexist advertising, literature, dating practices, norms of child-rearing, workplace practices, codes of dress, public policy and the manner it was made, and countless other supposedly trivial and frivolous elements of behaviour. There may be disagreement on the merits of the changes, the way they were brought about, and how much has changed, but there can be no disagreement that the feminist movement has significantly decentred the dominant male culture that existed in the 1950s and 1960s and before.

People of colour have also critiqued aspects of the dominant white culture and promoted their own cultures. African North Americans, in particular, have managed to carry out a cultural revolution by confronting the stereotypes and norms imposed on them by the dominant culture and by exerting their own dress, music, jewellery, speech, politics, hairstyles, foods, literature, and history. Many of these cultural products and expressions, previously suppressed, devalued, and even ridiculed by white society, are now sought out and enjoyed by members of all racial and ethnic groups.

Other subordinate groups who have been defined as the Other, the different, and the deviant have also politicized culture. Groups such as old people, First Nations persons, and disabled individuals have organized and asserted the positive aspects of their specific experiences and culture. Suzanne Pharr (1988: 66), for example, writes about the experience of lesbians surviving in the face of oppression by building community and celebrating lesbian culture:

> Despite the harsh damaging effects of homophobia, we have created a magnificent lesbian culture of books and music and crafts and film and paintings and newspapers and periodicals. We have created social communities in cities, lesbian land communities in rural areas, and retirement communities for older lesbians. With little support except from other lesbians, we have created lesbian counselling centers, support groups for chemically dependent lesbians, coffee houses, lesbian retreats and art festivals and music festivals, healing centers, outdoor clubs, support groups for lesbian survivors of battering, rape and incest, rituals for our passages, and our spirituality support groups for lesbian mothers, lesbians of color, differently abled lesbians, Jewish lesbians. The list goes on and on.

Members of subordinate groups need to experience consciousness-raising in order to develop, promote, and celebrate alternative or countercultures. Group members must, of course, first reclaim their own authentic identity before they can promote the culture associated with it. As Young (1990: 124) says, 'The dissolution of cultural imperialism . . . requires a cultural revolution which also entails a revolution of subjectivity.'

Resistance

Resistance to subordination, exploitation, and alienation has been alluded to throughout this book. For Foucault (1990) resistance is an aspect of relations of power that takes on local forms. Political and economic power tends to be concentrated among the dominant group, particularly among the elite of the dominant group. This type of power may be used to constrain or oppress subordinate group members in various ways, as outlined in previous chapters. Early radical social work tended to focus almost exclusively on the major apparatuses of power and domination—the abstractions of the state, capitalism, mass culture, and even the welfare state—searching for cracks and contradictions from which to mobilize collective resistance. Leonard (1997) argues that we must shift our attention from an exclusive focus on these macro systems and examine the micro processes of power relations. In other words, we must identify the diverse everyday experiences of heterogeneous subjects as they struggle with the relationships among determining social structures, the internalization of dominant discourses, and what remains of their own autonomy. Resistance is also a form of power, which may be manifest in the everyday ways that oppressed groups and individuals struggle against domination. Foucault (1990: 95) asserts that 'where there is power, there is resistance.'

Resistance can occur on an individual or collective basis and it can take the form of micro or macro processes. A service user disrupting the order of a social agency by not keeping or being late for appointments may be an example of an individual exercising resistance to the power and control that the agency has over that person. A social movement is an example of resistance at the macro level where large-scale change is sought. Everyone has the ability and agency to exercise personal or micro resistance to domination. This type of resistance is often viewed as sabotage by its target, but is a protest by the individual to exploitative or discriminatory or unfair treatment (i.e., oppressive treatment). An industrial example might help to clarify the matter. In the large automobile manufacturing plants in Detroit in the 1970s people worked on assembly lines and had to carry out small, routine, mundane, boring, and repetitive tasks. The work had no job satisfaction and was associated with high absenteeism and alcohol and drug abuse. One out of many acts of resistance to this situation was for the workers to place empty soda pop bottles inside the door panels of expensive cars before they rolled off the assembly line. Of course, the bottles would roll around inside the panels, making a terrible noise as soon as the car was driven. This action, which was labelled 'industrial sabotage' by the automobile manufacturers, was not a planned social action strategy of the workers. It is an example of the micro resistance of everyday life, one that in this case eventually forced the manufacturers to make changes to the assembly line, reducing its mind-numbing and soul-destroying aspects.

One aspect of micro resistance is that it is usually an individual act whereby individuals engaging in it are often unaware that others are doing likewise. If the anti-oppressive social worker becomes aware of behaviour that may be a form of micro resistance, he or she should not write it off as irresponsible behaviour. Rather, it should be explored with the individual and other similarly oppressed individuals to assess its full meaning. It is also incumbent on the anti-oppressive social worker to encourage and promote wider and more organized forms of collective resistance based on alternative ideologies and knowledge claims that confront, challenge, and attempt to change dominant discourses. Thompson (1998: 54) states, 'As power operates primarily through discourse (ideas, assumptions, knowledge, frameworks of understanding), such dominance can be challenged through acts of resistance, through the use of countervailing power to undermine dominant discursive practices.' Pease (1999) argues that for subordinate groups to resist dominant discourses and their places within them, it is helpful if they have alternative discourses available to them. However, even if alternative discourses are not in circulation it is still possible to resist dominant discourses by working on their internal contradictions (Weedon, 1987, cited in Pease, 1999) and using them as a basis for developing new discourses.

Alternative Discourses

Dominant discourses contradict and submerge the interests of subordinate groups, as was discussed in Chapter 4. A crucial anti-oppressive practice, then, will be to challenge and confront oppressive discourses. Consciousness-raising helps subordinate groups become aware of the oppressive features of dominant discourses. One way of resisting, confronting, and attempting to change dominant discourses is to develop and/or promote alternative or counter-discourses that, in themselves, provide powerful critiques of dominant discourses. If, as Peter Leonard (1997) asks, the object of collective resistance is to challenge dominant discourse, against what targets might such resistance be mounted? The simple answer is that resistance should be mounted against any discourse that oppresses, directly or indirectly, any social group of people.

Although more than a discourse, feminism (all schools) is regarded as an alternative discourse that resists and challenges the hegemony of male domination, and it has significantly modified the dominant discourse of patriarchy. Similarly, the dominant discourse of white supremacy has been challenged by black nationalists, black liberation philosophers and theologians, black academics, and black activists. Eurocentric discourses have been challenged by Afrocentricity,[7] Orientalism,[8] and post-colonial discourses. The dominant discourse of heterosexuality has been confronted by the discourses of the gay, lesbian, and bisexual movement. Capitalism, as the dominant economic discourse, has been challenged by a number of alternative economic discourses, including those of different schools of socialism and Marxism. Almost all (if not all) major discourses that are dominant and oppressive have been challenged in varying degrees by alternative or counter-discourses.

Even discourses within larger discourses have been confronted by alternative discourses. For example, the discourse of 'welfare dependency' that forms part of the larger discourse of welfare and capitalism has been challenged by a discourse of 'interdependency' (Bulhan, 1985; Leonard, 1997). Traditional discourses of work and the family and the current discourse on the inevitability and economic determinism of global capitalism, all of which are parts of the larger discourse on capitalism and the welfare state, have also been challenged by counter-discourses (Leonard, 1997). As noted in Chapter 4, the oppressive aspects of professional or expert discourses have been exposed and confronted by many writers, such as Margolin (1997) and Leonard (1997), and those of social agency discourses have been challenged by many writers as well, including Mullaly (1997a), Rose and Black (1985), and Thompson (1998).

In resisting and challenging dominant discourses, it is helpful to have knowledge of more than one discourse and to recognize that meaning is plural (Pease, 1999). A major role and task of the anti-oppressive worker is to be knowledgeable about existing alternative discourses and skilled in analyzing and deconstructing oppressive discourses as well as in developing (or assisting with the development of) alternative discourses. An important component of alternative discourse work is confronting stereotypes that form parts of the dominant discourse. It is this task to which I now turn.

Confronting Stereotypes

Every subordinate group has certain stereotypes imposed on it by the dominant group, which function to justify the oppression experienced by subordinate groups. One of the goals of consciousness-raising, as noted above, is for members of subordinate groups to be able to self-define their own identity, and for this to occur stereotypes must be exposed, challenged, and rendered unacceptable. Subordinate groups and those who work with them may confront and attempt to counteract negative stereotypes in various ways.

One approach to challenging and overcoming stereotypes is to develop a positive image among members of subordinate groups. 'Black is beautiful' was a slogan of African Americans in the 1960s that not only contributed to a cultural revolution among the black population of North America, but also unsettled the dominant white body aesthetic, which previously (stereo)typed black bodies as ugly and inferior. Similarly, Afro hairstyles replaced hairstyles treated with various straighteners among black North Americans and were actually adopted by a number of white North Americans. The African-American feminist, bell hooks (1993), argues that developing a positive black-centred body image is necessary for black persons to confront the many ways that socialization has instilled self-hatred, alienation from black culture and spirituality, unrealistic standards, negative emotional patterns, and racist stereotypes.

A positive image can be developed through the identification of strong role models among the subordinate population. For example, several years ago, the First Nations people in Canada waged a war against the use of drugs by their children by having prominent and high-profile First Nations adults, such as athletes, artists, politicians, and academics, speak out against drug and alcohol abuse. The women's movement has had many prominent women to draw upon as role models. For example, Geraldine Moane (1999) talks about how the former President of Ireland, Mary Robinson, was a very important source of encouragement and inspiration for women. It was not so much her achievements that made Mary Robinson such a positive role model, but her personal integrity and her courage in speaking out for women as a feminist. Fictional characters can also be used as role models to promote a positive image, as evidenced by the frequent citing by black feminist writers of characters in the writings of Toni Morrison and Alice Walker, whose characters often embody strength, compassion, and agency (hooks, 1993, cited in Moane, 1999).

A sense of history is helpful in highlighting the culture and achievements of the subordinate group. This history, in turn, helps to break down the inferior stereotypes of the oppressed group. The novel *Roots* (Haley, 1977) reflects the history of black North Americans from the time when they were enslaved and brought from Africa. It and the subsequent television series based on the novel became a source of pride for North American black people as it was a story of resistance to oppression, of the struggle for survival of a people who had suffered immensely under slavery and oppression. (The later revelation that Alex Haley had 'invented' significant parts of his panoramic saga rather than having based it on documentary and genealogical research perhaps said more about the need for the dominant white discourse to devalue its tremendous impact than it did about the 'authenticity' of the *Roots* saga.) Many oppressed groups such as women, First Nations people, and gay and lesbian persons have drawn pride, support, and inspiration from histories of resistance, from the knowledge that every oppressed group has always resisted its oppression, and from the perseverance and ingenuity that are intrinsic to stories of resistance. However, we should not assume that historical reclaiming or remembering is an easy task for oppressed persons. Homi Bhaba (1994: 63), a post-colonial writer, cautions us against adopting a cavalier attitude towards a process of intense discovery and disorientation that is involved with 're-membering'. Building on Fanon's work of linking the psychological with the political in developing (re-membering) an authentic cultural identity among colonized peoples, he says, 'Remembering is never a quiet act of introspection or retrospection. It is a painful re-membering, a putting together of the dismembered past to make sense of the trauma of the present.'

Another way of countering negative stereotypes is to develop or draw upon positive or affirmative stereotypes associated with the subordinate group. Leela Gandhi (1998) cites scholarship that argues that anti-colonial nationalist movements regularly draw upon affirmative Orientalist stereotypes to define an authentic cultural identity in opposition to that imposed by Western civilization. For example, the resistance led by the revolutionary Mahatma Gandhi against Britain depended on a cultural image of India as corporate, spiritual, and consensual. Consequently, enthusiastic Indian nationalists responded to pejorative stereotyped images of East Indians as caste-dominated, despotic, and patriarchal with reformist zeal and energy (Fox, 1992, cited in Gandhi, 1998). The affirmative stereotypes were instrumental in India becoming a Utopian alternative to the aggressive capitalism and territorialism of the West, visited by countless scholars, spiritualists, writers, and travellers.

Gandhi and a Very Good Idea

Journalistic legend has it that once when Mahatma Gandhi was visiting England, he was asked by an earnest young reporter, 'Mr. Gandhi, you have been in England now for several days. What do you think about modern civilization?' In some versions of this story, Gandhi laughed, and in others he became pensive before answering, 'I think it would be a very good idea.' (Leela Gandhi, 1998: 22)

The First Nations people of North America and Australian Aborigines have also drawn upon and developed affirmative or positive stereotypes that are more in accordance with their authentic identities than those imposed on them by Eurocentric groups. Aboriginal people have developed a positive image of living in harmony with nature and of practising a spirituality that has certain mystical properties. Many white people today are attracted (often to the point of cultural appropriation) to these aspects of Aboriginal culture, viewing them as alternatives or solutions to such problems as environmental devastation, alienation, existential meaninglessness, cynicism with government and organized religions, individual and corporate greed, and cutthroat competition. Affirmative stereotypes such as these would seem to have the potential to act as a countervailing force to negative stereotypes.

Negative stereotypes also can be confronted by a reversal technique whereby the characteristics that form a negative stereotype of a particular group are turned around and applied to the dominant group. A group of poor people in Vancouver calling itself 'End Legislated Poverty' has used such a technique. Tired of being stereotyped as lazy, dependent, chronically unemployed welfare bums, the group developed a discourse about rich people that included the same negative concepts. In other words, 'End Legislated Poverty' applied the same negative stereotype to wealthy people that they had imposed upon them. Some examples are:

- Wouldn't the wealthy feel better about themselves if they worked for their money rather than inheriting it?
- Wealthy people are too dependent on the tax system. How can we change it to make them more independent?
- Would counselling help break the culture or cycle of wealth?
- Is greed intergenerational? And, if so, would closing tax loopholes help break intergenerational wealth?
- Are wealthy people too dependent on wealth?
- If tax loopholes were closed, would the wealthy lose the incentive to work?

Young argues that when oppressed groups assert the value and specificity of their own cultures, the dominant culture becomes relative or is 'relativized'. In other words, it becomes more difficult for the dominant group to present its norms, values, and patterns of thinking as neutral and universal. When women, gay and lesbian persons, people of colour, and other oppressed groups assert the validity, positive values, self-development, and traditions of their particular cultures, the dominant culture is forced to see itself as a specific culture (i.e., Anglo, white, straight, Christian, masculine) among many. Young (1990: 166) elaborates on this point: 'By puncturing the universalist claim to unity that expels some groups and turns them into the Other, the assertion of positive group specificity introduces the possibility of understanding the relation between groups as merely difference, instead of exclusion, opposition, or dominance.'

Conclusion

An overview of anti-oppressive social work practice at the personal and cultural levels was presented in this chapter. The primary tasks of anti-oppressive social work practice at the individual level are to repair or counteract the intrapsychic damages associated with oppression and to build strengths in the individual for developing solidarity with others in order to take action against their oppression. Critical analysis and consciousness-raising are the major means for carrying out these tasks. Consciousness-raising is also an integral part of anti-oppressive social work at the interpersonal level, as are a number of other liberating practice elements that were presented. Just as culture is a site of oppression, so, too, can it be a site of challenge and conflict. Promoting alternative cultures, developing strategies of resistance, challenging dominant discourses with alternative discourses, and confronting negative stereotypes are some of the anti-oppressive social work practices at the cultural level.

Chapter Nine

Anti-Oppressive Social Work at the Structural Level and Selected Principles of Anti-Oppressive Social Work

Introduction

This final chapter looks at anti-oppressive social work practice at the structural level. It focuses on both confronting and changing those social institutions, policies, laws, and economic and political systems that operate in a way that benefits the dominant group at the expense of subordinate groups. As well, several principles of anti-oppressive social work practice are presented that are relevant at all levels of practice and to all social workers who have committed themselves to anti-oppression in both their professional and personal lives. Finally, I present what I consider to be the most important element in challenging oppression in any form, in any area, at any level, and with any group or individual—the constructive use of anger.

Anti-Oppressive Practice at the Structural Level

Anti-oppressive social work practice at the structural level attempts to change those institutional arrangements, social processes, and social practices that work together to benefit the dominant group at the expense of subordinate groups. Size, reasonableness, and militancy are not the criteria for structural change. Rather, it is the nature of the change that determines whether or not it is structural, that is, whether or not it contributes to a fundamental change in or transformation of the social or economic or political system. Social reform is not a part of social transformation unless it represents one step in a long-range strategy for more fundamental change. For example, an unemployment insurance scheme may be put in place to assist unemployed workers on a personal level, but it does nothing to eliminate the structural factors that caused the unemployment in the first place. Another example is that a policy of affirmative action may be legislated to assist women or people of colour or persons with a disability in obtaining employment, but the policy does nothing to eliminate sexism, racism, or ableism. Although such measures may ameliorate problems, they also tend to cover over issues of oppression by making a sexist, racist, and ableist society appear to be humane.

I emphasize here that the distinction between structural and cultural is somewhat arbitrary. Rather than a clear boundary between them, there is some degree of overlap. For example, although the discourses on capitalism and the welfare state were mentioned in the previous chapter, obviously they are discourses about structures. Thus they could have just as easily been placed in this chapter. Given the overviews and analyses of social, economic, and political structures presented in Chapter 5, this section will focus on a number of forms, strategies, and processes of anti-oppressive social work aimed at transforming these structures. Specifically, it will look at alternative services and organizations, new social movement theory and coalition-building, critical social policy practice, and revitalization of the political sector.

Alternative Services and Organizations

One way for anti-oppressive social workers to contribute to social transformation is to create, develop, and/or support alternative social service organizations that serve and are operated by members of particular oppressed groups. Just as anti-oppressive workers support and, if appropriate, work with consciousness-raising groups of oppressed people, so, too, do they support and work with alternative or group-specific services and organizations. These alternative services and organizations are usually established because traditional, mainstream social services are set up by the dominant group and tend to operate in accordance with dominant norms, values, and expectations. In other words, mainstream services and organizations are culturally specific (i.e., to the dominant culture) and sometimes will unintentionally contribute to the oppression of subordinate groups.

> If a cohesive radical movement is to emerge, focus on an alternative human services policy and program could serve an important integrating function. Because the recipients of human services are overwhelmingly poor and/or female and/or people of colour and/or young or old, it is an issue which creates bridges between the 'narrow' interests of pivotal oppressed groups. Because human services implicate economic and political and social issues, radical alternatives could create a 'cutting edge' in efforts to achieve comprehensive change. (Wineman, 1984: 20)

In other words, alternative services and programs are counter-systems to mainstream social agencies and can be used ultimately to establish 'a base from which larger social changes can be eventually effected' (Moreau, 1979: 87).

Alternative services and organizations are founded on different principles, values, and ideals than our traditional services and organizations. Attempts are made to institutionalize more egalitarian forms of social relationships by incorporating community control, mutual support, and shared decision-making as key features. Alternative services usually spring from the work of a specific oppressed community or movement such as people living in poverty, women, Native people, gay, lesbian, and bisexual people, and social service users. Examples of alternative services are welfare rights groups, tenants associations, rape crisis centres, transition homes for battered women and their children, off-reserve Native friendship centres, gay and lesbian associations, groups of former psychiatric patients, Alcoholics Anonymous, and prisoners' societies.

Anti-oppressive social workers understand that alternative services represent attempts by oppressed people to connect the personal with the political and to gain control over their own destiny. Workers may support alternative services in a variety of ways: by becoming involved with them to the extent that they can without endangering their employment in mainstream agencies; by providing material resources since alternative organizations are usually strapped for funds (e.g., money, stationery, photocopying); by providing inside information from one's own organization (e.g., notice of a pending policy that will negatively affect the alternative organization so that it can prepare to rebut or fight it); by referring users of a mainstream service to an alternative service (e.g., most persons applying for public assistance would benefit from membership within a welfare rights group); and by encouraging the formation of such services or organizations where none exist.

Anti-oppressive social workers must be careful not to romanticize alternative organizations. Anyone who has ever been associated with such an organization will know how difficult it is to work collectively and co-operatively and to share all decision-making when we, in the West, have been socialized into working and living in social institutions where hierarchy, specialization, and an overreliance on rules prevail. Withorn (1984) cautions us that old habits die hard, our expectations for alternative services are often too grand, and we may not always be clear on what an anti-capitalist, anti-racist, feminist practice is. In addition, Carniol (2000) warns those workers who have developed a critical awareness and are involved with alternative services against becoming arrogant and self-righteous and forgetting the importance of listening to and learning from the very groups we see as most oppressed. Most writers on the subject of alternative services point out the problem of funding these services because of a strong push towards co-optation by establishment funding agencies such as United Way and government departments.

Peter Leonard views alternative organizations as a prefigurative form of postmodern organization. He asserts that an alternative service is a minority, unstable, and often transitory form of organization, but one that has continued to survive as a vehicle for identity politics. It engages in a 'struggle to achieve, for specific populations of the Other—women, cultural and racial minorities, gays and lesbians, people living in poverty—justice, equality and welfare' (Leonard, 1997: 111). Leonard points to an inherent political problem with alternative organizations, however. Although their aim is usually to challenge the state and its dominant discourses to recognize and respond to *difference*, they, themselves, tend to be relatively *homogeneous*. Members tend to share a common set of beliefs and experiences on the basis of a shared culture, race, gender, or other social characteristic. Although these organizations may be committed to the value of diversity, their membership is often homogeneous. The political problem is how do such organizations form long-term alliances with other organizations

Whose Ethics?

I once worked with a welfare and tenants rights group (an alternative organization) that operated in the neighbourhood in which I grew up. I had known most of the members of this group all my life. Although most lived on the edge of the law, they were deeply concerned about the living conditions in the neighbourhood and were able to employ their considerable 'street smarts' in using the organization to obtain services and benefits for neighbourhood residents and to defend their rights. Some of the tactics and strategies, although ingenious and effective, will never be found in standard community organization textbooks (unfortunately). I remember one occasion when the executive of the organization was to present a brief on housing to City Council (this neighbourhood had some of the worst slum housing in Canada—dirt floors, holes in roofs, busted water pipes in the winter, no lights in dark stairwells, rats as big cats, etc.). It was not so much the brief that the executive was counting on, but the fact that the stationery room of City Hall was located around the corner from the council chambers. When the group went into the council chambers to present their brief, a few members stayed back. One went into the stationery room while two others kept guard outside. The person in the stationery room took a stack of stationery (and maybe a few supplies) with the city letterhead (Office of the Mayor) on it. After the Council meeting the group went back to its neighbourhood office and used the stationery with the city letterhead to type letters to slum landlords who owned many of the buildings in the neighbourhood. The content of the letters was to the effect that the landlords had 30 days to fix-up their buildings and, if they didn't, they would be prosecuted to the fullest extent of the law. Before the scam was realized, the group estimated that about 30 houses were repaired and that approximately 100 families had close to adequate housing for the first time in a long, long time. I remember one of my bourgeois colleagues asking me once when they learned of this tactic if I thought it was ethical. My initial reaction was to suggest that the person ask that question to the families who lived in the firetraps. However, I responded by asking this person a question: Would it have been ethical not to do it?

and build solidarity that transcends difference? An attempt to answer this question is made below.

New Social Movement Theory and Coalition-Building

Social movements before the onset of global capitalism tended to be initiated by the working class to counter the worst excesses of industrial capitalism. Unions were organized around class issues and promoted social democracy as the countervailing ideology to capitalism. Both unions and social democracy played a crucial role in the development of the Keynesian welfare state. Leaders of these working-class movements tended to be disaffected bourgeois intellectuals (ibid.). The major political goal was to gain state power, which would then be used in the interests of subordinate populations.

Fisher and Kling (1994) have identified two inherent weaknesses of these old social movements involved in resisting capitalism. First, those in power within the movements developed an increasingly parochial and self-serving agenda as prosperity weakened identification with the working class. Second, the old social movements may have achieved power as the voice for disadvantaged workers, but they also silenced the voices of women, minorities, and young people just entering the workforce. As well, the global economy without national regulation and control has undermined the old-style social movements. New social movements concerned with such issues as gender, race, sexuality, the environment, and human rights have replaced the old class- and workplace-based movements as forms of collective resistance to developments in late (i.e., global) capitalism (Fisher and Karger, 1997; Leonard, 1997).

Five characteristics differentiate new from old social movements (Fisher and Karger, 1997). First, they are organized around geography or communities of interest and much less often at the workplace. Second, they are organized around cultural identities, such as people of colour, gay men, lesbian women, students, and ecologists, so that labour becomes one constituency among many. Third, the predominant ideology is that of a neo-populist view of democracy that rejects hierarchy, communism, or nationalism. Fourth, the struggle over culture and social identity plays a greater role in community movements than it did in the work-based movements of the past. Fifth, new social movement strategies focus on empowerment and community autonomy, thus seeking independence from the state rather than state power. 'Identity, community and culture become the contexts through which people come to construct and understand political life' (Fisher and Kling, 1994: 9). Most importantly, the new social movements give voice to those who were previously silenced in the old social movements.

As noted earlier, a political problem arises from the formation of multiple identity groups and their associated social movements. How do they form alliances and build solidarity that transcends (rather than subjugates) their differences? An important part of social transformation work is to develop and/or participate in social movements. However, social movements usually require alliances or coalitions of different groups, especially if large-scale fundamental social change is the goal. A major obstacle to building coalitions is that many groups with potentially shared political interests will focus solely on their respective single issues. This tendency has some obvious problems, which Biklen (1983) delineates in his discussion of self-help groups: (1) social issues are defined in a narrow parochial fashion; (2) single-issue groups often fail to make alliances with other groups whose interests they share because there is no awareness of the common causes of the oppression that each group experiences; (3) when single-issue groups focus on single issues they may even compete with each other for resources, attention, acceptance, and political dominance; and (4) even when a single-issue group effects change in a particular area it is not likely to bring about broad social change.

Wineman (1984: 159) contends that the biggest obstacle to coalition-building is the ability of the current socio-economic-political system 'to create and sustain deep divisions among oppressed people'. This segmentation of oppression has historically been manifest in perceived conflicts of interest running along lines of class, gender, race, age, sexual orientation, and so on. With this segmentation each group is prone to analyzing society along parochial lines wherein a single but different basic source of oppression is identified by each group. For example, conventional Marxist analysis places economic organization and class oppression as the fundamental societal problem; black persons, Aboriginal people, and other people of colour may identify racism as the fundamental source of oppression; women's organizations may identify patriarchy as the fundamental source of oppression.

As Wineman points out, the problem with each oppressed group identifying a single source of oppression is 'that it at once fails to create a basis for unity which respects the dignity and felt experience of all the oppressed . . . who are supposed to become unified, and it fails to generate a practical strategy . . . [to] challenge all forms of oppression' (ibid., 163). Without unity a competition emerges among oppressed groups for resources and attention. And, with any competition, there are winners and losers. Overcoming the imposed divisiveness among oppressed groups and other barriers to coalition-building requires a number of actions and strategies. Four such actions and/or strategies originally developed by Wineman are presented below.

First, an essential element of successful coalition-building is to create a *'mutual expression of solidarity'* (ibid., 182). This does not mean that one oppressed group must submerge its perceived interests in the name of unity. Rather, members of groups oppressed in one way will identify with members of groups who are oppressed in other ways, regardless of the severity (but not pretending that all oppressions are equally severe). This kind of mutual identification is necessary to overcome competing claims of who is more oppressed and to bring about the unity required for successful creation of a broader-based movement.

Second, it is important to understand that mutual identification of one another's oppression, by itself, may only lead to sympathetic understanding unless it is recognized that all forms of oppression are related. 'Different oppressions intersect at innumerable points in everyday life and are mutually reinforcing, creating a *total system* of oppression in which one [category of oppression] . . . cannot be addressed in isolation from all the others' (ibid., 169). It may be true that sexism is at the base of gender inequality, that racism is at the base of racial inequality, and that classism is at the base of economic inequality, but it is also true that inequality is a value and an established practice in our present society. It makes no political sense for workers to demand economic equality but ignore gender inequality as someone else's problem or for women to demand gender equality but ignore racial inequality. Although each oppressed group may fight oppression on its own front, the recognition that we live in a society that requires inequality for its very survival will help to cultivate coalitions among groups by providing them with a common goal—the transformation of our present society based on inequality to one based on true equality, not just equal opportunity.

Third, related to a goal of social transformation is a shared political analysis as a prerequisite for coalition-building. Whatever the original causes of various forms of oppression, the fact is that they have become culturally ingrained into our society and have themselves become mutually reinforcing. Coalition-building for purposes of broad structural change becomes more crucial but more realistic when oppressed people understand that the same political and economic elite that allows the devastation of our environment for profits is also responsible for the immoral and gross inequalities of living conditions between rich and poor; that the same political and economic elite that promotes imperialist policies abroad for economic gain is also responsible for policies at home that discriminate against the poor, women, people of colour, gays and lesbians, and so on; and that the same political and economic elite that promotes militarism for political and economic domination is also responsible for consumerism whereby people measure their own and others' worth and social standing in terms of what they own. This kind of awareness makes it imperative for anti-oppressive social workers to join with the women's movement, the peace movement, the environmental movement, the human rights movement, and any other movement seeking a transformation of society in order to end oppression of any kind.

Fourth, an important dynamic of oppression that should facilitate coalition-building is that 'no category of oppression, however distinct, creates an irreducible group which is only oppressed in one way' (ibid., 167). Chapter 7 asserted that oppression does not occur in a single-strand fashion; rather, oppression is a multiple social phenomenon where various forms of oppression intersect each other (see Figure 7.2). Racism does affect people of colour, but people of colour include the working class, women, gays and lesbians, the young and old, and the disabled. In turn, classism affects the working class, but the working class consists of women, people of colour, gay and lesbian people, young and old persons, and disabled persons. Most oppressed people are multiply oppressed. This dynamic should help oppressed groups overcome any tendency towards single-constituency movements and assist in developing within a subordinate group what Wineman calls 'a flowering of internal caucuses based on sex, race, class, sexual orientation, age, disability, and various combinations of these characteristics' (ibid., 220). An internal caucus is a recognition of the fact that people bring their gender, race, class, sexual orientation, and other characteristics with them into various struggles. A caucus of women within an anti-poverty group's struggle against economic exploitation becomes a link between women's organizations and poor people's organizations. An Aboriginal women's caucus within an anti-poverty group becomes a link between First Nations, women's, and anti-poverty organizations. These internal caucuses not only manifest overlapping oppressions among single-constituency organizations but become the points of contact between various oppressed organizations and spearhead common goals and joint actions.

Social work could develop internal caucuses within its own professional associations or union branches. There are members of all subordinate groups within social work. A caucus of gay, lesbian, and bisexual social workers could be established within a professional association or union of social workers along with caucuses of social workers of colour, social workers with disabilities, unemployed social workers, older social workers, female social workers, resource-poor (presently or in the past) social workers, those of non-English-speaking background, and so on. These internal caucuses would serve two functions: (1) to keep the membership of the social work union or association sensitive to and informed about issues of oppression from their own colleagues; and (2) to communicate and interact with various outside organizations and groups of subordinate persons, which effectively ensures that social work is linked to the network of oppressed groups.

Critical Social Policy Practice

David Gil (1998) outlines from an anti-oppressive perspective a number of limitations of conventional social policy analysis, development, and advocacy. First, conventional policy practice tends to focus on single issues such as homelessness, hunger, domestic violence, and crime. This approach is based on the mistaken assumption that these single issues are separate problems rather than different symptoms of underlying common causes (i.e., domination, exploitation, oppression, and injustice), but unless these causes are addressed the problems are unlikely to be overcome. Second, major aspects of the prevailing cultural and institutional realities tend to be treated as fixed realities or constants rather than as dynamic, contested, and changing variables. Thus, conventional social policy tends to maintain the status quo. Third, conventional policy frequently lacks causal or explanatory theories for the problems targeted for intervention, which results in policies being formulated on the basis of symptoms rather than causes (e.g., build more jails and hire more police to deal with crime). And, fourth, policies are often formulated and pursued on the basis of their political feasibility, even when the policy practitioners know that they are unlikely to deal effectively with the targeted problems.

Gil (1998, 1992) outlines an alternative approach to social policy analysis, development, and advocacy, which seems to be more in accordance with an anti-oppressive approach. He bases his approach on a number of assumptions that are different from those underpinning conventional social policy. Gil argues that radical or anti-oppressive social policy must use a holistic approach that views social problems as interacting and related symptoms of a larger system characterized by oppression, and that real changes will require transformations of entire policy systems rather than marginal adjustments of specific policies. He also contends that anti-oppressive social policy must understand that the institutional and cultural contexts of human societies are the transient results of interactions among people throughout history rather than a consequence of fixed or unchangeable situations. This means that these transient conditions are subject to change by the interactions of people living now and in the future. The conceptual foundation of Gil's theory of social policy lies in 'the essential *operating* and *outcome variables* of social life and of policy formulation'. He elaborates:

> This theory derives from the study of the human condition in nature and from the realization that, as a result of biological evolution, the human species is genetically less programmed than other species. Humans are born without genetically fixed patterns of life, but with capacities to create, transmit, and transform such patterns, through interaction and communication with each other based on reflection and critical consciousness, and through interaction with the natural environment from which they derive their means of existence. (Gil, 1998: 119)

What Gil means by operating and outcome variables of social life are 'resources, work, rights, governance, and reproduction; and the circumstances and power of people and social classes, the quality of their relations, and the basic overall quality of life. The ability of people to meet their basic needs depends always on the way these variables are shaped by their societies' (ibid., 120). Gil believes that the attention given to these operating and outcome variables will give social policy a radical or anti-oppressive edge. The implications of any policy for the structure of society need to be discerned in terms of expected and actual changes to these operating and outcome variables of social life, that is, changes in the relative circumstances and power of individuals and social groups and in the relations among them.

The Revitalization of Political Life

In the first edition of *Structural Social Work* (1993) I called for social work to become involved in electoral politics, and I repeated this call in the 1997 edition. I took to task all social workers who perceived involvement in party politics as either a personal (not a professional) choice or as unprofessional, and proposed that the proper role of social work with respect to politics was to lobby governments for particular social policies. I argued then that social work was not politically neutral and that, if it removed itself from the political arena as a force for change, in effect it was supporting the status quo. In view of the fact that governments ultimately decide on the nature, shape, size, and quality of social programs, it hardly makes sense for social work not to involve itself in attempting to get elected the political party most sympathetic to progressive social policy and social change. If political decisions determine the fate of the welfare state and, in a major way, the nature of social relationships, anti-oppressive social workers must involve themselves in the political arena. They must align themselves with oppressed groups and other groups and organizations that share similar emancipatory goals. This includes supporting political parties committed to social, economic, and political justice for all and not just for a privileged minority. It makes no sense for anti-oppressive social workers not to resist bourgeois political parties or, worse yet, to support them. To support them would be similar to supporting an arsonist's bid for the job of fire chief.

The above call for involvement in electoral politics reflects one of the strategies of the old social movements mentioned above—to win state power and to use that power to transform society. The limitations of the old social movements have already been presented in terms of silencing the voices of many of the subordinate groups that were part of them (i.e., women, people of colour, etc.). As well, postmodernists and others have presented a legitimate concern with any proposal that the state provide the leadership, structure, and resources to meet the common needs of people. The modern nation-state, which was originally established as the collective expression of those ideals of universal reason and order, resulted in structures of domination, control, exclusion, homogenization, and discipline (Leonard, 1997).

Given these criticisms of old social movements and any attempt to gain state power, why would I suggest this strategy? It is because I agree with several contemporary writers (e.g., Fisher and Karger, 1997; Fisher and Kling, 1994; Leonard, 1997) who have argued that at some point we must turn our attention to the state and attempt to re-legitimize it. Contrary to neo-conservative dogma, the demands of the global economy require more rather than less government involvement in social, economic, and human affairs. The resources, structure, and legislation needed to ensure that the common needs are met can only be provided, at this point in our history, by the state. Despite its relative weakening in the face of global capitalism, no other institution has the capacity or the resources necessary to rebuild our neglected social and public infrastructure. The promised benefits of a global economy have not been delivered. 'Without a legitimate public sector there are no public citizens, only private consumers' (Fisher and Karger, 1997: 177). Government policies of privatization have undermined government legitimacy and responsibility, which has resulted in fewer public services and loss of access to a potentially accountable and responsible public sector.

If the issue of state power is revitalized, two questions must be addressed. (1) Who would be involved in attempting to win state power as part of the collective resistance to the developments of global capitalism that adversely affect the well-being of large numbers of people? (2) Would the winning of state power by a progressive political party (supported by oppressed groups) necessarily be a step towards the emancipation of these groups? With respect to the first question, it would seem that the old social movements based on the identities of class, trade unions, and the ideals of socialism seem to have lost the will and resources to mount an effective resistance to the New Right and global capitalism (Leonard, 1997). Are the new social movements in any better position to mount this resistance? Peter Leonard points out a number of political limitations of new social movements that would interfere with a project of resistance. First, they tend to focus on the different, the local community, and the specific need of a particular social group rather than on some universal claim to rectify large-scale injustices. Second, given the focus on diversity, group identity, and the specific needs of particular groups, there is little opportunity to establish solidarity among the new social movements. Third, because they tend to be community-based and because the workplace can rarely be thought of as a community, the new social movements lack the traditional trade union movement conflict with capital and its owners. Finally, strategies of the new social movements have focused on empowerment and community autonomy, thus have sought autonomy from the state rather than state power.

What could help new social movements overcome these limitations and become an effective political force for change? The response of several writers (e.g., P. Leonard, 1997; S. Leonard, 1990; Mullaly, 1997a; Young, 1990) to this question is for new social movement groups to incorporate a 'politics of difference' with a 'politics of solidarity' to overcome the limitations of identity politics. The former would help to ensure that diversity was respected and the latter would help to ensure that the commonality of oppression, along with a common interest in developing policies that benefited all the diverse groups (i.e., women, people of colour, workers, etc.), was at the fore. The elements of coalition-building discussed above should facilitate this process. Leonard (1997: 176) argues that 'this organized solidarity would need to aim for the winning of state power through the electoral process', which might or might not require the formation of a new political party, depending on specific circumstances.

The aim of winning state power brings us to the second question posed above. 'Would the winning of state power by a progressive political party (supported by oppressed groups) necessarily be a step towards the emancipation of these groups?' The experience to date with respect to social change and social policy outcomes from left-wing governments in the Western world has been less than satisfactory. Instead of attempting to transform capitalism into some form of socialism, most socialist or social democratic or labour governments have brokered deals with big business and labour, which included the development of the welfare state as an attempt to humanize capitalism. During the recessions of the 1980s and early 1990s, they adopted the same retrenchment policies as their bourgeois political counterparts (e.g., cutting back on social spending rather than reforming the tax system). Contemporary national leftist political parties such as Labour in the UK and Australia and the New Democratic Party in Canada, as well as the liberal Democratic Party in the US, have all adopted 'third-way' policies, which are essentially bourgeois policies couched in progressive rhetoric. State and provincial political parties on the Left have not adopted any policies different from those of their national counterparts. Although there is widespread popular cynicism towards the political system today (Fisher and Kling, 1994), people concerned with issues of social justice are especially disillusioned by the behaviour and dismal performance of governments and political parties supposedly on the Left with respect to these issues. Why, then, would we expect any more from governments and political parties formed by or supported by coalitions of new social movements? To help answer this question, I again turn to Peter Leonard, one of the most respected writers of progressive social work and social welfare in the English-speaking world.

Leonard (1997: 176–7) avoids the term 'coalition' because it implies to him a political organization too unstable and transitory to serve the purpose of winning state power in the interests of oppressed groups. He prefers instead the term 'a confederation of diversities' in which member organizations would join together to express (rather than subjugate) their separate identities in solidarity with each other. To make this confederation work for all members it would be based on dialogical communication at every level between those who experience different forms of domination and exploitation. It would also be committed to an internal culture that resisted the urge to homogenize, encouraged discourses of difference, and sought to reclaim previously hidden narratives of subordination and exclusion all the while it continued to build solidarities. Leonard asserts that a political organization cannot emerge spontaneously but must be constituted from certain already existing economic and political conditions. Three such conditions outlined by Leonard are: (1) shifts in economic circumstances that impinge on the consciousness of subordinate groups, such as dramatic increases in disparities between rich and poor, increased unemployment and underemployment, and increased exploitation of labour; (2) the realization that state power cannot be won on the basis of working-class movements themselves; and (3) a recognition that identity politics, although necessary, is not sufficient to meet the demands of human welfare—a confederation of solidarity is also needed.

The above is no guarantee that a political party established by a confederation of diversities, including oppressed groups, will assume the difficult task of social transformation. It would seem, however, that a shift in the discourse that drives the state apparatus is a prerequisite for such fundamental social change, which makes achieving state power an emancipatory imperative. We do know that contradictions within global capitalism continue to grow—increasing disparities of wealth, concentration of political power, persistent high levels of unemployment and underemployment, the Asian and Russian economic crises, falling currency values, and, more recently, budget surpluses. Leonard (1997) argues that pressure is increasing to explore new forms of politics as the existing ones become discredited. Although there is no guarantee that the current critical situation will lead to a formation of political parties committed to solidarity in defence of diversity, social justice, and equality, he reminds us that the future is determined by acts of human will. Quoting Marx, Leonard says that 'human subjects act, "but not in circumstances of their own choosing" ' (ibid., 178). It is worth noting that the current world situation came about by the actions of the corporate elite, not because of some law of economic determinism or principle of social evolution. What was made by a small elite group of people can be unmade or remade.

Selective Principles of Anti-Oppressive Social Work Practice

This final section of the book presents a number of principles to help guide the anti-oppressive social worker in his or her practice. I have chosen the principles outlined here because some of them helped me to clarify my teaching and my writing of progressive forms of social work practice and have informed my social activism over the past 15 years. Other principles have recently been added to my inventory through the course of my work in reading, thinking, and writing in the area of oppression and anti-oppression. These principles are not presented in any order of importance or priority.

A Goal of Social Transformation

Gil (1998: 68–85) outlines the following conceptually distinct but overlapping dimensions of social work practice:

- *Amelioration*: alleviating suffering resulting from systemic oppression and injustice by providing some material goods in a paternalistic (charitable) manner.
- *Control*: controlling, regulating, and monitoring members of subordinate groups and enforcing change in their behaviours because they are considered immoral and responsible for their own problematic situation, due to supposedly personal defects and inadequacies.
- *Adaptation*: counselling and treatment of oppressed persons to help them adjust to, cope with, and fit into the 'realities' of unjust and oppressive societies.
- *Reform*: advocating for, initiating, and implementing 'top-down' minor changes in the system (system-tinkering) to reduce the severity of injustice and oppression, but not eliminating their root causes.
- *Structural transformation*: involvement in consciousness-raising concerning the realities of oppression and joining with other social workers, members of oppressed groups, and their allies in acts of resistance and social movements to overcome the fundamental causes of injustice and oppression.

Anti-oppressive social workers will, for the most part, work within the dimension of structural or social transformation. This is not to say that anti-oppressive social workers will never engage in any of the other dimensions, but that amelioration, adaptation, reform, and control are not ends or goals in themselves but part of a larger strategy of social transformation. An attempt should be made to link everyday practice at whatever level at which one is working to the goal of social transformation. One of the purposes of this book has been to show how anti-oppressive social work practice can (and must) occur at the personal, group, cultural, and structural levels.

Realistic Expectations

There are no quick and easy strategies for eliminating oppression. Some social workers equate social transformation with overnight revolution and believe that the absence of militant or cataclysmic or large-scale changes is proof that fundamental social change is unrealistic and that progressive forms of social work are ineffective. Gil reminds us that oppressive institutions have evolved over many centuries and, therefore, are often perceived to be natural, normal, legitimate, and inevitable. Dominant groups will often defend established structures and relationships because they believe that they are fair and/or compatible with their interests. As well, as we have seen, almost everyone occupies at least one position of dominance and, therefore, benefits in some way (in spite of one's overall position) from the present system. 'In other words, nearly all people are now part of the problem, regardless of personal philosophy, and would have to change their ways of life to become part of the solution' (ibid., 130). Consistent with this assertion is the argument I have made in previous chapters that personal or self-transformation is part of the larger task of social transformation.

The social transformation of a society characterized by oppression will require a lengthy and difficult process, one that could take decades or centuries. This does not mean that we have to tolerate the status quo. It merely means that we have to be realistic about the outcomes of anti-oppressive social work. The question is not, 'How can I start the revolution to end oppression?' Rather, it is, 'How can I can contribute to undermining and resisting oppression in my everyday practice?' Our task is to contribute to social transformation in any way we can— in our professional practices and in our personal lives. Although complete social transformation may not occur in the lifetimes of most of us, we will see some fundamental changes. Changes resulting from the women's movement are evidence of this. One of the changes coming from this movement is the common usage today of gender-inclusive language as opposed to the male-dominated of a couple of decades ago. This change, of course, is much greater than a simple vocabulary alteration. It has both symbolic and real effects. Language is part of culture. It reflects and contributes to dominant-subordinate relationships. One way of helping to change the culture is to change the language.

Everyone in her or his day-to-day living experiences can contribute to language changes. For example, instead of using the term 'client', which denotes a relationship of inequality between the social worker (the helper) and the 'helpee', many social workers today use the term 'service user'. An example of where an anti-oppressive social worker can make a contribution to undermining some of the oppressive aspects of social work practice is in the area of case recordings and agency files. Traditionally, case recordings were written in a diagnostic discourse that tended to pathologize the service user by attributing problems to deficiencies of the individual, family, subculture, and so on. These recordings were guarded like Fort Knox and could only be seen by selected agency personnel. The anti-oppressive social worker could help to de-pathologize the experiences of service users by attributing the problems to racism, sexism, classism, or other forms of oppression rather than use some victim-blaming explanation. Service users could also have access to their files and be provided with the opportunity to disagree with what is written and to offer their own narratives. Some agencies have a policy of co-authorship of a joint narrative about problems, needs, and claims (Leonard, 1997). This practice recognizes that narratives are open to interpretation and that the service user's knowledge is just as valuable as is some piece of universal expert knowledge, which by itself has a tendency to homogenize people within a professional narrative.

Critical Self-Reflection

Critical self-reflection is an element of the critical social theory tradition, which

Leonard (1997) argues provides a connection to postmodern critique. Because we all internalize to varying degrees parts of the dominant ideology, it is important to develop reflexive knowledge of the dominant ideology to see how it constrains us and limits our freedom. Reflexive knowledge, derived mainly through critical self-reflection, is knowledge about ourselves. It helps us to understand how our identities are largely determined by the dominant ideology. Reflexive knowledge is knowledge about our location within the social order, that is, the forms and sources of our positions of both domination and oppression, and how we may exercise power in our professional and personal lives to either reproduce or resist social features that limit others' agency. It is also knowledge about the source and substance of our social beliefs, attitudes, and values. Such understanding may help us to free ourselves from self-imposed constraints that are derived from the massive legitimating power of the dominant ideology. An ideology is embedded within a particular discourse. Schon (1983: 163) has developed a social work practice (i.e., reflective practice) wherein the practitioner carries out a 'reflective conversation with the situation'. This technique can be used to identify oppressive traces of the dominant ideology or discourse that may be present in our narratives of domination and subordination or in our social work practices. Critical self-reflection is a form of 'internal criticism', a never-ending questioning of our social, economic, political, and cultural beliefs, assumptions, and actions. It is also a political practice (Leonard, 1997) that allows scope for greater sensitivity to issues relating to power, injustice, and oppression and avoids dogma and orthodoxy (Thompson, 1998), including stereotypes.

Critical Self-Reflection Needed Here!

John is a member of the Mi'kmaq First Nation, which is scattered along the east coast of Canada. He is a first year MSW student in a social work program that publicizes and prides itself as possessing an anti-oppressive curriculum. One day the class was discussing the concepts of 'essentialism' and 'homogeneity'. Many comments and questions were made about how ridiculous it was to assume that a group of people would be the same in every respect or to think that they would all have an essential human nature. Variations on the theme that 'Of course people are different, even if they belong to a certain social category' were espoused by several class members. Then John spoke. He asked, 'So, is essentialism or homogeneity like when people (staff and students) in this program always ask me "What do Aboriginals think about this?" or "What is the Native position on that?" Do you really think that First Nations people are so similar that I or any other Aboriginal person can speak for all of them?'

Peter Leonard (1997) discusses an aspect of critical self-reflection that is highly relevant to those, including anti-oppressive social workers, concerned with social justice. He argues that without critical self-reflection there is a danger of not discovering those parts of oppressive discourses embedded in our consciousness. However, he also points out that critical self-reflection is no guarantee of discovering those oppressive aspects of ourselves. For example, as a white person I have benefited and continue to benefit from institutional or structural racism. Thus I can never claim to be non-racist. I can claim, however, that I am anti-racist, which means that I am committed not only to fight external forms of racism but also to struggle, through critical self-reflection, against the racism that I have internalized. Similarly, I cannot claim to be feminist because, as a man, I have benefited from institutional and cultural sexism. I can, however, claim to be pro-feminist as long as I fight against external forms of sexism and struggle, through critical self-reflection, against those elements of the dominant discourse on gender that I have internalized.

The other example that Leonard presents that highlights the importance of critical social reflection is the meaning of democracy. We may think of democracy as an element of emancipation, but deeply embedded in the dominant discourse of democracy are bourgeois and patriarchal assumptions about leadership, representation, majority rule, dissent, and diversity.

Gil (1998) provides us with a beginning list of areas for critical self-reflection:

- the images of social reality that we presently hold;
- the ideas, beliefs, and assumptions we now take for granted about people, society, and the relationship between the two;
- the perceptions we hold of individual and collective needs and wants, which underpin the actions, thoughts, and social relations of most people;
- our values and ideologies, which derive from our perceptions of needs and interests, and affect our choices, actions, thoughts, and social relations.

Anne Bishop discusses the importance for anyone who wishes to become an ally of oppressed groups to reflect on his or her own experiences as a member of an oppressed group and as a member of an oppressor group. She asserts that learning about one's own oppression is much different from learning about oneself as an oppressor, because the process of becoming an oppressor is hidden from the person. That is, the oppressor role is equated with normalcy, universal standards and values, and political and cultural neutrality. Nothing adverse is perpetrated on the oppressor to make him or her aware of the role of oppressor: 'Becoming a member of an oppressor group is to be cut off from the ability to identify with the experience of the oppressed. . . . When the oppression is not part of your own experience, you can only understand it through hearing other's experiences, along with a process of analysis and parallels' (Bishop, 1994: 95). Bishop argues that oppressed persons always know a great deal more about the oppressor group than the oppressor group knows about oppressed groups. Understanding one's position as an oppressor requires an understanding that one is a member of a particular social group or collective reality and not just an individual member of society. Bishop asserts that it is more difficult to reflect on one's own role as oppressor than it is on one's role as oppressed because the former involves a sense of guilt while the latter involves a sense of anger. It is more difficult to confront guilt than anger because the latter may actually assist in the process of liberation from oppression by releasing energy and propelling the process forward. Guilt, on the other hand, is more likely to inhibit the process of liberating oneself from the position of oppressor. Anti-oppressive social workers will engage in ongoing critical self-reflection of their roles as oppressor and oppressed in both their personal lives and their social work practice.

Support and Study Groups

Gil (1998: 123) articulates a risk that all progressive social workers face because their perspectives and practices derive from a critique of our current social institutions and dominant culture as interfering with the needs satisfaction and development of subordinate group members, and the real solutions to social problems lie in the transformation of these institutions and culture. 'Many social workers and administrators of social services reject this critique and consider the perspectives of radical [including anti-oppressive] social workers, and their approach to practice, unprofessional, unrealistic, and utopian.' As a result of these negative attitudes towards them, anti-oppressive social workers may experience isolation, persecution, and ridicule in their workplace unless opportunities for mutual support and co-operation are available.

Studies on the experiences of many graduates from progressive social work programs in Canada show that practices and strategies of resistance are useful in challenging the dominant discourse that blames individuals for all their problems (Lecomte, 1990; Moreau and Leonard, 1989). There is consensus in the progressive and anti-oppressive social work literature (Baines, 1997; Carniol, 2000; Galper, 1980; Gil, 1998; Mullaly, 1997a) and among progressive social work practitioners that the most important element in successfully carrying out acts of resistance and in protecting oneself from the risks that are an inherent part of such practice is to establish and work with caucuses or support groups of like-minded colleagues (see Mullaly, 1997a, and Thompson, 1998, for discussions of ways for progressive social workers to protect themselves).

Gil (1998: 124–5) outlines several functions that support groups carry out for their members and for anti-oppressive social work practice in general. First, they can serve as settings for non-hierarchical, co-operative, mutually caring relationships among anti-oppressive practitioners who feel isolated and alienated because their views, values, assumptions, theory, and practice differ from those of co-workers and from that espoused within the work setting. Second, they can confirm the realism and sanity of anti-oppressive social workers, which are sometimes questioned by co-workers and administrators because of their unconventional views. Third, they can serve as settings for co-operative and critical study and discussion of the anti-oppressive practice and activism of members, thus enabling members to enhance their critical awareness and to push the existing boundaries of anti-oppressive social work theory and practices. Finally, members of study and support groups can recruit new members, initiate the establishment of new groups, and organize networks of such groups.

An example of a study and support group is provided by one progressive social worker in a public hospital in a culturally diverse, impoverished inner-city community in the United States who was part of such a group:

> Jokingly referring to ourselves as 'the conspiracy,' we shared stories and our outrage over lunch. Without the support of these colleagues, I would have found it difficult to resist the dominant discourse that blames individuals for all their problems. Instead, we continually reframed our problems and our clients' problems to be the result of structural and systemic forces and sought solutions that went beyond those just for individual cases. (Baines, 1997: 314)

The Constructive Use of Anger

Obviously, anti-oppressive social work practice will not be easy. It requires an examination and deconstruction of social work's most cherished assumptions so that we can learn and become part of the resurgence of social critique in the newer forms of political movements that challenge the dominant order in the name of equality and diversity (Leonard, 1997). It requires a view of the reality of oppression, not as a closed world from which there is no exit, but as a limited situation that can be transformed (Freire, cited in Rees, 1991). It also requires an understanding of the nature and causes of the new social, economic, and political conditions of globalization and the current worldwide reactionary political climate. We cannot theorize and analyze from a distance, however, because most of all, anti-oppressive social work requires a personal and collective commitment to social justice. It is not enough to know that we should involve ourselves in struggle or even to want to become involved in social struggle.

But what is it that would drive a person to take on such an onerous commitment to literally change the world as we now know it? The answer, I think, is to capitalize on a feeling that most social workers concerned about social injustice (at least the ones I know) possess—anger at the degrading material and social conditions experienced on a daily basis by millions of people in the less-developed countries and in capitalist countries; anger at governments that cater to the wishes of the wealthy at the expense of women, children, visible minorities, and other marginalized groups; anger at a social welfare system that homogenizes, controls, and monitors people who are forced to go to it for assistance and that has proletarianized its workers; and anger at the discrimination, exploitation, and blocked opportunities that so many people experience today, not because of anything they might have done or who they are as individuals, but simply because they belong to particular social groups, which for the most part they did not choose.

Two old community development principles state that: (1) the most effective way to overcome apathy and passivity in organizing and mobilizing groups is to identify the major sources of discontent within a community, stimulate that discontent, and turn it into anger so that community members want to do something about their situation; and (2) channel the anger onto the source of the discontent and develop long- and short-term strategies to change the situation. Surely, progressive social workers have no shortage of discontent and anger today.

Feminists have used the construction of anger as a catalyst to attack sexism and patriarchy. According to feminist therapy, women need to get in touch with their anger and turn it outward, rather than inward (Goldhor-Lerner, 1985), as the latter results in depression, despair, and anxiety, which, in turn, reproduce women's traditional roles of passivity and submission under patriarchy (Baines, 1997). A similar dynamic is operative for social workers who internalize their anger caused by social and workplace injustice.

Peter Leonard argues that a sense of moral outrage at the structures of domination and oppression manufactured and reproduced within the current set of oppressive social arrangements provides the basis for progressive discourses and practices. 'Not intellectual detachment but anger is the human attribute which has the most possibility of generating the kind of individual and collective resistance which is a necessary precondition of emancipation' (Leonard, 1997: 162). Thompson (1998) issues an important caution about anger, however. He asserts that anger can be a positive force for change if it is channelled constructively, but if it gets out of control or is misdirected or used as a blanket approach to struggles for liberation, it can be used ideologically by the dominant group to pathologize and stigmatize subordinate group members and their anti-oppressive allies.

Anger is a gift (Lim, 1996, cited in Leonard, 1997). It has been the driving force behind all great social movements. It can move oppressed people and their allies from feelings of 'helpless fury' to 'righteous indignation' (Herman, 1992: 189). Leonard (1997: 162) argues that anger can be mobilized from internalization as anxiety and depression into externalization as collective resistance: 'Collectively, anger emerges as a moral protest at injustice.' Bishop (1994: 84) identifies anger as a source of power if it is used as 'an expression of our will directed against injustice'.

Anger is what will enable those of us who are committed to anti-oppressive social work to translate our social justice ideals into practice and to continue the struggle for liberation. This struggle can be painful and discouraging at times, but anyone who has participated in it knows that it also brings great comradeship, which is deeply rewarding. If we do nothing about oppression, we lose our basic humanity. If, in our personal lives and in our social work practice, we assist in making oppression acceptable by helping people to cope with it or adjust to it, we not only fail them, we fail ourselves and we become part of the problem. Social workers who are committed to social justice must join the struggle against oppression in all its forms and at all levels at which it occurs. There is no choice.

Conclusion

Maintain the rage (but use it wisely).   – bob m.

Notes

Chapter 1

1. A subsequent analysis by this author of British (Coulshed and Orme, 1998) and Australian (O'Connor et al., 1998) introductory social work textbooks revealed the same lack of discussion of social problems as a concept in both books. Each of these textbooks was the only one in its respective country considered to be an introductory book with respect to the criteria used in the American textbook study.

2. Use of the term 'conflict' is problematic as it is used by different writers to refer not only to a perspective but also to a theory or to a paradigm as well as to other constructs that have a critical element. The term 'perspective' is adopted here because many different conflict theories are based on the conflict perspective, and to call a perspective a theory is to confuse the two. The position adopted here is that a perspective has descriptive and analytical qualities but no prescriptive component. Theory emanates from a perspective but includes a prescription.

3. The conflict theorist recognizes that there are personal difficulties, issues, or problems (e.g., relationship difficulties, marriage breakdown) that are not directly attributable to structural factors. However, a social problem, by definition, affects large numbers of people and usually has a social cause.

4. One of the earliest concepts of critical social theory that was developed to answer the question 'why do people seemingly accept social structures that dominate, exploit, and oppress them?' is that of 'false consciousness'. Today, this term raises the ire of many (but not all) postmodernists, post-structuralists, and feminists because it suggests that not only is there a false consciousness, but there must also be a 'true consciousness', and who is to say or judge what is true or false for other people. Although I personally think that this dichotomous 'true-false' criticism is a distortion of what critical social theorists mean by the term, I do understand that it does not have the same meaning outside a Marxist discourse as it does within. For this reason I will use terms such as 'acceptance of' and 'resignation to' to refer to the phenomenon whereby people seemingly support a society that oppresses them and whereby they appear to participate willingly in their own oppression.

5. This is not to say that ideologies are totally internally coherent. As Thompson (1998: 21) points out, 'it is not uncommon for ideologies to encompass a range of contradictory or logically incompatible ideas—the need for ideology need not rest on rational argument.' See also Hall (1986).

Chapter 2

1. Thompson (1998) argues convincingly that use of the word 'tolerance' with respect to differences is problematic because it conveys that something is 'wrong with' or 'negative about' the particular difference. The position taken in this book is that group and cultural differences should be promoted and celebrated, not just accepted or tolerated.

Chapter 3

1. Woman's beauty, narrowly defined by men, was an important category of physical beauty, but deviated from the notion of 'ideal beauty' because it was associated with inferior qualities of weakness, delicateness, emotionality, etc.

Chapter 4

1. For a succinct and insightful discussion of 'culture' in the contexts of modernity and

postmodernity, see Leonard (1997: ch. 3). For an overview of the 'cultural studies movement', see Agger (1992) and Grossberg et al. (1992).

2. Biklen echoes Gitlin's (1980) contention that members of social action and subordinate groups, among others, tend to be naive in their dealings with the media in that they seem unmindful of the media's tendency to promote dominant social values. To help counter this tendency Biklen discusses the following strategies in preparing for media exposure. (1) Speak as a representative of a group, as individuals without a group affiliation will generally be perceived as oddballs or deviant (unless they are perceived to be experts). (2) Ensure that the group defines the issue in clear and simple terms (preferably emphasizing one point only). Otherwise, the media will define the issue from the dominant perspective. (3) Plan to control the issue/message by developing 10 different ways to say it. Otherwise, the media are apt to get the group off track with questions that do not relate directly to the group's message. (4) Because there is considerable competition for news publicity, make the event or issue newsworthy (i.e., give it entertainment value or present it as an issue that affects a large number of people or as an issue that involves a significant injustice or an issue that is supported by (or will receive support from) authoritative circles (experts, intellectuals, formal organizations, influential people, etc.). (5) Know the opposing view in order to critique it when the media ask the group to respond to it. (6) Develop a list of media outlets and reporters who are sympathetic to the cause or issue and will treat it fairly.

3. For a complementary view of hegemony, see Laclau and Mouffe (1985), who trace the concept from the late nineteenth-century debates on working-class unity to the contemporary emergence of new antagonisms and forms of emancipatory struggle. This work develops the concept of hegemony beyond the essentialism and universalism of classical Marxist thought; 'it (the discourse of the universal) has been replaced by a polyphony of voices, each of which constructs its own irreducible discursive identity' (ibid., 191).

4. I am not convinced that social work must organize itself along professional lines to achieve these ends, but I accept that others do. For a discussion of this issue, see Mullaly (1997a: 194–9).

Chapter 5

1. Potocky (1998) notes that the dominant theory of multicultural social work in the United States is that of cultural sensitivity (my experience in social work in Canada and Australia has convinced me that the situation is similar in both these countries). The aim of this theory is to increase worker and agency sensitivity to different cultural norms, and to decrease (but not eliminate) institutional racism. Cultural sensitivity enables white social workers to better establish a 'helping relationship' with other races and cultures so as to make services more accessible and to advocate for the enactment of equal rights legislation. Although the cultural sensitivity model represents an advance over the earlier colour-blind and assimilationist (melting-pot) approach to issues of race and culture, it can actually, although unintentionally, allow racism to persist, but in a more respectable form (Ahmed, 1991; Thompson, 1997). The cultural sensitivity model ignores the fact that cultures and races are ranked in order of perceived merit and it ignores the power relations between people of colour and white people in history and in the present (Ahmed, 1991; Williams, 1989).

2. 'Multiculturalism' as a concept and as a public policy issue dates back to the 1970s in most Western industrialized countries; there have been many progressive activists and supporters of multiculturalism. However, Agger contends that the concept of multiculturalism has been appropriated to some extent by some schools of postmodernism and consequently a change in meaning has occurred. It has also been appropriated by social work, as outlined above in note 1. Basically, Agger argues that multiculturalism is a recognition and acceptance of cultural pluralism, but it does nothing to change the situation of there being one dominant culture with all others subordinate to it. The argument of earlier multicultural activists that there not be a hierarchy of cultures is part of the position of the 'politics of difference' approach today.

3. The interpretation of these events, of course, varies (see Mullaly, 1997a). Conservatives view welfare capitalism as governments pandering to the working class and

other subordinate groups (e.g., minorities, feminists) in exchange for political popularity. Liberals view it as a genuine attempt to humanize capitalism for all groups, both dominant and subordinate. Critical social theorists, including Marxists, feminists, and social democrats, view welfare capitalism as a social institution that reinforces capitalism by disguising the true oppressive nature of capitalism and by 'conning' the general public into thinking that the government is acting in their best interests first (O'Connor, 1973).

4. For a fuller discussion on the nature of human beings (i.e., whether they are political or apolitical by nature) and its relationship to politics and political theory, see Berry (1986).

5. The book by Sidanius and Pratto is used here because: it is relatively recent, it brings together an impressive amount of international empirical evidence, and it focuses on social inequalities as forms of institutional discrimination and structural oppression. There is a vast literature on social inequality, including national and international accounts, studies, and analyses. All nations are characterized by social inequality, although it varies from country to country in terms of how great the discrepancies are between dominant and subordinate persons. For example, among Western democracies the United States has the greatest discrepancies in levels of living between dominant and subordinate groups, whereas the Scandinavian countries are among those having the least. The purpose here is to show how these inequalities help to maintain and reproduce oppression and how this oppression has violent consequences. The evidence presented in this chapter is meant to be illustrative rather than exhaustive.

6. I am indebted to Rosalie Chappell, *Social Welfare in Canadian Society* (1997), for many of the references in this section documenting the situation of Canadian First Nations people.

Chapter 6

1. For an overview of the psychology of oppression and liberation from a critical point of view, see Moane (1999). It is from her book that I draw much of the material for this section on the psychology of oppression.

2. Individuals may also shape (within limits) their social environment. They have some choices (e.g., how to interpret particular discourses and mediate their impact and who to interact with). They can influence their birth family and the families they establish themselves. And they may choose to resist and fight oppression rather than resign themselves to it.

3. Shulman (1992) notes that the central idea of gaining one's sense of self by exploitation of others can be seen in many different oppressive relationships with which social workers deal—the abusing parent and abused child, the battering husband and his partner, the straight society's repression of gay, lesbian, and bisexual persons, the discrimination of people of colour by white society, and so on.

4. Agger (1998) describes interpretive social theory as that set of theories that seeks to understand the meanings that people attach to their actions in everyday life. Unlike critical theory, interpretive theories do not attempt to mobilize social action, and unlike positivist theory they do not attempt to produce social laws.

5. Gil does not condemn all religions. He points out that many religions place primacy on social justice, equality, and liberation from oppression as values (e.g., liberation theology).

6. I am indebted to Hussein Bulhan (1985) for his succinct and insightful explanation of Fanon's theory of a Manichean psychology.

Chapter 7

1. Mutual oppression occurs in the form of different oppressed persons or groups oppressing each other.

2. I am aware that the globalization of the economy has meant the loss of some state government autonomy to the corporate sector. The extent of corporate influence and coercion over national governments is a debatable issue, but certainly most govern-

ments all over the world have aligned themselves with the corporate agenda at the expense of the social services sector. In fact, many of the world's elected leaders come from or aspire to become part of the corporate elite.

3. Lena Dominelli (1997), among others who write in the area of race relations, contends that race is a social construction because there is only one race of people—*Homo sapiens*.

4. See Williams (1989) for a discussion of these differences.

Chapter 8

1. For a discussion of the concept and use of 'dialectic' in progressive social work, see Mullaly (1997a).

2. Some writers (e.g., Bishop, 1994; Butler, 1978) speak of liberation as a journey where one starts out as a victim, moves to being a survivor, and ends up as a warrior or activist fighting against oppression. This should not be interpreted as a linear, forward-moving, and uninterrupted journey, however.

3. For an insightful and informative discussion on power, see Thompson (1998).

4. This concept of normalization is very different from Foucault's notion of 'normalization'. The latter refers to standards of acceptable social behaviour and the mechanisms or systems of rewards and punishments put in place to promote adherence to these standards.

5. Ruth's description is that oppressed persons in this stage never accept the dominant discourse and never act subservient again. This, in my view, is completely unrealistic.

6. This was a common expression used by many white people in the southern US during the civil rights movement in the early to mid-1960s, which concentrated on obtaining basic civil and political rights for the black population.

7. Afrocentricity is a 'philosophical model predicated on traditional African assumptions that reflect the "original" cultural values (i.e., interdependency, collectivity, and spirituality) of Africans before the advent of European and Arab influences' (Schiele, 1994: 13). Today, Afrocentricity, as a world view, is increasingly being used by black people (one of the largest groups of 'diaspora') all over the world as a counter-discourse to Eurocentricity.

8. Orientalism refers to the processes by which the 'Orient' was, and continues to be, constructed in European thinking and discourse. Popularized by Edward Said (1978), Orientalism is the way in which the West deals with the Orient—making statements about it, authorizing views about it, studying it, describing it, teaching it, settling it, and ruling over it. In short, it is a Western way of dominating, restructuring, and having authority over the Orient (or over any Other). The relationship between the West (or the Occident) and the Orient is one of power, domination, and a complex hegemony (Ashcroft et al., 1998). Being aware of how Orientalism works is a tremendous step for the people of the Orient to resist it and to develop counter-discourses.

Bibliography

Adam, Barry D. 1978. *The Survival of Domination: Inferiorization and Everyday Life.* New York: Elsevier.

Agel, Jerome, ed. 1971. *The Radical Therapist.* New York: Ballantine Books.

Agger, Ben. 1989. *Socio(ontology): A Disciplinary Reading.* Urbana: University of Illinois Press.

———. 1991. 'Critical Theory, Poststructuralism, Postmodernism: Their Sociological Relevance', *Annual Review of Sociology* 17: 105–31.

———. 1992. *Cultural Studies as Critical Theory.* London: Falmer Press.

———. 1998. *Critical Social Theories: An Introduction.* Boulder, Colo.: Westview Press.

Ahmad, B. 1990. *Black Perspectives in Social Work.* Birmingham: Venture.

Ahmed, S. 1991. 'Developing Anti-Racist Social Work Education Practice', in CD Project Steering Group, ed., *Setting the Context for Change.* London: CCETSW.

Albert, M., L. Cagan, N. Chomsky, R. Hahnel, M. King, L. Sargent, and H. Sklar. 1986. *Liberating Theory.* Boston: South End Press.

Alexander, David. 1987. 'Gendered Job Traits and Women's Occupations', Ph.D. thesis, University of Massachusetts.

Althusser, Louis. 1969. *For Marx.* London: Allen Lane.

Anleu, Sharyn L. Roach. 1999. *Deviance, Conformity and Control.* South Melbourne: Longman.

Anthias, F., and N. Yuval-Davis. 1992. *Radicalized Boundaries: Race, Nation, Colour, Class and the Anti-Racist Struggle.* London: Routledge.

Apter, M.J. 1983. 'Negativism and the Sense of Identity', in Breakwell (1983: 75–90).

Arnowitz, Stanley. 1992. *The Politics of Identity: Class, Culture, Social Movements.* New York: Routledge.

Ashcroft, Bill, Gareth Griffiths, and Helen Tiffin. 1998. *Key Concepts in Post-Colonial Studies.* London: Routledge.

Astbury, Jill. 1996. *Crazy for You: The Making of Women's Madness.* Melbourne: Oxford University Press.

Bachrach, P. 1969. *The Theory of Democratic Elitism.* London: University of London Press.

Bailey, Roy, and Mike Brake, eds. 1975. *Radical Social Work.* New York: Pantheon Books.

Baines, Donna. 1997. 'Feminist Social Work in the Inner City: The Challenges of Race, Class, and Gender', *Affilia* 12, 3: 29–33.

———. 2000. 'Everyday Practices of Race, Class and Gender: Struggles, Skills, and Radical Social Work', *Journal of Progressive Human Services* 11, 2: 5–27.

———. 2001. 'Race, Class, and Gender in the Everyday Talk of Social Workers: The Ways We Limit the Possibilities for Radical Practice', *Race, Gender and Class* (special issue on Social Work) 9, 1.

Banton, M., and J. Harwood. 1975. *The Race Concept.* Buckingham: Open University Press.

Barbour, Rosaline S. 1984. 'Social Work Education: Tackling the Theory-Practice Dilemma', *British Journal of Social Work* 14: 557–77.

Barker, Robert L. 1987. *The Social Work Dictionary.* Silver Spring, Md: National Association of Social Workers.

Bartky, S.L. 1990. *Femininity and Domination: Studies in the Phenomenology of Oppression.* London: Routledge.

Baudrillard, J. 1983. *Simulations.* New York: Semiotext(e).

Baughman, E. Earle. 1971. *Black Americans: A Psychological Analysis.* New York: Academic Press.

Bauman, Zygmunt. 1992. *Intimations of Postmodernity.* London: Routledge.

———. 1998. *Work, Consumerism and the New Poor.* Philadelphia: Open University Press.

Beagley, J.M. 1989. 'Gender Issues in Child Abuse: She Must Have Known What Was Happening', *Child Abuse Review* 3, 2.

Beauvoir, Simone de. 1961. *The Second Sex.* New York: Bantam.

Berger, Peter L., and Thomas Luckmann. 1966. *The Social Construction of Reality.* New York: Doubleday.

Berry, Christopher J. 1986. *Human Nature.* Atlantic Highlands, NJ: Humanities Press International.

Best, S., and D. Kellner. 1991. *Postmodern Theorizing.* London: Macmillan.

Bhaba, Homi K. 1994. *The Location of Culture.* London: Routledge.

Biklen, Douglas P. 1983. *Community Organizing: Theory and Practice.* Englewood Cliffs, NJ: Prentice-Hall.

Bishop, Anne. 1994. *Becoming an Ally: Breaking the Cycle of Oppression.* Halifax: Fernwood.

Black, Rita Beck. 1995. 'Diversity and Populations at Risk: People with Disabilities', in Frederic G. Reamer, ed., *The Foundations of Social Work Knowledge.* New York: Columbia University Press, 391–416.

Blumenfeld, W.J., and D. Raymond. 1988. *Looking at Gay and Lesbian Life.* Boston: Beacon Press.

Brake, M. 1980. *The Sociology of Youth Culture and Youth Subcultures: Sex, Drugs 'n' Rock and Roll.* New York: Routledge.

Breakwell, Glynis M., ed. 1983. *Threatened Identities.* Chichester: Wiley.

———. 1986. *Coping with Threatened Identities.* London: Methuen.

Brittan, Arthur, and Mary Maynard. 1984. *Sexism, Racism and Oppression.* Oxford: Blackwell.

Brodribb, S. 1992. *Nothing Mat(t)ers: A Feminist Critique of Post-Modernism.* New York: New York University Press.

Bromley, D., and C.F. Longino, Jr. 1972. *White Racism and Black Americans.* Cambridge, Mass.: Schenkman.

Bulhan, Hussein A. 1985. *Frantz Fanon and the Psychology of Oppression.* New York: Plenum Press.

Burr, V. 1995. *An Introduction to Social Constructionism.* London: Routledge.

Butler, Sandra. 1978. *Conspiracy of Silence: The Trauma of Incest.* San Francisco: Volcano Press.

——— and C. Wintram. 1991. *Feminist Groupwork.* London: Sage.

Canadian Advisory Council on the Status of Women. 1990. *Women and Labour Market Poverty.* Ottawa: CACSW.

Carlen, P., and A. Worral, eds. 1987. *Gender, Crime and Justice.* Milton Keynes: Open University Press.

Carniol, Ben. 1979. 'A Critical Approach in Social Work', *Canadian Journal of Social Work Education* 5, 1: 95–111.

———. 1992. 'Structural Social Work: Maurice Moreau's Challenge to Social Work Practice', *Journal of Progressive Human Services* 3, 1: 1–20.

———. 2000. *Case Critical,* 4th edn. Toronto: Between the Lines.

Chappell, Rosalie. 1997. *Social Welfare in Canadian Society.* Scarborough, Ont.: Nelson.

Chevigny, P. 1995. *Edge of the Knife: Police Violence in the Americas.* New York: New Press.

Clarke, G. 1990. 'Defending Ski-Jumpers: A Critique of Theories of Youth Subcultures', in S. Frith and A. Goodwin, eds, *On Record.* New York: Pantheon, 81–96.

Clarke, Michelle. 1991. *Fighting Poverty Through Programs: Social and Health Programs for Canada's Poor Children and Youth.* Ottawa: Children*Enfants*Jeunesse*Youth (CEJY).

Clough, Patricia Ticineto. 1994. *Feminist Thought: Desire, Power, and Academic Discourse.* Cambridge, Mass.: Blackwell.

Coates, John. 1991. 'Putting Knowledge for Practice Into Perspective', *Canadian Social Work Review* 8, 1: 82–96.

Cole, D.P., and M. Gittens. 1995. *Report of the Commission on Systemic Racism in the Ontario Criminal Justice System.* Toronto: Queen's Printer of Ontario.

Cole, Thomas R. 1986. 'Putting Off the Old: Middle Class Morality, Antebellum Protestantism, and the Origins of Ageism', in David Van Tassel and Peter N. Stearns, eds, *Old Age in a Bureaucratic Society.* New York: Greenwood.

Collins, Barbara G. 1986. 'Defining Feminist Social Work', *Social Work* 31, 3: 214–19.

Collins, P. 1990. *Black Feminist Thought.* London: Unwin Hyman.

Coulshed, Veronica, and Joan Orme. 1998. *Social Work Practice: An Introduction.* Basingstoke: Macmillan.

Curtis, James, Edward Grabb, Neil Guppy, and Sid Gilbert. 1988. *Social Inequality in Canada: Patterns, Problems, Policies.* Scarborough, Ont.: Prentice-Hall Canada.

Dahl, Robert. 1970. *Modern Political Analysis*, 2nd edn. Englewood Cliffs, NJ: Prentice-Hall.

Daly, Mary. 1984. *Pure Lust: Elemental Feminist Philosophy.* Boston: Beacon Press.

Dalrymple, Jane, and Beverley Burke. 1995. *Anti-Oppressive Practice: Social Care and the Law.* Buckingham: Open University Press.

Day, Lesley. 1992. 'Women and Oppression: Race, Class and Gender', in Langan and Day (1992: 12–31).

Dekeseredy, Walter S., and Ronald Hinch. 1991. *Woman Abuse: Sociological Perspectives.* Toronto: Thompson Educational Publishing.

Denzin, Norman K. 1991. *Images of Postmodern Society: Social Theory and Contemporary Cinema.* London: Sage.

Dominelli, Lena. 1997. *Anti-Racist Social Work*, 2nd edn. London: Macmillan.

———— and Eileen McLeod. 1989. *Feminist Social Work.* Hampshire, UK: Macmillan Education.

Donald, J., and S. Hall, eds. 1986. *Politics and Ideology.* Milton Keynes: Open University Press.

Du Bois, W.E.B. 1969. *The Souls of Black Folk.* New York: New American Library.

Ebony. 1986. Special Edition on Black Families, August.

Emberley, J.V. 1993. *Thresholds of Difference.* Toronto: University of Toronto Press.

Eyerman, Ron. 1981. *False Consciousness and Ideology in Marxist Theory.* Atlantic Highlands, NJ: Humanities Press.

Eysenck, H.J. 1971. *Race, Intelligence and Education.* London: Temple Smith.

————. 1973. *The Inequality of Man.* London: Temple Smith.

Fanon, Frantz. 1967. *Black Skin: White Masks.* New York: Grove Press.

————. 1968. *The Wretched of the Earth.* New York: Grove Press.

Featherstone, B., and B. Fawsett. 1994. 'Oh No! Not More Isms: Feminism, Postmodernism, Poststructuralism and Social Work Education', paper presented at the IASSW Congress, Amsterdam.

Featherstone, Mike. 1991. *Consumer Culture and Postmodernism.* London: Sage.

Fischer, Joel. 1978. *Effective Casework Practice.* New York: McGraw-Hill.

Fisher, Robert, and Howard J. Karger. 1997. *Social Work and Community in a Private World: Getting Out in Public.* White Plains, NY: Longman.

———— and Joe Kling. 1994. 'Community Organization and New Social Movement Theory', *Journal of Progressive Human Services* 5, 2: 5–24.

Fleras, Augie. 2001. *Social Problems in Canada: Conditions, Constructions and Challenges.* Toronto: Prentice-Hall.

Foucault, Michel. 1976. *The Archaeology of Knowledge.* New York: Harper and Row.

————. 1977. *Discipline and Punish.* New York: Pantheon.

———. 1980. *Power/Knowledge: Selected Interviews and Other Writings 1972–77*, ed. C. Gordon. Brighton: Harvester Press.

———. 1988. *Politics, Culture, Philosophy: Interviews and Other Writings 1977–1984*. New York: Routledge.

———. 1990. *Introduction*, vol. 1 of *The History of Sexuality* (1978). Reprint, New York: Random House.

Fox, D.R., and I. Prilleltensky, eds. 1997. *Critical Psychology: An Introduction*. London: Sage.

Fox, R. 1992. 'East of Said', in Michael Sprinker, ed., *Edward Said: A Critical Reader*. Oxford: Blackwell, 144–56.

Freire, Paulo. 1994 [1970]. *Pedagogy of the Oppressed*, 2nd edn. New York: Continuum Publishing.

Fromm, Erich. 1966. *The Heart of Man*. New York: Basic Books.

Frye, Marilyn. 1983. *The Politics of Reality: Essays in Feminist Theory*. Trumansburg, NY: Crossing Press.

Galper, Jeffry. 1975. *The Politics of Social Services*. Englewood Cliffs, NJ: Prentice-Hall.

———. 1980. *Social Work Practice: A Radical Perspective*. Englewood Cliffs, NJ: Prentice-Hall.

Galtung, Johan. 1990. 'Cultural Violence', *Journal of Peace Research* 27, 3: 291–305.

Gandhi, Leela. 1998. *Postcolonial Theory: A Critical Introduction*. St Leonards, New South Wales: Allen and Unwin.

Geertz, C. 1986. 'The Uses of Diversity', *Michigan Quarterly Review* 25, 1: 105–23.

George, Usha. 2000. 'Towards Anti-Racism in Social Work in the Canadian Context', in Agnes Calliste and George J. Sefa Dei, eds, *Anti-Racist Feminism*. Halifax: Fernwood, 111–22.

——— and Sarah Ramkissoon. 1998. 'Race, Gender, and Class in the Lives of South Asian Women in Canada', *Affilia* 13, 1: 102–19.

Giddens, A. 1995. *A Contemporary Critique of Historical Materialism*, 2nd edn. London: Macmillan.

Gil, David G. 1976a. 'Social Policies and Social Development: A Humanistic-Egalitarian Perspective', *Journal of Sociology and Social Welfare* 3, 3: 242–63.

———. 1976b. *The Challenge of Social Equality*. Cambridge, Mass.: Schenkman.

———. 1992. *Unravelling Social Policy*, 5th edn. Rochester, Vt: Schenkman.

———. 1994. 'Confronting Injustice and Oppression', in Frederic G. Reamer, ed., *The Foundation of Social Work Knowledge*. New York: Columbia University Press, 231–63.

———. 1998. *Confronting Injustice and Oppression: Concepts and Strategies for Social Workers*. New York: Columbia University Press.

Gitlin, Todd. 1979. 'Prime Time Ideology: The Herpmanic Process in Television Entertainment', *Social Problems* 26, 3: 251–66.

———. 1980. *The Whole World Is Watching*. Berkeley: University of California Press.

Goldhor-Lerner, H. 1985. *The Dance of Anger*. New York: Harper & Row.

Gould, K. 1987. 'Life Model Versus Conflict Model: A Feminist Perspective', *Social Work* (May–June): 346–51.

Gramsci. Antonio. 1971. *Selections from the Prison Notebooks*. London: Lawrence and Wishart.

Greenberg, David. 1988. *The Construction of Homosexuality*. Chicago: University of Chicago Press.

Grossberg, Lawrence, Cary Nelson, and Paula Treichler, eds. 1992. *Cultural Studies*. New York: Routledge.

Guillou, J. 1996. '60 doms varje ar for valdtakt', *Aftonbladet*. Available at: < http://www.aftonbladet.se.nyheter/guillou9.html > .

Habermas, Jürgen. 1975. *Legitimation Crisis*. Boston: Beacon Press.

Haley, Alex. 1977. *Roots*. London: Hutchinson.

Hall, S. 1986. 'Variations of Liberalism', in Donald and Hall (1986: 34–69).

———. 1988. *The Hard Road to Renewal: Thatcherism and the Crisis of the Left*. London: Verso.

———, C. Critcher, T. Jefferson, J. Clarke, and B. Roberts. 1978. *Policing the Crisis: Muggings, the State and Law and Order*. London: Macmillan.

Haney, Eleanor H. 1989. *Vision & Struggle: Meditations on Feminist Spirituality and Politics*. Portland, Maine: Astarte Shell Press.

Hardy, Jean. 1981a. *Values in Social Work*. London: Routledge & Kegan Paul.

———. 1981b. *Values in Social Policy: Nine Contradictions*. London: Routledge & Kegan Paul.

Hartman, Heidi. 1981. 'The Unhappy Marriage of Marxism and Feminism', in Lydia Sargent, ed., *Women and Revolution*. Montreal: Black Rose Books, 1–41.

Harvey, David. 1989. *The Condition of Postmodernity: An Enquiry into the Origins of Cultural Change*. Cambridge, Mass.: Basil Blackwell.

Head, S. 1996. 'The New, Ruthless Economy', *The New York Review* 43, 4 (29 Feb.).

Health Canada. 1989. *Issues: Drug Use by the Elderly*. Ottawa: Health Protection Branch, 20 Sept.

———. 1994. *Suicide in Canada: Update on the Report of the Task Force on Suicide in Canada*: Ottawa: Health Canada.

Health and Welfare Canada. 1991a. *Health Status of Canadian Indians and Inuit*. Ottawa: Minister of Supply and Services Canada.

———. 1991b. *Services to Elderly Patients with Mental Health Problems in General Hospitals: Guidelines*. Ottawa: Health and Welfare Canada.

———. 1992. *Aboriginal Health in Canada*. Ottawa: Health and Welfare Canada.

Healey, Joseph F. 1995. *Race, Ethnicity, Gender and Class*. Thousand Oaks, Calif.: Pine Forge.

Healy, Karen, and Peter Leonard. 2000. 'Responding to Uncertainty: Critical Social Work Education in the Postmodern Habitat', *Journal of Progressive Human Services* 11, 1: 23–48.

Hebdige, D. 1979. *Subculture: The Meaning of Style*. London: Methuen.

———. 1988. *Hiding in the Light: On Images and Things*. New York: Routledge.

Hegel, G.W.F. 1966 [1807]. *The Phenomenology of Mind*. London: Allen and Unwin.

Heidegger, Martin. 1971. 'Building, Dwelling, Thinking', in Heidegger, *Poetry, Language, Thought*. New York: Harper and Row.

Heller, Agnes. 1987. *Beyond Justice*. New York: Basic Books.

Herman, J.L. 1992. *Trauma and Recovery*. New York: Basic Books.

Herrnstein, R.J. 1971. *IQ in the Meritocracy*. Boston: Little, Brown.

Hobsbawm, E.J., and T. Ranger, eds. 1993. *The Invention of Tradition*. Cambridge: Cambridge University Press.

Hodges, Andrew, and David Hutter. 1974. *With Downcast Gays: Aspects of Homosexual Self-Oppression*. London: Pomegranate.

hooks, bell. 1990. *Yearning: Race, Gender and Cultural Politics*. Boston: South End Press.

———. 1993. *Sisters of the Yam: Black Women and Self-Recovery*. Boston: South End Press.

Horton, John. 1966. 'Order and Conflict Theories of Social Problems as Competing Ideologies', *American Journal of Sociology* 72 (May): 701–13.

Howe, David. 1987. *An Introduction to Social Work Theory*. Aldershot, UK: Wildwood House.

———. 1994. 'Modernity, Postmodernity and Social Work', *British Journal of Social Work* 24: 513–32.

Ife, Jim. 1996. *Rethinking Social Work*. Lance Cove, New South Wales: Addison-Wesley Longman.

Jamrozik, Adam, and Luisa Nocella. 1998. *The Sociology of Social Problems: Theoretical Perspectives and Methods of Intervention*. Cambridge: Cambridge University Press.

Jay, Martin. 1973. *The Dialectical Imagination*. Boston: Little, Brown.

Jensen, A.R. 1969. 'How Much Can We Boost IQ and Scholastic Achievement?', *Harvard Educational Review* 39: 1–23.

Johnson, Allan G. 2000. *The Blackwell Dictionary of Sociology: A User's Guide to Sociological Language*, 2nd edn. Malden, Mass.: Blackwell.

Jones, J.H. 1993. *Bad Blood: The Tuskegee Syphilis Experiment*. New York: Free Press.

Jost, J.T. 1995. 'Negative Illusions: Conceptual Clarification and Psychological Evidence Concerning False Consciousness', *Political Psychology* 16: 13–15.

Junger, M., and W. Polder. 1992. 'Some Explanations of Crime among Four Ethnic Groups in the Netherlands', *Journal of Quantitative Criminology* 8: 51–78.

Kanuha, V.K. 1999. 'The Social Process of "Passing" to Manage Stigma: Acts of Internalized Oppression or Acts of Resistance?', *Journal of Sociology and Social Welfare* 26, 4: 27–46.

Karl, M. 1995. *Women and Empowerment, Participation and Decision-Making*. London: Zed Books.

Keller, Evelyn Fox. 1986. *Reflections on Gender and Science*. New Haven: Yale University Press.

Kellner, Douglas. 1989. *Critical Theory, Marxism, and Modernity*. Baltimore: Johns Hopkins University Press.

———. 1990. *Television and the Crisis of Democracy*. Boulder, Colo.: Westview Press.

Kitzinger, C., and R. Perkins. 1993. *Changing Our Minds: Lesbian Feminism and Psychology*. London: Onlywomen.

Kogan, M.D., M. Kotelchuck, G.R. Alexander, and W.E. Johnson. 1994. 'Racial Disparities in Reported Prenatal Care Advice from Health Care Providers', *American Journal of Public Health* 84: 82–8.

Kojeve, A. 1969. *Introduction to the Reading of Hegel*. New York: Basic Books.

Kovel, Joel. 1984. *White Racism: A Psychohistory*, 2nd edn. New York: Columbia University Press.

Krieger, N., and S. Sidney. 1996. 'Racial Discrimination and Blood Pressure: The CARDIA Study of Young Black and White Adults', *American Journal of Public Health* 86: 1370–8.

Kuhn, Thomas S. 1970 [1962]. *The Structure of Scientific Revolutions*, 2nd edn. Chicago: University of Chicago Press.

Laclau, E., and C. Mouffe. 1985. *Hegemony & Socialist Strategy: Towards a Radical Democratic Politics*. London: Verso.

Langan, Mary, and Lesley Day, eds. 1992. *Women, Oppression and Social Work*. London: Routledge.

Laursen, Kay. 1975. 'Professionalism', in Harold Throssell, ed., *Social Work: Radical Essays*. St Lucia, Queensland: University of Queensland Press, 47–71.

Lecomte, Roland. 1990. 'Connecting Private Troubles and Public Issues in Social Work Education', in Brian Wharf, ed., *Social Work and Social Change in Canada*. Toronto: McClelland & Stewart, 47–71.

Lees, Ray. 1972. *Politics and Social Work*. London: Routledge & Kegan Paul.

Leonard, Peter. 1984. *Personality and Ideology: Towards a Materialist Understanding of the Individual*. London: Macmillan.

———. 1994. 'Knowledge/Power and Postmodernism', *Canadian Social Work Review* 11, 1: 11–26.

———. 1995. 'Postmodernism, Socialism and Social Welfare', *Journal of Progressive Human Services* 6, 2: 3–19.

———. 1997. *Postmodern Welfare: Reconstructing an Emancipatory Project*. London: Sage.

Leonard, Stephen T. 1990. *Critical Theory in Political Practice*. Princeton, NJ: Princeton University Press.

Lerner, G. 1986. *The Creation of Patriarchy*. Oxford: Oxford University Press.

Lewontin, Richard C., Steven Rose, and Leon J. Kamin. 1984. *Not in Our Genes: Biology, Ideology, and Human Nature*. New York: Pantheon Books.

Lim, O. 1996. 'Anger is a Gift', unpublished research paper, McGill University.

Littleton, Christine. 1987. 'Reconstructing Sexual Equality', *California Law Review* 75 (July): 1279–1337.

Longres, John. 1986. 'Marxian Theory and Social Work Practice', *Catalyst* 5, 4: 13–34.

—— and Eileen McLeod. 1980. 'Consciousness Raising and Social Work Practice', *Social Casework* 61, 5: 267–76.

Lukacs, G. 1971. *History and Class Consciousness*. London: Methuen.

Lyman, Stanford M., ed. 1995. *Social Movements: Critiques, Concepts, Case-Studies*. New York: New York University Press.

Lyotard, J.F. 1988. *The Differend: Phrases in Dispute*. Minneapolis: University of Minnesota Press.

McCarthy, John, and William Yancey. 1971. 'Uncle Tom and Mr. Charlie: Metaphysical Pathos in the Study of Racism and Personal Disorganization', *American Journal of Sociology* 76 (Jan.): 648–72.

McDaniel, Susan A., and Ben Agger. 1984. *Social Problems Through Conflict and Order*. Don Mills, Ont.: Addison-Wesley.

Macey, Marie, and Eileen Moxon. 1996. 'An Examination of Anti-Racist and Anti-Oppressive Theory and Practice in Social Work Education', *British Journal of Social Work* 26: 297–314.

McFarland, Joan, and Robert Mullaly. 1996. 'NB Works: Image vs. Reality', in J. Pulkingham and G. Ternowetsky, eds, *Remaking Canadian Social Policy: Staking Claims and Forging Changes*. Halifax: Fernwood, 202–19.

McGregor, Craig. 1997. *Class in Australia*. Sydney: Penguin.

McRobbie, A. 1981. 'Settling Accounts with Subcultures: A Feminist Critique', in T. Bennett et al., eds, *Culture, Ideology and Social Process*. London: Batsford, 111–24.

Mannoni, O. 1962. *Prospero and Caliban: The Psychology of Colonization*. New York: Praeger.

Maracle, Lee. 1990. *Sojourner's Truth and Other Stories*. Vancouver: Press Gang.

——. 1996. *I Am Woman: A Native Perspective on Sociology and Feminism*, 2nd edn. Vancouver: Press Gang.

Marchak, M. Patricia. 1981. *Ideological Perspectives on Canada*, 2nd edn. Toronto: McGraw-Hill Ryerson.

Margolin, Leslie. 1997. *Under the Cover of Kindness: The Invention of Social Work*. Charlottesville: University Press of Virginia.

Marshall, M. 1990. *Social Work with Old People*, 2nd edn. London: Macmillan.

Martin-Baro, Ignacio. 1994. *Writings for a Liberation Psychology: Essays, 1985–1989*, ed. A. Aron and S. Corne. Cambridge, Mass.: Harvard University Press.

Marx, K., and F. Engels. 1967. *The Communist Manifesto*. New York: Pantheon.

—— and ——. 1978. *The Marx-Engels Reader*. New York: Norton.

Memmi, Albert. 1963. *Portrait of a Jew*. London: Eyre and Spottiswoode.

——. 1967. *The Colonizer and the Colonized*. Boston: Beacon Press.

——. 1968. *Dominated Man*. Boston: Beacon Press.

——. 1973. *The Liberation of the Jew*. New York: Viking.

Merchant, Carolyn. 1978. *The Death of Nature*. New York: Harper & Row.

Meszaros, I. 1970. *Marx's Theory of Alienation*. New York: Harper & Row.

Midgely, James. 1982. *Professional Imperialism: Social Work in the Third World*. London: Heinemann.

Miller, Alice. 1980. *For Your Own Good: Hidden Cruelty in Child-rearing and the Roots of Violence*. New York: Farrar, Straus and Giroux.

Miller, Jean Baker. 1986. *Toward a New Psychology of Women*, 2nd edn. London: Penguin.

Minow, Martha. 1985. 'Learning to Live with the Dilemma of Difference: Bilingual and Special Education', *Law and Contemporary Problems* 48 (Spring): 157–211.

————. 1987. 'Justice Engendered', *Harvard Law Review* 101 (Nov.): 11–95.

Moane, Geraldine. 1999. *Gender and Colonialism: A Psychological Analysis of Oppression and Liberation*. New York: St Martin's Press.

Moreau, Maurice J. 1979. 'A Structural Approach to Social Work Practice', *Canadian Journal of Social Work Education* 5, 1: 78–94.

———— and Lynn Leonard. 1989. *Empowerment Through a Structural Approach to Social Work*. Ottawa: Health and Welfare Canada.

Mosse, George. 1985. *Nationalism and Sexuality*. New York: Fertig.

Mullaly, Robert. 1995. 'Workfare: Participation or Persecution of the Poor?', *Perception* 18, 3–4: 8–13.

————. 1997a. *Structural Social Work: Ideology, Theory, and Practice*, 2nd edn. Toronto: Oxford University Press.

————. 1997b. 'The Politics of Workfare: NB Works', in E. Shragge, ed., *Workfare: Ideology for a New Underclass*. Toronto: Garamond Press, 35–57.

————. 2001. 'Confronting the Politics of Despair: Towards the Reconstruction of Progressive Social Work in a Global Economy and Postmodern Age', *Social Work Education* 20, 3: 303–20.

———— and Eric Keating. 1991. 'Similarities, Differences and Dialectics of Radical Social Work', *Journal of Progressive Human Services* 2, 2: 49–78.

Mulvey, C. 1994. *Evaluation Report on the Allen Lane Foundation's Funding Programme in Ireland, 1989–1991*. Dublin: Allen Lane Foundation.

Nandy, Ashis. 1983. *The Intimate Enemy*. Delhi: Oxford University Press.

National Council of Welfare. 1996. *Poverty Profile 1994*. Ottawa: Minister of Supply and Services.

Ng, R. 1993. 'Racism, Sexism, and Nation-Building in Canada', in C. McCarthy and W. Crichlow, eds, *Race, Identity, and Representation in Education*. New York: Routledge, 50–9.

Nicholson, L.J., ed. 1990. *Feminism/Postmodernism*. London: Routledge.

Nietzsche, F. 1967. *The Birth of Tragedy and the Case of Wagner*. New York: Vintage.

————. 1969. *On the Genealogy of Morals*. New York: Vintage.

Oberle, Peter. 1993. *The Incidence of Family Poverty on Canadian Indian Reserves*. Ottawa: Indian and Northern Affairs Canada.

O'Connor, Ian, Jill Wilson, and Deborah Setterlund. 1998. *Social Work and Welfare Practice*, 3rd edn. South Melbourne: Longman.

O'Connor, James. 1973. *The Fiscal Crisis of the State*. New York: St Martin's Press.

Parton, C., and N. Parton. 1989. 'Women, the Family and Child Protection', *Critical Social Policy* 24.

Pateman, C. 1970. *Participation and Democratic Theory*. Cambridge: Cambridge University Press.

Patterson, O. 1982. *Slavery and Social Death: A Comparative Study*. Cambridge, Mass.: Harvard University Press.

Pease, Bob. 1999. 'Deconstructing Masculinity—Reconstructing Men', in Pease and Fook (1999: 97–112).

———— and Jan Fook, eds. 1999. *Transforming Social Work Practice: Postmodern Critical Perspectives*. London: Routledge.

Pharr, Suzanne. 1988. *Homophobia: A Weapon of Sexism*. Inverness, Calif.: Chadron Press.

Pitkin, Hannah. 1981. 'Justice: On Relating Public and Private', *Political Theory* 9 (Aug.): 327–52.

Potocky, M. 1998. 'Multicultural Social Work in the United States: A Review and Critique', *International Social Work* 40: 315–26.

Powell, Gloria. 1973. 'Self-Concept in White and Black Children', in C. Willie, B. Kramer, and R. Brown, eds, *Racism and Mental Health: Essays*. Pittsburgh: University of Pittsburgh Press.

Pritchard, Colin, and Richard Taylor. 1978. *Social Work: Reform or Revolution?* London: Routledge & Kegan Paul.

Radway, J. 1984. *Reading the Romance: Women, Patriarchy and Popular Literature.* Chapel Hill: University of North Carolina Press.

Ramazanoglu, Caroline. 1989. *Feminism and the Contradictions of Oppression.* London: Routledge.

Reasons, Charles E., and William D. Perdue. 1981. *Ideology of Social Problems.* Scarborough, Ont.: Nelson Canada.

Rees, S. 1991. *Achieving Power: Practice and Policy in Social Welfare.* North Sydney, Australia: Allen & Unwin.

Reich, Michael. 1975. *The Mass Psychology of Fascism,* trans. V.R. Carpagno. Harmondsworth: Penguin.

Reynolds, Paul Davidson. 1971. *A Primer in Theory Construction.* New York: Bobbs-Merrill.

Riley, Mark. 2001. 'Slavery in our times', *The Age* (Melbourne), 4 June, 1, 13.

Rojek, C. , G. Peacock, and S. Collins. 1988. *Social Work and Received Ideas.* London: Routledge & Kegan Paul.

Rose, Stephen M., and Bruce L. Black. 1985. *Advocacy and Empowerment: Mental Health Care in the Community.* Boston: Routledge & Kegan Paul.

Rose, Steven, ed. 1982. *Against Biological Determinism: The Dialectics of Biology Group.* New York: Allison and Busby.

———. 1998. *Lifelines: Biology beyond Determinism.* New York: Oxford University Press.

Rosen, Michael. 1996. *On Voluntary Servitude: False Consciousness and the Theory of Ideology.* Cambridge: Polity Press.

Rosenberg, Morris, and Roberta Simmons. 1971. *Black and White Self-Esteem: The Urban School Child.* Washington: American Sociological Association.

Round Lake Treatment Centre. 1992. *The Next Generation: Native Adolescent Substance Abuse Treatment Model.* Armstrong, BC: Round Lake Treatment Centre.

Rubington, Earl, and S. Martin Weinberg, eds. 1995. *The Study of Social Problems,* 5th edn. New York: Oxford University Press.

Rushton, J. Philippe. 1988. 'Race Differences in Behaviour: A Review and Evolutionary Analysis', *Personality and Individual Differences* 9, 6: 1009–24.

Ruth, Sean. 1988. 'Understanding Oppression and Liberation', *Studies: An Irish Quarterly Review* (Winter): 434–43.

Ryan, W. 1976. *Blaming the Victim,* 2nd edn. New York: Vintage Books.

Said, Edward. 1978. *Orientalism.* New York: Pantheon.

Schiele, Jerome. 1994. 'Afrocentricity as an Alternative World View for Equality', *Journal of Progressive Human Services* 5, 1: 5–25.

Schon, Donald A. 1983. *The Reflective Practitioner.* London: Temple Smith.

———. 1987. *Educating the Reflective Practitioner.* San Francisco: Jossey–Bass.

Schriraldi, V., S. Kuyper, and S. Hewitt. 1996. *Young African-Americans and the Criminal Justice System in California: Five Years Later.* San Francisco: Center on Juvenile and Criminal Justice.

Schumpeter, J. 1950. *Capitalism, Socialism and Democracy.* London: Allen & Unwin.

Scott, Joan. 1988. 'Deconstructing Equality-versus-Difference: Or the Uses of Post-Structuralist Theory for Feminism', *Feminist Studies* 14: 33–50.

Seager, J. 1997. *The State of Women in the World Atlas.* London: Penguin.

Seidman, Steven. 1998. *Contested Knowledge: Social Theory in the Postmodern Era.* Malden, Mass.: Blackwell.

Sennett, Richard, and Jonathan Cobb. 1972. *The Hidden Injuries of Class.* New York: Vintage.

Shulman, Lawrence. 1992. *The Skills of Helping Individuals and Groups,* 2nd edn. Itasca, Ill.: Peacock.

Sibeon, R. 1991. 'The Construction of a Contemporary Sociology of Social Work', in Martin Davies, ed., *The Sociology of Social Work*. London: Routledge, 17–67.

Sidanius, Jim, and Felicia Pratto. 1999. *Social Dominance: An Intergroup Theory of Social Hierarchy and Oppression*. Cambridge: Cambridge University Press.

Sills, David, ed. 1968. *International Encyclopaedia of the Social Sciences*, vol. 12, 'Pluralism'. New York: Macmillan and the Free Press.

Smith, T. 1993. 'Postmodernism: Theory and Politics', *The Activist* 3, 7: 31–4.

Spector, M., and J.I. Kitsuse. 1987. *Constructing Social Problems*. New York: de Gruyter.

Spender, Dale. 1990. *Man Made Language*, 2nd edn. London: Pandora.

Stainton, Tim, and Karen Swift. 1996. "Difference" and Social Work Curriculum', *Canadian Social Work Review* 13, 1: 75–87.

Staples, R. 1988. *Black Masculinity: The Black Man's Role in American Society*. San Francisco: Black Scholar Press.

Starhawk. 1987. *Truth or Dare*. San Francisco: Harper & Row.

Statistics Canada. 1993. *The Violence against Women Survey*. Ottawa: Ministry of Industry, Science and Technology.

Tajfel, H. 1981. 'Social Stereotypes and Social Groups', in J.C. Turner and H. Giles, eds, *Intergroup Behaviour*. Oxford: Blackwell, 144–67.

Taylor, Charles. 1985. *Philosophy and the Human Sciences*. Cambridge: Cambridge University Press.

Taylor, Rupert J. 1991. 'Catalogue of Failure', *Canada and the World* (Feb.): 14–19.

Thompson, Neil. 1997. *Anti-Discriminatory Practice*, 2nd edn. London: Macmillan.

———. 1998. *Promoting Equality: Challenging Discrimination and Oppression in the Human Services*. London: Macmillan.

Wachholz, Sandra, and Robert Mullaly. 1993. 'Policing the deinstitutionalized mentally ill: Toward an understanding of its function', *Crime, Law and Social Change* 19: 281–300.

——— and ———. 2000. 'The Politics of the Textbook: A Content Analysis of Feminist, Radical, and Anti-Racist Social Work Scholarship in American Introductory Social Work Textbooks Published Between 1988 and 1997', *Journal of Progressive Human Services* 11, 2: 51–75.

Wagner, David, and Marcia B. Cohen. 1978. 'Social Workers, Class and Professionalism', *Catalyst* 1, 1: 25–55.

Walker, J. 1994. 'The Overrepresentation of Aboriginal and Torres Strait Islander People in Prison', *Criminology Australia*, 6: 13–15.

Walker, S., C. Spohn, and M. Delone. 1996. *The Color of Justice: Race, Ethnicity, and Crime in America*. San Francisco: Wadsworth.

Walkerdine, V., ed. 1996. 'Social Class', special issue of *Feminism and Psychology* 6, 3.

Wasserton, Richard. 1980. *Philosophy and Social Issues*. Notre Dame, Ind.: Notre Dame University Press.

Weedon, Chris. 1987. *Feminist Practice and Poststructuralist Theory*. Oxford: Blackwell.

———. 1997. *Feminist Practice and Poststructuralist Theory*, 2nd edn. Oxford: Blackwell.

West, Cornel. 1982. *Prophesy Deliverance! An Afro–American Revolutionary Christianity*. Philadelphia: Westminster.

———. 1993. *Race Matters*. Boston: Beacon.

Wharf, Brian, and John Cossom. 1987. 'Citizen Participation and Social Policy', in Shankar A. Yelaja, ed., *Canadian Social Policy*, 2nd edn. Waterloo, Ont.: Wilfrid Laurier University Press, 266–87.

Wilkinson, S., ed. 1996. *Feminist Social Psychologies*. Buckingham: Open University Press.

Williams, Fiona. 1989. *Social Policy: A Critical Introduction—Issues of Race, Gender and Class*. New York: Basil Blackwell.

Williams, Frank P., and Marilyn D. McShane. 1988. *Criminological Theory*. Englewood Cliffs, NJ: Prentice-Hall.

Williams, R. 1981. *Culture*. Cambridge: Fontana.

Willis, P. 1977. *Learning to Labour: How Working Class Kids Get Working Class Jobs*. Aldershot: Gower.

———. 1978. *Profane Culture*. London: Routledge & Kegan Paul.

Wilson, Elizabeth. 1993. 'Is Transgression Transgressive?', in J. Bristow and A.R. Wilson, eds, *Activating Theory: Lesbian, Gay, Bisexual Politics*. London: Lawrence and Wishart.

Wineman, Steven. 1984. *The Politics of Human Services*. Montreal: Black Rose Books.

Withorn, Ann. 1984. *Serving the People: Social Services and Social Change*: New York: Columbia University Press.

Young, Iris Marion. 1990. *Justice and the Politics of Difference*. Princeton, NJ: Princeton University Press.

Index